*f*P

FORCES OF FORTUNE

THE RISE OF THE
NEW MUSLIM MIDDLE CLASS
AND WHAT IT WILL MEAN
FOR OUR WORLD

A Council on Foreign Relations Book

Vali Nasr

FREE PRESS
New York   London   Toronto   Sydney

The Council on Foreign Relations (CFR) is an independent, nonpartisan membership organization, think tank, and publisher dedicated to being a resource for its members, government officials, business executives, journalists, educators and students, civic and religious leaders, and other interested citizens in order to help them better understand the world and the foreign policy choices facing the United States and other countries. Founded in 1921, CFR carries out its mission by maintaining a diverse membership, with special programs to promote interest and develop expertise in the next generation of foreign policy leaders; convening meetings at its headquarters in New York and in Washington, DC, and other cities where senior government officials, members of Congress, global leaders, and prominent thinkers come together with CFR members to discuss and debate major international issues; supporting a Studies Program that fosters independent research, enabling CFR scholars to produce articles, reports, and books and hold roundtables that analyze foreign policy issues and make concrete policy recommendations; publishing *Foreign Affairs*, the preeminent journal on international affairs and U.S. foreign policy; sponsoring Independent Task Forces that produce reports with both findings and policy prescriptions on the most important foreign policy topics; and providing up-to-date information and analysis about world events and American foreign policy on its website, www.cfr.org.

The Council on Foreign Relations takes no institutional position on policy issues and has no affiliation with the U.S. government. All statements of fact and expressions of opinion contained in its publications are the sole responsibility of the author or authors.

*f*P

Free Press
A Division of Simon & Schuster, Inc.
1230 Avenue of the Americas
New York, NY 10020

First Free Press hardcover edition September 2009

FREE PRESS and colophon are trademarks of Simon & Schuster, Inc.

For information about special discounts for bulk purchases, please contact
Simon & Schuster Special Sales at 1-866-506-1949 or business@simonandschuster.com.

The Simon & Schuster Speakers Bureau can bring authors to your live event.
For more information or to book an event contact the Simon & Schuster Speakers Bureau
at 1-866-248-3049 or visit our website at simonspeakers.com.

Designed by Julie Schroeder

Manufactured in the United States of America

1   3   5   7   9   10   8   6   4   2

Library of Congress Cataloging-in-Publication Data is available.

ISBN 978-1-4165-8968-6
ISBN 978-1-4165-9194-8 (ebook)

To

JOHN ESPOSITO
LEILA FAWAZ
MYRON WEINER

Scholars, Teachers, and Friends

[Commerce] rouses men from their indolence; and presenting them the gayer and more opulent part of the nation with objects of luxury, which they never have dreamed of, raises in them a desire of a more splendid way of life than what their ancestors enjoyed.

—David Hume
Political Discourses

CONTENTS

FORCES OF
FORTUNE

CHAPTER 1

THE POWER OF COMMERCE

It all happened quickly. The Muslim world changed dramatically in the short thirty-two months that separated the Ayatollah Khomeini's return to Iran on February 1, 1979, and the assassination of Anwar Sadat in Cairo on October 6, 1981. During that time of remarkable upheaval the forces of Islamic revolution seized Iran; Pakistan proclaimed itself an Islamic state; the Soviet Union touched off a jihad by invading Afghanistan; and Egyptian president Anwar Sadat was assassinated by radical fundamentalists. Since those fateful years, many more violent revolts, deadly clashes, terror attacks, and bloody suppressions have followed, along with deepening conservative Islamic attitudes and anti-Americanism across a vast swath of countries from North Africa to Southeast Asia. Extremism has come of age in this cauldron, giving rise to al-Qaeda, and its cult of violence and dark vision of the future.

In the face of all of this tumult, and in response to the rise of terrorism, America's most abiding objective in the Middle East since 1979 has been to contain and defeat Islamic fundamentalism. That object has determined how America sorts its allies from its adversaries, which fights it has taken on, and whether in pursuing its interests it will champion reform, promote democracy, or look to dictators and military solutions. It has also led America perilously close to reducing everything in the Middle East to the fight against fundamentalism, and to seeing every expression of Islam as a threat. The U.S. leadership has seen the fundamentalist challenge largely as a new kind of cold war. That sort of

---

1

clarity can be a great help, but it can also grossly oversimplify, obscuring vital aspects of the situations within countries and regions that provide opportunities for improving relations.

Looking at the Middle East as it is today—caught in the web of violent conflicts, seething with anger and anti-Americanism, and vulnerable to extremist ideas—it is difficult to have hope for the future. But, however difficult, that is just what we must do. In his perceptive book *The Age of the Unthinkable*, the strategist Joshua Cooper Ramo argues that by intensely focusing on that which is before us, we miss important trends—some barely detectable—that will shape the future.[1] The paradigms that dominate today may matter little tomorrow. We will do ourselves a disservice if we think of our future with the Muslim world only in terms of today's conflicts. These conflicts are serious, and we must prevail in them, but we should also recognize that there are other forces at work in the Muslim world and they too deserve our attention—they may ultimately matter more to us.

Take the case regarding the paradox of Iran, a brutish theocracy lording over a restless population that is also a rising power with ambitions to match its glorious ancient history, and a keen sense of purpose honed by decades of confrontation with the West. An examination of the ironies of Iranian power, and the fault lines within the country—on display in the recent presidential election—offer a particularly revealing starting point for rethinking the true challenges, and prospects, in transforming relations with the Muslim world. Iran's saber-rattling, and the Bush administration's hard-line stance—now being softened by the Obama administration—have diverted attention from important truths that belie the received wisdom regarding the Iranian threat, and those truths speak volumes about opportunities around the wider region.

The recent history of Iran's relations with the West is surely deeply troubling.[2] Iran's revolution empowered a particularly uncompromising brand of Islam that has turned anti-Americanism into an article of faith in much of the Muslim world, and Iran's rulers have steadily supported terrorism with money, training, and weaponry. Iran also now openly seeks great-power status and is building a nuclear program. Making matters worse in recent years was the more antagonistic approach to dealing with Iran that was adopted by the Bush administration, and the badly managed prosecution of the wars in Iraq and Afghanistan.

For much of the past three decades, the United States and Iran were locked in a stalemate, with no diplomatic relations, but also not much in the way of direct confrontation. America was content to isolate Iran as much as possible while waiting for the clerical regime to succumb to perceived inevitable internal pressures for change. In the wake of 9/11 that approach changed. The Bush administration believed it could nudge history along. Veterans of Reagan era cold war politics—the so-called neoconservative hawks who gathered around Vice President Dick Cheney and Secretary of Defense Donald Rumsfeld—drew confidence from what they perceived as the U.S. role in helping to toss communism onto the ash heap of history. They believed the toppling of Saddam Hussein and the rise of a reasonably stable, democratic new Iraq next door to Iran would stir Iranians into revolt and sufficiently unnerve the country's clerical rulers to provide that opening. The bitter irony was that when American troops showed up in Iraq, the grip of Iran's ruling clerics was strengthened.

By breaking the Taliban regime in Afghanistan in late 2001, toppling Saddam, and then uprooting Baathism in Iraq, the United States removed local rivals that had contained Iranian power to its east and west. Since the Shah's time and more so after the Islamic Revolution, Saddam's military had been the main barrier to Iran's expansionist aims. Today there is no indigenous military force in the Persian Gulf region capable of containing Iran. What's more, in the political vacuum that followed Saddam's fall, Shia Iran quickly extended its reach into the predominantly Shia lands of southern Iraq. Many of Iraq's new leaders had spent years of exile in Iran and relied on Iranian support during the dark years of Saddam's rule. It was no coincidence that Iran was the first of Iraq's neighbors to recognize its new government and to encourage Iraqis to participate in the political order established by the United States. Now Iran runs extensive intelligence and political networks that give the Islamic Republic influence at every level of Iraq's bureaucracy, clerical and tribal establishments, and security agencies—impacting election results, the flow of trade, and the tempo of violence.

Iranian leaders are keenly aware of how their regional influence has grown since 2001, and especially since 2003.[3] Former president Muhammad Khatami, the onetime great hope of the reformers in Iran, captured this sentiment when I asked him in 2007 about how he assessed Iran's place in the region. "Regardless of where the United States changes regimes," he observed, "it is our friends who will come to power."[4] True enough, Tehran has more impact on Arab politics—especially in the critical zones of Iraq, Lebanon, and Palestine—than it did ten years ago. Not only does Iran's influence in Iraq far exceed that of any Arab government, but since the war between Hezbollah and Israel in the summer of 2006, Iran has gained more say in Lebanon's domestic politics as well—pushing for Hezbollah's interests and constricting politicians favored by the United States or Iran's Arab rivals. The clerical regime has also kept up, if not jacked up, its meddling in Palestinian politics through its support for the extremists of Palestinian Islamic Jihad and Hamas, as well as cultivating ties with Syria. By excoriating Israel and taking advantage of Arab frustration with the lack of progress in the peace process, Iran seems to curry more favor these days on the Arab street than the tired old Arab dictatorships in charge. So it is that Iran's Supreme Leader confidently boasted that no problem can be solved in the Middle East without Iran's consent and help.

Iran's hubris was fueled by soaring oil prices in 2007 and the first three quarters of 2008, which eventually topped out at close to $150 a barrel. Flush with petrodollars, Iran's rulers were confident they could afford their shopping spree for influence in the Palestinian Territories, Lebanon, and Iraq by supplying their allies and clients with funds, weapons—including rockets and missiles—and training. There is worry across the Middle East that all this activity will only increase if Iran goes nuclear. Then Tehran will have little fear of reprisal for its boldly aggressive policies, which is one reason why a host of Arab nations now contemplate nuclear programs of their own to temper Iran's surging influence.

Talk of military action against Iran was rife in the Bush administration throughout 2007 and 2008, but the United States had too much on its plate in Iraq and Afghanistan, not to mention the deepening political crisis in Pakistan, to take any such step. All of this seems to indicate that Iran has become a juggernaut. But as the recent upheaval shows, the reality is more complex.

For the West, the most often used measure of Iran's regional influence is the flow of arms and influence from Tehran to its allies and clients. In order to gauge how much weight Iran is throwing around, America looks to metrics such as those above about the dollar amount Tehran promises Hamas, the volume of weapons it smuggles to Hezbollah, and the numbers of those trained in terrorist tactics by the Iranian Revolutionary Guards' shadowy Quds Brigade. There is plenty of this activity to alarm America and its Arab allies, and worse, those ties are becoming stronger. If Iran goes nuclear there is no telling what havoc might be wreaked by means of Iran's minions. There is no denying, then, that Iran's hard power and influence have been growing. But viewing Iranian power from that angle alone makes it look more inevitable and ominous than it really is.

Economics has more to do with determining the pecking order in the Middle East than the region's miasmic tumult of feuds, wars, and saber rattlings would lead one to believe. The Middle East is not just a zone of clashing extremist ideas and zealous terrorist armies. It is also a place of struggling and thriving economies, where new classes and business elites are elbowing their way higher in the power structures of many countries, changing religious, social, and political life on the way. Other contenders for great-power status in recent memory, Brazil, China, or India, all rose to prominence not on the back of hard power but as economic stars driving growth in the regions around them. That is not the case with Iran. Iran is not going the way of the so-called BRICs (to use the somewhat misleading acronym that lumps petro-dependent Russia in with the more diversified economies of Brazil, India, and China). Iran's economy is the 151st most isolated in the world (that is out of 160) and sixteenth most isolated in the Middle East (out of seventeen).

Iran's drive for regional power lacks an economic underpinning. And that makes gauging Iran's regional power a tricky business. Hard power is not its most effective means to greater influence.

Iran has most influence where it does most trade; where that influence is backed by economic and business relations. While Iran has deep ties to Lebanon's Hezbollah and a long-running alliance with Syria, its most certain sphere of influence is far closer to home, in an arc that runs from Central Asia in the north and east down through western Afghanistan and on into the Persian Gulf and southern Iraq to the south and west. "When you go to Central Asia these days" remarks *The Atlantic Monthly*'s Robert Kaplan, "you feel you are in greater Iran."[5] It is in this arc where Iran does most of its regional business, selling agricultural products, electricity (a big-ticket item in this air-conditioning-hungry region), natural gas, and even manufactured goods.

The trade between Iran and the five Central Asian 'stans was worth well over $1 billion in 2008 (up from $580 million in 2001). The Iranian rial changes hands there as easily as local currencies. Counting the unaccounted for cross-border trade, Iran does about the same amount of business with Afghanistan (up astronomically from a paltry $52 million in 2001). Trade with Iraq topped $4 billion in 2008 and with the United Arab Emirates reached $14 billion—a figure that does *not* include all the black-market trading that goes on across the Gulf. In fact, Iran has such a vital interest in this trade that the regime has created banking and financial ties and invested infrastructure projects in these countries ranging from roads, railways, and piers to pipelines and electricity pylons. Businesses of all kinds have grown in these countries on the back of this trade.

In so many ways, Iran is well qualified to become a true economic powerhouse driving wider growth in the region. Its nearly 70 million people give it a population about the same size as Turkey's. It has vast oil and gas reserves, plus a strong industrial base by regional standards. Labor is cheap but the literacy rate is high, over 75 percent. As the country's thriving art scene and internationally acclaimed movie industry suggest, Iranians are also far better plugged into world culture than is the norm in the region.

Iranians are Web- and mobile-savvy (Persian is the world's third most widely used language online, the country boasts the most bloggers per capita anywhere in the world, and almost two-thirds of the country—some 48 million people—are mobile phone users). They are also technically adept: The country's leading technical school, Sharif University of Science and Technology in Tehran, turns out world-class engineers and scientists. Stanford regularly admits Sharif alumni into its graduate programs in engineering, and according to one Stanford professor and former department chair, "Sharif now has one of the best undergraduate electrical-engineering programs in the world."[6]

This sort of human-capital development can make Iran a player in the competitive global economy. The degree of ingenuity and skill already present is attested to, ironically, by the nuclear program, which is run by homegrown experts. Iran's rulers even like to claim—despite great skepticism in most Western quarters—that the nuclear drive and rocket program will be Iran's ticket to economic globalization's cutting edge.[7] And it is not just splitting atoms that is supposed to catapult Iran into global status, the country is also investing in space research and biotechnology. Research outfit Iran Cord Blood Bank, created in 2003 with the Supreme Leader's blessing, has committed $2.5 billion to human embryonic stem cell research to help cure a range of ailments from heart disease to multiple sclerosis.[8] The initiative has surged ahead taking advantage of the fact that a fetus is not considered a human in Islamic law before the end of the first trimester of a pregnancy.

In a more down-to-earth vein, Tehran mayor and former Revolutionary Guards commander Muhammad Baqer Qalibaf talks of development in terms of economic reform, private sector growth, and globalization. When he ran for president in 2005, he fashioned himself as the Islamic Republic's version of the maverick state-builder and founder of the Pahlavi monarchy, Reza Shah, turning heads with his colorful feel-good campaign posters that promised growth and prosperity. The same themes crop up routinely in Qalibaf's speeches and interviews as the can-do mayor of Tehran.

Such hopeful talk from the higher-ups falls flat, though, before the reality of an Iran where inflation is running at double digits and about a quarter of the workforce is jobless. The problem is not a lack of enterprise or fundamental potential. Iran has a dynamic private sector and the middle class to go with it. The economist Djavad Saleh-Isfahani estimates that around half of Iran's population of 70 million is middle class or above—counting their possessions, disposable income, level of education, and family size—with the kind of social attitudes that are needed to support robust consumption habits and modernizing change.[9] The problem is that Iran's private sector is shackled by a corrupt and inefficient state that dominates 80 percent of the economy. The state grew to its current size after the revolution by devouring large parts of the private sector—nationalizing businesses, banks, and industries. It prioritizes spending on the poor above achieving economic growth, and therefore sees no problem in stifling entrepreneurship with red tape, starving businesses of resources, and taxing them dry. It is top-down centralized economic management at its worst.

When it comes to the economy, Iran is not a regional leader but a regional laggard, dawdling in the soggy bottomlands of suffocating statism. This economic stagnation was a powerful driver of the vehement opposition to Ahmadinejad in the recent election. The thing to watch in Iran over the next few years is the private sector and the middle class tied to it—the same class that in the aftermath of the June 2009 election led millions to ask "where is my vote?" The great battle for the soul of Iran—and for the soul of the region as a whole—will be fought not over religion but over business and capitalism. At issue will be whether the state will free the economy and let this dynamic society reach its full potential.

The deeper truth about Iran's power is that playing the anti-American and pro-Palestinian cards is not going to bring Iran lasting influence. As a senior Iranian official once told me, "When push comes to shove, the Palestinians will be the first to turn on Iran." Iran will not be able to truly dominate the region if it does not do a better job of developing its economic clout. Great-power status presupposes economic leadership, and that Iran is not currently providing. This is the key to Iran's quest for nuclear capability; the Iranian rulers think they need the threat of nuclear aggression or retaliation in order to forestall Western pressure for regime change and to intimidate neighbors, but even more important to punch above their weight. After all, Iran's GDP is about the same as that of Massachusetts. It spends only $6 billion a year on its military. That is less than a third of Saudi Arabia's military expenditure of $21 billion a year, and close to half of Turkey or Israel's annual military spending.[10] Before the revolution, Iran's military expenditure was as high as 18 percent of GDP; today it is a paltry 3 percent. How can a country with an economy the size of Massachusetts and the lowest military expenditure in its neighborhood take on the United States and claim great-power status? The answer in Tehran is that only nuclear capability will address Iran's glaring economic and military deficits. And if Iranians had any doubts that nuclear capability will raise their stock, America's near obsession with the issue over the past six years has convinced them.

But even with nuclear capability, the kind of status that Iran covets will elude it. Both India and Pakistan started down the nuclear path in the 1970s, but only one of them emerged as a regional great power in the 1990s. It was not nukes that turned India into a rising power, but rather its economic growth rate, newfound friendliness to free markets, and ability to integrate into the global economy. Iran today rallies the alienated and rouses the dispossessed, but those seeking progress and prosperity have to look elsewhere for inspiration. If Iran wants to be a great power, it will have to further nurture its economy so that it serves as the engine of growth for the region that it could be. That would mean bringing itself into concert with a vital economic transformation underway all around the region—the rise of a new middle class that is the key to more fully integrating the Middle East into the global economy, and to the building of better relations with the West. It is to this rise of a new middle class that leaders in the United States and around the West should turn attention—to fuel its potential—rather than allowing the chimerical power of fundamentalism to dictate so much of the approach to the region.

The great irony of the fundamentalist threat is that the two years from 1979 to 1981 in which Islamic fundamentalism shook the world and terrified the West were also its high point of power. That is not to say, of course, that after fundamentalism won Iran, turned Pakistan, and destabilized Egypt it just died out; fundamentalists are too vocal, active, well organized, and well funded for that. Fundamentalism most definitely remains a worry, and its extremist edge a serious threat. Extremism that has been festering in the innards of Pakistan's society is surging, laying claim to vast swaths of its territory, and those extremist forces are waging a two-pronged war against not only foreign troops but the governments of both Afghanistan and Pakistan. The thought of nuclear-armed Pakistan, with its 175-million-plus population—deeply divided along ethnic lines, and with a troubled economy and weak government—unraveling before the extremist onslaught is unnerving to say the least. A failed Pakistan in the clutches of extremism or plunged into civil war, and with no safeguards locking down its nuclear arsenal, would be deeply destabilizing for the region and the world.

The larger truth about fundamentalism's drive to power, though, is that since 1980 it has toppled no more dominoes. The Taliban visited horror on Afghanistan, but this rag-tag army of religious zealots and tribal warriors amounted to no more than an incomplete insurgency in a broken corner of the Muslim world—an antique badland even before decades of war ravaged it. There have been no additional Irans, and the prospect that another Islamic state will arise—whether through peaceful means or violent ones—has been steadily declining.

The West must remain vigilant against fundamentalism, but that should not stop Western policymakers and publics from seeing the "whole picture" in the Middle East, and a vital truth of the region is that the fundamentalist strain of Islam is not practiced by the vast majority of the population, and is *not* on the rise. What is true is that since 1980, a broader wave of Islamic resurgence has swept across the Middle East, and fundamentalism has surfed that wave rather than fueling it. The

Islamic resurgence is much larger, deeper, and more complex. The vast majority of Muslims are moderate and pragmatic when it comes to religion, balancing law and piety with a healthy dose of mystical practices and folk religion.

It is not fundamentalism that accounts for the ubiquity of Islamic influence across the region today; rather it is the other way around: Widespread Islamic fervor—which can, but does not have to, take on a fundamentalist form—has allowed fundamentalism to survive past its prime. It would of course be foolish to ignore fundamentalism and the extremists associated with it, but it is also imprudent to consider fundamentalism the end-all and be-all of what we need to know about Islam and the Middle East. It is time that we take a good look at the vitality of the energetic blending of Islamic piety and capitalist fervor that is flourishing in many pockets around the region.

In November 2006, when Pope Benedict XVI visited Turkey, he made a stop at the seventeenth-century Blue Mosque, so called for the more than twenty thousand handcrafted cobalt-blue Iznik tiles that adorn its interior. A testament to Ottoman grandeur, the great mosque is an architectural marvel of unrivaled beauty. At one point, the gently strolling pontiff stopped and looked up at a large black tableau with ornate white calligraphy, etched into an arch at the mosque's main exit, and asked his guide what the flowing script said. They were the words of the Prophet, he was told: "A merchant is the beloved of God" (al-kasib habiballah).

Benedict's visit to Turkey was historic, his first to a Muslim country. It was also a hastily organized damage-control mission. Two months earlier, His Holiness had caused a furor when, in a speech in his German homeland, he had evoked the criticisms of Islam made by fourteenth-century Byzantine emperor Manuel II Paleologus, who led the empire during its last days, as the Ottoman Turks steadily encroached on its power, eventually seizing Constantinople. Manuel had written a "Refutation of Islam," in which he argued that Islam was an irrational

religion, an evil falsehood that had been spread by the sword.[11] Making
the reference worse was the fact that Manuel, in his desperate efforts
to obtain support for the fight against the Turks, had made an alliance
with the pope in Rome. By quoting Manuel, the current pope seemed
to be saying that Islam was essentially driven by jihad and was at odds
with Western values—not only Christian values, but those of modernity altogether.

How ironic, then, that on that day at the Blue Mosque, the pope discovered that for centuries, the last words worshippers read when leaving
the mosque were a call to commerce. Not only was commerce important
to the seventeenth-century Muslim world, it is even more important to
that world today. Washington is certainly not entirely unaware of this.
The United States has been supporting economic reform and business
initiatives in the Muslim world, but with too much focus on working
with government planners and the top-level business elite. Change will
not come from this upper crust—it has too much invested in the status
quo and depends too heavily on the state. It is business with small "b"
that should hold our attention.

All across the region, a whole new economy is rising, mixing local
values with surging consumption and building ever richer ties to the
global economy, and this trend is not only every bit as powerful and
important as the threat of fundamentalism, it is more so.[12]

In the spring of 2009, I met in Dubai with a group of Middle Eastern businessmen. Only a short time earlier, the little emirate had been
swept to dizzying heights of wealth and prosperity, and these businessmen had done quite well for themselves. Now the discussion was more
somber, focused not surprisingly on the global financial crisis. After
much talk about failing banks and falling real estate prices, I asked the
group how they were responding.

"Money is flying to Beirut," one of them explained. "Everyone is
putting what they can in Lebanese banks."

Lebanese banks?

Why were these very savvy businessmen prepared to trust their substantial assets and investments to banks in a country with a reputation for

war and instability—the Hezbollah-land that so worries the West? Were they making a political statement with their money, sending a further message to the West about their willingness to support their cause even in a time of financial trouble? Or was I missing their point altogether?

"Why Lebanon?" I finally asked sheepishly.

"Well, the interest rate is much higher in Lebanon than here," one answered, while another pointed out what was already obvious to the rest of the group: "Lebanese banks sit outside the global financial system. They have no toxic assets to worry about. Nor are they threatened with collapse or government takeover, as are banks in New York and London."

Why had I needed to be reminded that capitalism is alive and thriving in the Middle East? There are signs of it everywhere, from the actions of these businessmen to protect their assets to the staggering rate at which shopping malls and modern retail establishments of all kinds have gone up in the Muslim world, and not just in Kuala Lumpur or Dubai, where one sees extravagant Rodeo Drive–style malls. In war-torn Beirut and fundamentalist-dominated Tehran, glitzy malls are filled on holidays with shoppers eager to buy the latest electronics or fashionable home furnishings.

This capitalist flowering has had clearly definable cultural ramifications as well. A quick glance at rooftops in any Arab city will leave little room for doubt that satellite television has mesmerized the Arab world, to the chagrin of its dictators and their censors. There are some 280 channels to choose from, and the more popular ones, such as al-Jazeera or al-Arabiya, claim viewership in the tens of millions. It is also on these airwaves that some of the most interesting religious debates take place. Clerics are not the only ones who draw the big audiences. They must now compete with a new breed of televangelists, who preach modernity- and business-friendly Islam.

Internet use too is steadily growing. About 40 percent of Iran's population surfs the Web, with the ranks of first-timers swelling constantly, as opinion and information flow briskly into and out of social networking websites and chat rooms, and then get further interpreted on blogs. Even clerics maintain active websites, blogs, and Facebook pages, and have Twitter followings. Those two social networking sites took over the presidential campaign of 2009, upending traditional media to make way for new political dynamics in the country. The government has tried its hand at restricting and censoring the Net, but it is King Canute ordering back the tide. And even if the hard-line ayatollahs and their minions could strangle the Internet, what would they do about the explosion of cell phones and mobile texting? In 2000, fewer than a million Iranians had a cell phone. Now some 48 million—about two-thirds of the country—have one. Even people too poor to obtain a regular mobile subscription can buy cheap prepaid phones to start talking and texting. And it is not just Iran: Next door in war-ravaged Afghanistan, the close of 2008 found eight million mobile phones in use—about one quarter of the population. Pakistan's numbers are even more impressive; in 2008, 78 million were using mobile phones; up from a mere 750,000 in 2001.

A vital characteristic of this flourishing capitalism is that it goes so much hand in hand with the resurgence of traditional Islamic belief. All over the Middle East, piety is shaping consumption. Those who live by Islam also demand Islamic goods; not just *halal* food and headscarves, but Islamic housing, haute couture, banking, education, entertainment, media, consumer goods (such as Europe-based alternatives to Coke and Pepsi, Mecca Cola and Qibla Cola), and even vacations—Islamic cruises are a growth industry in Turkey, and the governor of Najaf in southern Iraq has been thinking of ways to market pilgrimage vacation packages in order to coax some of the million-plus Iranians who visit the sacred sites in his city every year into staying longer and spending more. Some offerings mix the taste for Islam with that for globalization, as, for example, The Caprice, a luxury hotel with a distinctly French name that caters to the Islamically conscious vacationing on Turkey's western coast.

This upwardly mobile class consumes Islam as much as practicing it, demanding the same sorts of life-enhancing goods and services as middle classes everywhere. Their preference that those goods have an Islamic flavor makes Islam big business. A booming economic sector around the region is catering to this exploding demand, and these rising Islamic consumers comprise as much as a sixth of humanity, spread across a vast expanse from Morocco to Malaysia, with notable toeholds from Detroit to Düsseldorf and São Paulo to Singapore.

Americans are easily dazzled by the size of China's economy, the speed of its growth, and the room it has to expand. In recent years, India's economy has also made remarkable strides. Thinking of the notional "Muslim-world economy" provides an interesting basis for comparison. The global Muslim population of a billion-plus is about the same size as both India and China's populations. In 2008 the GDP of the economies of five of the largest countries in and around the Middle East—Egypt, Iran, Pakistan, Saudi Arabia, and Turkey, with a combined population of 420 million—was $3.3 trillion, the same size as that of India, which has three times the population.

The bottom line is: A billion consumers have clout. Across economies as diverse as those of Mali, Dubai, and Indonesia—and outside the Muslim-majority countries, in the Muslim diasporas—the demand for Islamic goods and services is strong and growing, and it has already created waves in global markets. This is perhaps best demonstrated by the boom in Islamic finance, which is doing good work in further integrating the economies of the Muslim world and the global economy.

———

For Americans, seeing the words "Islamic" and "finance" in the same sentence tends to conjure up worries about terrorism.[13] The need to identify and cut off terrorists' money flows is entirely legitimate, but "Islamic finance" has nothing to do with funding extremism or violence; rather the term refers to banking and other financial services— such as insurance, mutual funds, equities, bonds, credit cards, and even derivatives—that are compatible with shariah rules and regulations. Shariah requires neither collecting nor paying interest on bank deposits or loans, and in the case of bonds, limiting the amount of debt a company takes on in issuing bonds to the value of assets on its books. Islamic finance also means avoiding investment in ventures that may violate the shariah, such as businesses that serve alcohol, involve gambling, produce devices that can promote immorality, or in some cases, even the use of mannequins or bareheaded women in advertising.[14]

In place of charging interest, Islamic finance relies on forming partnerships that demand that borrowers, lenders, and investors jointly take an equity position in business ventures, sharing in the risk and reward of those investments.[15] The whole thing works better in theory than in practice, and Islamic financiers have had to develop entrepreneurial ways of working around these restrictions to make the system work. For instance, car dealerships will simply add the amount they would make in interest for a loan to the cost of a car, and offer buyers a deferred payment schedule.

Although Islamic finance remains a fledgling, niche market in the vast global financial-services industry, it has lately been growing at the rate of 15 to 20 percent per year.[16] The American consulting firm McKinsey & Co. estimates that by 2010, assets held by Islamic financial houses will total $1 trillion, a fivefold growth in five years.[17] The Western ratings agency Standard and Poor estimates that these assets could ultimately grow to as much as $4 trillion.[18] The 2008 global financial crisis may in fact give a good boost to these numbers as more Muslims may decide to pull their money from traditional investments for the perceived security of the Islamic alternative.

There are some three hundred Islamic banks and investment firms operating in more than seventy-five countries. By the end of 2006, some 218 shariah-compliant mutual funds were managing an estimated $14 billion.[19] Iran accounts for the most shariah-compliant assets ($155 billion in 2007), followed by Saudi Arabia and Malaysia ($69 and $65 billion each) and then Kuwait and U.A.E. ($38 and $35 billion each).[20] These banks oversee banking services totaling close to $500 billion and an Islamic bond market worth $82 billion—a mere one-tenth of one percent of the global bond market, but expanding fast. The total investment in these bonds grew by an eye-popping 250 percent in 2006, and growth continued even with the global financial downturn.[21]

Three large Middle Eastern players dominate Islamic finance: the Faysal Group, al-Baraka, and the Kuwait Finance House. The most active hub for Islamic finance has for many years been Kuala Lumpur—where Southeast Asia's boom in the 1990s charted the way for the integration of Muslim Malaysia and Indonesia into the global economy—but Dubai and Bahrain now account for a growing share of the market. All of them now warily anticipate competition from the larger financial centers of London, Tokyo, Hong Kong, and Singapore.

As an indication of how this form of financing can serve to build ties between the Middle East and global economy, many global financial brands such as HSBC, Deutsche Bank, Barclays, Credit Suisse, Citigroup, and the UK's Black Rock are getting into the game. They are targeting a growing market of Muslims in the West for retail banking as well as more lucrative upscale financial services, such as private banking and wealth management, and looking to gain growing shares of the booming Islamic-bond market. Deutsche Bank, Barclays Capital, and BNP Paribas are now among the world's top five issuers of Islamic bonds. The equity markets in the West are also joining in. Dow Jones has indexes for both Islamic bonds and Islamic investment funds.[22] Research and analysis into Islamic finance is also going on at Moody's and Reuters, and the premier annual gathering of experts on the subject takes place at Harvard University's Forum on Islamic Finance.

London in particular has set its sights on becoming a major center for Islamic finance. The city saw its first Islamic bank open in 2004, and since then two more have opened and a fourth is on the way. The London stock market issued its first Islamic bond in 2007, and is well on its way to expanding into the sovereign Islamic-bond market. Competition is spurring legal reform and the creation of new regulatory mechanisms designed to encourage Islamic financial activity. So far that competition has favored Dubai, whose relatively hands-off regulatory environment is the most attractive to investors and borrowers, but there is no denying that increasingly Islamic finance is going global.

Arab Islamic banks are setting up shop in Europe and Southeast Asia, and European and Southeast Asian banks are providing Islamic banking in the Persian Gulf. Banks such as Saudi Arabia's al-Rajhi or Kuwait Financial House have been building branches across the Muslim

world and competing with local Islamic banks such as the Dubai Islamic
Bank or the Islamic Bank of Jordan, or the Islamic arm of local mainstream banks or global financial outfits like HSBC or Citigroup. Smaller
markets are converging into one global market ruled by the same regulations and standards, which mix Western business practices with Islamic
ones, all enforced by Islamic scholars and shariah-compliance boards.
Malaysia has tried to enforce standards by creating the National Shariah
Board, and there is a broader international effort aimed at creating common standards is in the works at Bahrain's Accounting and Auditing
Organization for Islamic Financial Institutions.[23]

Islamic scholars on lucrative retainers with financial institutions,
some in America, help design new Islamic financial products—and
even help bend the rules to sell finance to shariah-conscious customers.[24] One particularly influential one is Yusuf DeLorenzo, an American
convert from Brooklyn. In addition to advising twenty global financial
institutions and a few Muslim countries, the dapper sheikh is the chief
shariah officer (rhymes with chief financial officer) at Shariah Capital, a
Connecticut-based Islamic hedge fund. Meanwhile, many of these customers come from Turkey, Indonesia, and North Africa, where the religiously conscious middle class is growing.

When in 2006 the Dubai Port Authority acquired British Peninsu-
lar and Oriental Steam Navigation (which managed a number of U.S.
ports), some in the United States pointed to the $3.5 billion Islamic
bond that had financed the deal as proof of a threat to U.S. security.[25]
Islamic bonds were then unknown to most Americans, and the mere
mention of Islam with relation to financing was enough to ring alarm
bells. Yet a number of American companies had already dipped their
toes into these waters. In 2004, the Texas-based oil group East Cameron
Partners became the first American company to issue Islamic bonds.[26]
Recently, Ford Motor Company's $848 million sale of Aston-Martin
to the Kuwait-based Islamic bank Investment Dar required Islamic
financing. Caribou Coffee, America's largest specialty coffee chain after
Starbucks, is owned by a shariah-compliant private-equity firm based in
Bahrain.[27] In Europe, British developers have financed the multibillion-

dollar purchase of London's historic Chelsea Barracks complex with Islamic bonds,[28] while in 2004, the German provincial government of Saxony-Anhalt became the first non-Muslim sovereign entity to do so, raising 100 million Euros in the process.[29] France, China, Japan, and Thailand are all poised to follow.

Key to understanding the growth of Islamic finance, and the insight it offers into the up-and-coming mind-set of so many Muslims, is that it evolved due to the demands of average customers. Some observers ascribe the spectacular growth of the last few years to the oil boom, and the flow back to the region of an estimated $800 billion belonging to Muslims made nervous by post-9/11 financial regulations intended to clamp down on the laundering of money to fund terrorism. Surely those cash flows have greatly accelerated growth, but consider that this money that had been stashed away in America, Britain, or Switzerland before 9/11 could, when it "came home," just as easily have gone into regular banks and investment funds in the Middle East, which are plentiful. The directing of so much money into Islamic finance suggests a strong specific demand for this brand of the blending of capitalism and Islam.

Indeed shariah compliance has attracted many Muslims to investing who had previously shunned formal markets. One can think of Islamic finance in its early days as somewhat akin to microfinance, meaning the provision of small loans to those shunned by traditional bankers because of low income and little or no collateral to offer. When Bangladesh's Grameen Bank pioneered the idea, the intent was not so much to make profits but to lift people out of poverty. But over the past decade, microfinance has evolved into big business, with large banks and investment funds competing over what the business strategist C. K. Prahalad calls "the fortune at the bottom of the pyramid."[30]

Like microcredit, Islamic finance was a response to a moral imperative: to fulfill a demand for loans by those who wanted their business to be in compliance with the shariah. The largest Islamic financial institution, Saudi Arabia's al-Rajhi Bank, started operations as a small firm providing the interest-free equivalent of modest loans, and it grew largely by bringing in new, piously interest-averse investors. Whereas in

· 1978, savings accounted for only 10 percent of all deposits in Saudi Arabia,[31] thanks to Islamic banking, that number had grown to 53 percent by 2007.[32] In 2008 the three Islamic banks in the kingdom accounted for 45 percent of all bank-credit facilities, and al-Rajhi now has more branches—many located away from major cities—than any other bank in the kingdom, boasting an impressive $15 billion in deposits.[33] So popular was the opportunity to bank in this fashion that when Kuwait Finance House, now one of the world's largest Islamic banks and the holder of its country's largest single deposit pool, opened its doors, it attracted so many customers that it met the deposit goal for its whole first year within thirty days.[34]

There is no question that Islamic finance is now benefiting from an advantage in attracting deposits and investments from the growing wealth at the top of society, and in the government, in prospering Southeast Asia and the oil-rich Persian Gulf. Financiers in the West know very well about the kind of wealth that floats around at the top levels of these societies, especially the huge reserves of cash in government coffers and sovereign wealth funds—investment funds run by the government, with government money. But the growing ranks of newly cash rich individuals in the Muslim world, who come not from the traditional elite but from the rising classes, are strong consumers of Islamic finance too.

Their counterparts in Europe and the United States are also fans. Accenture, a global consulting company, estimates that demand among Muslims in Europe will drive the next phase of the growth. Half of all Muslim middle-class savings in the world belong to Muslims who live in the West.[35] American Muslims are more likely than their coreligionists in Europe or the Muslim-majority countries to enjoy middle-class status. According to Zogby polls, a majority of U.S. Muslims are educated and earn more than $50,000 a year. Pent-up demand among middle-class American Muslims has already made Islamic finance an instant success in Chicago. No sooner had that city's Devon Bank begun looking into the feasibility of Islamic banking in 2002 than local Muslims came to it in droves looking for shariah-compliant home mortgages and car loans.[36] Islamic finance will likely soon be as ubiquitous in the West as in the Muslim world, and if Islamic finance's market share were to reflect the Muslim's 20 percent share of world population, then shariah-compliant finance will be growing at a spectacular pace for some time.

Islamic finance is also attractive to many women who generate, own, inherit, or manage wealth, but who find themselves inhibited by law or custom from dealing with the mixed-sex environment of regular financial institutions. "Ladies only" banks have been a growth industry. Coutts, a private bank based in London, has been doing a brisk business in private banking services for wealthy Persian Gulf female residents.[37] The air of propriety surrounding shariah-compliant finance is attractive to women. There are fewer stigmas associated with walking into an Islamic bank or investing through Islamic investment arms without male supervision. To cater to this growing market, Islamic banks have been educating women in finance. The Kuwait Finance House, for example, holds classes for women. Islamic finance firms are also hiring more women than do regular banks. A third of financial-sector employees in Bahrain and two-fifths of those in Kuwait, for example, are women.

All of this is not to say that Islamic finance will in any way become dominant in the global economy, not by a very long shot. Limitations will rein in the growth of this business. Islam's ban on speculation, for example, means that transactions must be based on tangible assets, which makes it easy to do business in commodities and real estate, but much trickier to innovate financial products. Islamic finance could run out of assets to sustain its growth, and even short of that it may overemphasize investment in certain assets, such as real estate or retail, thereby increasing the risk of losses. The business may also suffer from squabbles over just what is properly Islamic. The Islamic bond market took a tumble—and along with it the value of properties funded by Islamic bonds—when in 2008 a group of clerics in Bahrain declared that most Islamic bonds are not Islamic because they fail to shift the ownership of collateral to bond holders. Without that transfer, they argued, a financial transaction isn't based on tangible assets and is therefore not Islamic.[38]

The cost of that religious ruling was high and the evidence that clerics can send the market tumbling was disconcerting to many investors. The question is also open whether Islamic finance can keep growing by tap-dancing around the matter of interest rates. Profit-sharing instruments, or other work-arounds such as providing indirect car loans, are relatively inefficient, incurring higher costs in putting deals together. [39] Islamic finance will need more innovation of clever strategies if it is to continue to grow market share by comparison to traditional finance. A great deal of money is being poured into research and development of schemes, but it's hard to know whether those efforts will yield results.

Given ample demand and all the windfall oil cash sluicing around the Middle East, Islamic finance will likely continue to ride high despite its inefficiencies, but it will eventually hit a glass ceiling. Nonetheless it has already become a notable part of global financial trade, and most important for our purposes here, it will serve as a vehicle for integrating the Muslim economy ever more into the world economy.

All this emphasis on morals in finance may not seem economically rational, but taking stock of the global financial crisis of 2008, there is something to be said for ethics in finance. Islamic financiers now brag that their ethics steered them away from the risky ventures that have caused so much havoc, and will make them more attractive to investors going forward.[40] Indonesia's President Susilo Bambang Yudhoyono recently told a gathering of Islamic bankers in Jakarta that they must educate the West in the merits of their enterprise.[41]

The reason, though, that all of this economic vitality around the blending of Islam and capitalism is so important for the West to take note of is that it reveals so much about the nature of the new middle class that is driving this growth, and is in turn growing ever larger and more influential. Some members of this new middle class are the children of the old *haute bourgeoisie*, their families tied to large, venerable industries and the type of state patronage that the West is familiar with. But a far larger percentage—and here is the key—comes from the provincial and lower social classes. These sons and daughters of the poor and the provinces who have made the jump to the middle class have done so by accepting the requirements of modern economies and latching on to the economic realities that define modernism. They have embraced the rules of the market, responding to its incentives, and are guided in their decisions by the desire to serve their economic interests. So energetic is their commitment to the capitalist credo that their activities now account for most of the real economic growth in the region. The consumerism of the general population is largely the result of their handiwork.[42] Ambitious and resourceful, they fill the ranks of the professionals, the entrepreneurs, the corporate businessmen, and the traders. It is they who have established for the next generation a new economic model of the good life here on Earth.

The interests that this economy is creating, and the ties with the global community that it is forging, offer ample opportunities for engaging this "critical middle" that has come to be the center of gravity in one Muslim-majority society after another. In coming years, that middle is only going to get bigger, and richer: In 2007, GDP grew at an annual rate of around 6.1 percent in the Muslim countries of Southeast Asia (Indonesia and Malaysia) and the Arab countries of the Persian Gulf rim (followed by robust but slightly lower rates in Egypt, Pakistan, and Turkey). Europe and the United States, by comparison, grew at around 2.2 percent that year. In 1970, only 4 percent of the professionals in Malaysia were Muslim; today, that figure is closer to 40 percent. Since 1970, Malaysia has emerged as a success story of globalization, one of the largest exporters of electronic goods to the United States and an integral part of the global supply chain for the computer and electronics industries. Globalization and rising middle classes with big wallets—and a continuing interest in living as observant Muslims—have gone hand in hand.

The crucial aspect of this "critical middle" that is difficult for those in the West to grasp is that for this population, Islam is a powerful supporter of the drive to modernity. The great majority of Muslims think that Islam improves their lives. They want heaven later, and wealth in the meantime—and think that handling the latter well can help lead to the former. As Pope Benedict learned at the Blue Mosque, Islamic piety is not only about things that the West fears; it is also about things that the West appreciates. This distinctive blending of Islamic values and economic vitality is a crucial development in the Muslim world that should shape our approach to building better relations with the region.

Will the Muslim businessmen of the coming century lead a capitalist revolution much as Protestant burghers did in Holland four centuries ago? We do not know yet, but it is possible. The mayor of the booming town of Kayseri in central Turkey, where many of the so-called Islamically conscious "Anatolian Tigers" come from, thinks so. "I had read Weber," he says, referring to the German sociologist who first credited Calvinist ethic for the rise of capitalism. The idea of "how Calvinists work hard, save money and then reinvest it into business" seems, he continued, "very similar to what was happening in Kayseri."[43] Reflecting on the words of the Prophet hanging in the Blue Mosque, the mayor of Hacilar, a deeply religious little boom town not too far from Kayseri, explained the business activity around him saying "opening a factory in Islam is a sort of prayer."[44] If there is going to be genuine capitalism in the Middle East, in the broad sense of the term as experienced by the West—where individuals working through markets account for growth and prosperity—it will come from these pious businessmen and not from state-led initiatives and the state-sponsored economic elites associated with them who have for much too long ruled the Middle Eastern economies.

If European history is any guide only this robust breed of capitalism will bring true modernizing change to the Muslim world. The modern world was invented by children of the Reformation, but it was not their puritanical and intolerant faith that transformed the world—far from it—but rather trade and commerce that took hold in unlikely backward corners of Europe like Scotland, home to the early Industrial Revolution and the likes of Adam Smith, David Hume, and Sir Walter Scott.[45]

If the Middle East is to be properly integrated into the global economy, turn to democracy, give women their rights, embrace values that transcend cultural divides, and keep extremism at bay, then it too will have to be transformed by the capitalist revolution. The most decisive battle for the future in the region will not be the one over religion—in which, as we shall see, the tide has already turned against extremism. Nor will it be the growing battle over political rights, as hopeful as that is. The key struggle that will pave the way for the decisive defeat of extremism and to social liberalization will be the battle to free the markets. If that battle is won by private-sector business leaders and the rising middle class tied to them, then progress with political rights will follow.

Even in Iran, the potential for opening, and an economically led entry into the world community, is strong. As the election protests vividly revealed Iran has a dynamic civil society. Women's right activists, students, labor unionists, journalists, bloggers, artists, and intellectuals have made up the backbone of the struggle for reform and continue valiantly to resist oppression, bad laws, and arbitrary rule, and their voices could be heard loudly and clearly during the election. During the presidency of the reformist Muhammad Khatami between 1997 and 2005, they seemed to hold the promise of being able to liberate Iran from theocratic oppression and set it on course for true democracy. That campaign and the effort to elect the reform candidate Hossein Moussavi faltered, for reasons that we will explore further later, but those who launched those movements are still around, and they still believe in freedom. The civil society that they represent grew in tandem with the private sector, relying on its economic health to energize demands for rights. For that energy to nudge Iran decisively in the direction of change and openness, private-sector dynamism must be reignited.

When China opened to the world, human rights and political reform were hardly the goals Communist leaders had in mind. In fact, booming China all too often seemed to feel that its success made it free to ignore outside pressures to yield to its dissidents, change its laws, or move in the direction of pluralism and democracy. Whatever change came to China in the form of gradual legal reform and greater civil society activism owed much to pressure from investors and traders. Deepening ties with global business forced China to change many laws and practices—to adopt what the American geostrategic writer Thomas P. M. Barnett calls the transparent modern "rule sets" of the world's developed and well-integrated "core."[46] None of the changes that China grudgingly made—often in response to embarrassing crises like scares over the SARS virus and tainted toothpaste and pet-food exports—was explicitly political in nature. Yet they represented significant progress nonetheless.

A legal system and bureaucracy forced to change in one area becomes more receptive to change in other areas as well. Fueling the activities of the Middle East's rising middle class, and working to bring the economies of the region more fully into the web of globalization, can push the status quo to the tipping point where national leaders have no choice but to embrace change and try to make the most of it. That is the key first step toward liberalization of the political systems. The road to human rights, social freedoms, and democracy runs through business growth and economic progress.

If we were to ponder how change in Iran can change the Middle East (as it did once before in 1979), and how the specter of a rising Iran could guide the region around it in a new direction we would have to conclude that things will go right when developments inside Iran align with the main trend that is afoot in the region. The strong interests of the West are in seeing Iran line up with, not against, the logic of economic change; to yield to a rising business sector and a new middle class that would change politics and religion and then amplify the same trend in the Arab world. But we are not going to be able to help Iranians get there, or leaders in the other critical nations of the region, until economics becomes as important to our thinking about policy as hard power. It is time to think less about civilizations clashing, and to recover the great insights—which lie very close to the foundations of classical liberalism and modern political thought—about the transformative power of markets and commerce. Commerce, as David Hume and the other great minds of the Scottish Enlightenment liked to point out, softens manners and makes a politics based on reason and deliberation, rather than fighting and romanticism, far more imaginable.

Through the course of this book, we will probe into the different prospects and challenges for the rising middle class in the countries whose fate is most pivotal for realizing this future in the Middle

East. Some, such as Dubai and Turkey, are forging ahead at astonishing speed, while others are caught in a vise of internal contradictions, such as Iran and Pakistan. Coming to appreciate why the stories of the countries are so different, and understanding the distinctive perspective and desires of this new class will also require delving into the history of subjugation and misguided reform that has held the capitalist potential of the region down for so long. Only by developing a fresh perspective on the struggles of the region—so different from the compelling but fundamentally flawed story of an intractable clash of civilizations—will the West understand how best to engage with these countries in order to precipitate reform and vastly improved relations.

CHAPTER 2

THE WORLD
ACCORDING TO DUBAI

The Mall of the Emirates is like no other shopping center in the world. A sprawling maze of marble and glass, it covers six and a half million square feet, catering to hordes of European tourists in T-shirts and shorts joined by throngs of Arab, Iranian, Uzbek, and Pakistani shoppers dressed in everything from Western attire to full *hejab*. Mall goers mingle in posh restaurants and a labyrinth of high-end boutiques amid jaw-dropping attractions like an indoor ski slope contained in a shiny tube that juts futuristically off the building into the sky. The overall effect is audacious and surreal; the kind of shock-and-awe mix of consumerism and entertainment for which Las Vegas is famous.

This Rhode Island–sized emirate, one of the seven nestled on the eastern edge of the Arabian Peninsula that form the United Arab Emirates (UAE), is a land of superlatives. Dubai boasts not only the world's tallest building but also its two biggest shopping malls, its largest airport, largest arched bridge, largest man-made archipelago, largest man-made harbor, and largest theme park, which is twice the size of Disney World. Until the global recession of 2008 slowed its stride, 80 percent of the world's water-dredging equipment was in use in Dubai, as were a fifth of the tallest cranes on earth. This emirate seeks to set world standards for luxury and consumerism, to be first in everything, especially the kinds of things the West appreciates.

The world's best-known architects have been testing the limits of their imaginations in Dubai, vying to define how we will live in the future.[1] Their designs include plans for innovative green buildings, such as a pair of rotating towers that can change shape and make energy in the process, as well as designs for dancing towers, twisting towers, towers made in the shape of a wheel, and an opera house built to look like a waterfall.

With the world in the grip of recession Dubai's growth all but ended, but in 2006 and 2007 it posted a dizzying 11 percent growth rate. Between 1995 and 2008 its GDP grew by 267 percent, average per capita income rose 126 percent, exports expanded by 575 percent, and the population grew by 186 percent. By 2005, five years ahead of time, the emirate had already met or surpassed ambitious goals it had set back in 2000 for growth of GDP, income per capita, and expansion of the service sector by 2010.

Nine years ago, the eastern edge of Dubai, where the financial district now sits, was desert; the four-lane road stretching from the city center simply vanished into the sand. Today, it is the world's largest construction site. At one manic point half a million laborers were working on an estimated $300 billion worth of building projects including towering skyscrapers such as the Bourj Dubai, which will be the world's tallest, and an entire financial city, along with hotels, shopping malls, and residential quarters. Nor is this the only large-scale construction project. Dubai expanded on the same scale in every direction, building a media city, a sport city, and an Internet city as well as health care, finance, and education centers. The scale and striking look of the physical transformation of the city is astounding, with a skyline that competes with those of New York and Shanghai; a world-class airport, served by the first-rate Emirate Airlines, and mega-sized Jebel Ali high-tech port; as well as more malls per capita than anywhere else in the world. In 2007 "Little Dubai," writes the author Afshin Molavi, attracted "more tourists than the whole of India, more shipping vessels than Singapore, and more foreign capital than many European countries."[2]

Seemingly overnight, Dubai became a magnet for American investors and business. The energy giant Halliburton moved its headquarters to Dubai. Leading Wall Street financial houses along with a slew of well-known American law firms, media outlets, corporations, and universities all set up shop in the city, in addition to a plethora of European and Asian firms. Twenty of the world's top twenty-five banks opened operations in the Dubai International Financial Center (DIFC), which for a time became one of the most expensive real estate markets in the world. Housing prices in the city rose 42 percent in the first three months of 2008 alone.[3]

Dubai may appear an extreme case of the manifestation of booming oil wealth, and it's true enough that the emirate profited greatly from the rise of oil prices in recent years. The petroleum-rich monarchies of the Persian Gulf, Saudi Arabia, Oman, Qatar, Kuwait, and the rest of the UAE earned more than $1.5 trillion from oil and gas exports between 2001 and 2007. Almost a third of that figure, $407 billion, came in 2007 alone—more than the combined exports of Brazil, India, Poland, and Turkey that year.[4] The oil princedoms may well accrue trillions more when oil prices inevitably rise again. By some estimates oil earnings will reach as high as $9 trillion by 2020.[5] At the height of the oil boom wealthy monarchies announced $1.9 trillion worth of building projects, a construction renaissance from the Oman's Arabian Sea shores to Saudi Arabia's Red Sea coast.[6] Nowhere was the building more manic than in Dubai, which moved faster and took more risks, assuming a debt load that by 2008 was worrisome: 148 percent of GDP.[7] Dubai's growth, though, has not been primarily fueled by oil production.

In fact, the growth was achieved even as the emirate's oil production shrank. Dubai pumps just a quarter of what it did in 1992. The share of GDP that the oil industry accounts for is down to barely 5 percent today from 43 percent in 1992. Services, including tourism, finance, real estate, education, media, and transportation, now account for more than 80 percent of GDP.[8]

Who would have thought Muslims had this in them: to reach so high and to condone, let alone revel in, so much capitalism? In 2005 the Arab world, with a population about the same size as America's, accounted for a measly 4 percent of world trade (5.5 percent of global exports, 90 percent of which was oil).[9] Its unemployment rates stand among the world's highest and per capita GDP is slipping to 1980s levels as its vast numbers of young people face bleak prospects. Dubai has emphatically bucked that trend. And a key reason is that Dubai has pioneered in offering a winning formula for blending Islam with capitalism.

Dubai has become the preferred imagined future—the dreamland—of the Muslim world, the most talked about and most favored destination for Muslim tourists and businessmen, and where most Muslims claim they would like to live, other than in their own country. They have been attracted to the city's distinctive merger of a relaxed social scene with a thriving nightlife and respect for a certain degree of Islamic decorum.

An Arab friend, a businessman who travels often to Dubai for work and even more often for pleasure, told me over dinner one night about how much he had enjoyed the experience of noontime prayer that day at the opulent Jumeirah Mosque, which sits in the shadow of massive high-rises in the city's upscale new financial district. He said, "If you are going to be a good Muslim, pray to God that you live in Dubai. The mosques are luxurious, immaculately clean, air-conditioned, and fitted with high-tech gadgets that make even ablutions pain-free. It is a pleasure to pray here. In Dubai you stay at five-star hotels and pray at five-star mosques." He then put a fine point on Dubai's appeal: "I like this place because I can shop, eat, enjoy luxury, and be a good Muslim too." Dubai allows Muslims to be Western-style consumerists, while still feeling true to their faith.

Beyond the glitzy high rises and the high-flying life style, Dubai is still very much an Islamic city, with laws against public display of affection between the sexes and scant clothing. Mosques dot the city's many neighborhoods and the call for prayer punctuates daily life, especially away from the hubbub of the tourist attractions and the business districts. The local Islam is a variation of the puritanical Islam of the Arabian Peninsula, but Dubai is also home to many other forms of Islam belonging to the many Muslim populations that now work and live in the city. The dream of becoming a business hub in the image of the West has ironically turned Dubai into a microcosm of the Muslim world.

The rise of Dubai has not only transformed the geography of global business; more important, it has transformed the mental map of the Muslim world. Behind the showmanship and glitz, Dubai is aiming to become the Singapore of the Middle East—and even to surpass Singapore on the world stage. To many Muslims who have worked and played in Dubai, or who admire its accomplishments from afar, it represents a new kind of progress, one that impresses the West but does not depend on secularism. The ability to stay true to Islamic values even while pursuing capitalist dreams is essential to its success. The Dubai experience builds on similar experiments in Malaysia and Turkey, where development has also relied on releasing the entrepreneurial energies of the new and pious middle class, through a blending of the values of Islam and capitalism. But Dubai has been more ambitious and grown faster. Its ambition and accomplishments forcefully demonstrate the economic potential of the critical middle in the Muslim world. To Muslims, Dubai's growth represents an enormously appealing new model of development, and the surging popularity of all things Dubai among the Muslim world's rising middle class is a striking testament to the potential for dramatic progress in the region. The tiny emirate's success could not have been more unlikely.

———————

Dubai's story begins in 1831 when the al-Maktoum family, the emirate's current rulers, took control of what was then nothing more than a poor, desolate village that barely survived on fishing, pearl diving, and trade. Those in Dubai learned early on that to get by they would need to survive on commerce, but the village had little to offer the world other than its location at the crossroads of the Persian Gulf and the Indian Ocean. Astute emirs realized that if they refrained from taxing traders heavily and sheltered them from the wrath of their own governments, perhaps those traders would find it expedient to set up shop in the little emirate. Generations of Indian and Iranian merchants who did business in the city then helped Dubai not only grow its economy, but develop a deep appreciation for free trade along with the necessary tolerance for diversity it requires.[10] All these years later, Dubai's vibrant nightlife, so popular with Muslim and European visitors, is every bit as important to its accomplishments as its economic planning.[11]

The emirate's economic growth took off, though, largely due to its enlightened ruler. Fifty years ago, Dubai was still a backwater town of mud houses and Bedouin tents, of camel caravans and wooden dhows that left for ports around the Indian Ocean basin.[12] In 1959 the emir, Sheikh Rashid al-Maktoum, borrowed money from Kuwait to dredge the narrow creek that was the emirate's only access to the Gulf in order to create a harbor for large boats. He built wharves and warehouses, roads and schools, daring to envision Dubai as a major port city. Sheikh Rashid was a humble tribal ruler, a man of the desert with little experience of the world beyond. But he was a doer, a ruler with a vision and the determination to realize it, and he was quick to change laws and regulations to woo merchants to his town.

An old Iranian merchant, veteran of many decades of trading in Dubai, told me of an exemplary experience with the able emir. In the 1960s, my interlocutor and some of his fellow Iranian merchants decided to build an Iran Club in Dubai. It was important to their business, and would attract more of their kind to the city. They bought the land where they thought a main road would be passing, but once the building was up, they learned that the British engineers in charge of the road were planning to site it elsewhere. The merchants formed a delegation and went to see Sheikh Rashid at his house, where he used to hold court. Local grandees and petitioners alike would sit shoulder to shoulder around a large room, sip tea and eat dates as they waited their turn to speak with the ruler about their concerns. The Iranians joined the local petitioners, drank several cups of tea and moved to chairs ever closer to the emir. When it was their turn, they told Sheikh Rashid about their problem, and explained that with the road going elsewhere their club would be neglected. The Sheikh got up and told the congregation to stay put until he got back. He then called for his car and headed to the construction site with the Iranians in tow. Inspecting the site, he asked about the road, and then summoned the British engineers in order to tell them that it would go where the Iranian merchants wanted it to, and that was that. Merchants brought business to Dubai; catering to their needs was job one.

Sheikh Rashid was unique among Middle Eastern rulers. At a time when better-known Arab leaders were preoccupied with grand social schemes and lofty political goals, he saw himself as a businessman. Echoing Calvin Coolidge, he would famously say "the business of Dubai is business."[13] The ruler of Dubai today is Sheikh Rashid's son, Sheikh Muhammad bin Rashid al-Maktoum, affectionately known as "Sheikh Mo" to the many foreign workers and businessmen who live in his emirate. Sheikh Muhammad has built on his father's vision since he inherited the emir's title in 1990, also running Dubai like a business, and fashioning himself as the "CEO Sheikh."[14]

That is the model that served Hong Kong and Singapore well, and Dubai has invested heavily in it. Sheikh Muhammad saw the accelerating globalization that took off in the 1990s as a golden opportunity. The Persian Gulf region was then in a recession; oil prices had tumbled in the mid-1980s, and along with them national and individual incomes, and he looked to the world economy to help Dubai escape the slump. Expanding world trade was changing the pattern of international business by connecting new markets, and that was opening up important gaps in transportation, logistics, and financial services that Dubai could fill.

The emirate got another boost after 9/11 when money that traditionally left the Middle East for the safety of Western financial markets began staying closer to home. New financial restrictions, combined with anger at Western policies, made New York or London less attractive to Muslim money, and that was good for local investments. A hub such as Dubai served an important need in a region that was accruing wealth, but where conflicts and political tensions combined with rickety infrastructure, bureaucratic inertia and red tape impeded the regular flow of business. Money escaping political troubles and economic stagnation in Iran and Pakistan was attracted to Dubai, as was a good deal of Saudi and Russian investment, along with money from China and India. All that money coming in generated demand for financial services and large volumes of trade, and soon turned Dubai into a regional investment hub. Dubai sits between the major financial centers of Europe and Asia—London and Singapore—perfectly placed to be a crossroads between Asia and Europe.

Though so much focus in the literature on globalization has been on the so-called BRIC economies (Brazil, Russia, India and China; or Big Rapidly Industrializing Countries), the prospects for fuller integration of the Gulf region into the global economy are also vital to understand. Globalization is seen largely as a tale of dissipating American economic might and the rise of China, with the pivotal relationship being between China and America, what the historian Niall Ferguson calls "Chimerica."[15] But that giant West-East axis is now intersecting with regional economies in all directions and increasingly the flow of business is through Dubai.

Just as Hong Kong and Singapore developed as entrepôts for a rising Asia, the emirate is positioning itself at the center of a rising Middle East and South Asia, a region of some 2.2 billion people with a combined GDP of $2.5 trillion, from Egypt to Iran to India. There is plenty of money in this region and Dubai has figured out the way to tap into it. Here too, growing trade is happening in a region with many insular economies, limited infrastructure, and underdeveloped financial markets. War has all but ended Beirut's ambitions to be a regional economic center, and Mumbai is prisoner to its debilitating poverty, sagging infrastructure, and big and bad government. Consider the fact that Mumbai's Jawaharlal Nehru Trust port, which handles 60 percent of India's container traffic, has berths for only nine cargo vessels as compared to seventy-one at Dubai's Jebel Ali port, which can accommodate 14 million containers and relieve ships of their cargo four containers at a time using state-of-the-art "quad-lift" cranes. Its rivals' failings have been Dubai's good fortune.

Connecting the many economies of the region to one another and then to the larger world economy, and providing them with critical financial and logistical services in the process, presents Dubai with the opportunity to generate wealth from trade at an unprecedented scale in the region. The author Robert Kaplan argues that the Indian Ocean will be at the heart of world trade in the twenty-first century. Half of the world containers on tankers and "70 percent of the total traffic of petroleum products passes through the Indian Ocean from the Middle East to the Pacific," and those numbers are only expected to grow further in the coming decades.[16] Dubai has tied its future to that trade.

Dubai's ports can particularly facilitate greater trade in the region through the reexport business—which is importing goods from different places with the specific aim of exporting them to other places (only Hong Kong and Singapore currently reexport more). Dubai serves as the transit point for large volumes of goods that must flow into and out of this large zone of two billion people. The Persian Gulf region, which by some estimates is the world's sixteenth-largest economic zone, is estimated by some projections to be the sixth-largest zone by 2030.

Equally important, Dubai provides trade and financial services that are otherwise unavailable to Iran, Pakistan, the Arab world, Central Asia, East Africa, and the Caucasus. These economies are not as large as those of those of the BRICs (to say nothing of the larger Western and Asian economies), but there is plenty of money to be made in building ties among them as well as between them and the larger global economies. That is what Dubai has been doing. In the words of Afshin Molavi, a long-time observer of Dubai's development, what has emerged is a new "Silk Road"[17] that begins in the West and runs through Dubai to Mumbai, Kuala Lumpur, and Shanghai, with many other large and small stops along the way, and with detours north and south.

The growing significance of the Persian Gulf to the emerging global economy is also evident in the increasingly prominent role that the region's so-called sovereign wealth funds and private investment pools have played. Eighteen months after America rebuffed Dubai Ports World, Wall Street turned to Persian Gulf investors to shore up its flagging banks as they struggled to make it through the subprime mortgage crisis. Abu Dhabi Investment Authority's $7.5 billion investment in Citigroup and $9 billion investment in England's Barclays Bank, as well as Dubai's purchase of 2.2 percent of the German Deutsche Bank and 20 percent of the NASDAQ stock exchange, declared loud and clear that an important axis of the world economy now ran through the Persian Gulf.

That axis now also runs in the other direction into the heart of Asia as well. Sovereign funds such as Kuwait Investment Authority and private funds such as the Saudi-based Kingdom Holding were among the top investors in the initial public offering of the Commercial Industrial Bank of China. "Chimerica" now has a Persian Gulf detour. Nor is it only banking and finance that confirm the Gulf's rising prominence. New York's Chrysler Building is an Abu Dhabi–owned property, and during a recent high-profile trip to India, Dubai's Sheikh Muhammad signed a $20 billion deal to create three townships on 40,000 acres in India's Maharashtra state.[18] Dubai along with other sovereign funds and private investors is making similar inroads into Pakistan, the Middle East, and Africa. Global recession will reduce these investments for a time, but they will inevitably resume.

As important as Dubai's role as an economic crossroads is the manner in which its economic flourishing has been achieved, by a pro-capitalist, public-private partnership. The idea of the state taking the facilitation of capitalism to be its mandate is a novelty in the Middle East, and what truly makes Dubai modern is not its consumerism or its construction boom, but its embrace of the idea of the capitalism-friendly state—the good *dirigisme* of Singapore.

This overturns a long history in the Middle East of state control and disdain for pure capitalism. Many states—Iran, Egypt, and Syria come to mind—have sought to protect their societies from capitalism, leading to a legacy of nationalizing industries, heavy taxing and regulation of the private sector, and the instilling of fear of foreign capital, trade, and businessmen in the citizenry. If these states have occasionally let the private sector take wing, it has been within strict limits and only so that the state could skim off revenue from business profits. Other states have sought to emulate capitalist growth but have smothered private business in state control, seeing businessmen as decidedly junior partners. Turkey under Ataturk, the Shah's Iran, and Saudi Arabia all fit this model, not actually disdaining capitalism, but not allowing business-men to operate freely.

Over the past two decades, in other regions when such constraints on capitalist development were loosened, impressive growth followed. For decades after its independence India was fearful of capitalism and given to socialism. When the country embraced markets and privati-zation wholeheartedly in the 1990s, it prospered greatly. Across Asia, Latin America, and Eastern Europe, shrinking states and growing pri-vate sectors transformed economies and societies in the same period. The Middle East has yet to make the transition, but Dubai may be lead-ing the way.

With Lee Kwan Yew's Singapore in mind, Dubai has reinvented the concept of Arab government, building an effective business infrastruc-ture, with a proper regulatory environment. The government bureau-cracy has been streamlined, and the financial markets have been opened to foreign ownership. The government has also created free-trade zones and industrial parks, and laid miles of fiber-optic cable, all of which has made it easier for businesses, both homegrown and foreign, to open up shop and prosper. In Dubai, a phone line or a passport can be obtained in a day—whereas in the rest of the Arab world such routine services take weeks and months. The Executive Office—the government of Dubai—has invested heavily in training its personnel and enhancing efficiency in managing relations with business.

Most of the countries of the Middle East have yet to accept the notion that the government must not stand in the way of capitalist growth, or try to make growth happen on its own in a top-down, state-driven fashion. Dubai can help the region come to believe in the value of unfettered entrepreneurship.

———

Dubai's boom has been driven primarily by large conglomerates that are government financed but not government run. Dubai Holdings, Dubai Ports World, Emirates Airlines, and construction giants Emaar and Nakheel (which recently refurbished the historic Hotel Washington in downtown D.C., just a block from the White House) have led the charge and emerged as world-class corporations.

The stunning 2,257-foot-tall Bourj Dubai is a project of the government-backed construction giant, Emaar, which along with Dubai Holdings and Nakheel has dominated the construction and development market in Dubai. Emaar was a trailblazer in the develop-ment market, eventually building entire new residential neighborhoods. The company began offering mortgages to buyers, and developed a spe-cialty in selling dream properties before they were built; the proceeds financed the actual construction. From those early beginnings, it grew to claim some of Dubai's largest marquee projects, including huge chunks of the two-square-kilometer new downtown around the Bourj Dubai.

Emaar's market capitalization in 2008 made it one of the world's largest real estate companies, and as such, it no longer looked for growth opportunities in Dubai alone. In 2006, Emaar raised $680 million to build a new city on Saudi Arabia's Red Sea coast sixty miles north of Jed-dah, the gateway to the Islamic holy city of Mecca.[19]

Muhammad Ali Alabbar is the chairman of Emaar, and his rags-to-riches life story is also the story of Dubai's renaissance. He is a standout representation of the aspirations, and enormous potential, of the new breed of Islamic capitalists, rising from rural, lower class roots. Alabbar comes from humble Bedouin origins, the oldest of twelve children. His father was a fisherman and his earliest memories are of subsistence-level living in a tent made of palm fronds. But Alabbar was a promising stu-dent and won a government scholarship to study in America, attend-ing business school in Seattle and returning to Dubai in 1981. For the next decade he held various government jobs, as a banker at the Central Bank of UAE, and as financier on government development projects. He was ambitious and hard-working, and quickly moved up the ladder, eventually being appointed head of the government-owned al-Khaleej Investments in Singapore. His years in Singapore at the height of that city-state's boom in the 1980s left a deep impression on Alabbar, and he returned to Dubai convinced that it too could be a global city if it modeled itself on Singapore.

Alabbar was fortunate that Sheikh Muhammad, then the crown prince, shared his vision, and Alabbar's star rose once Sheikh Muhammad became emir and led Dubai on its transformation. He was appointed head of the Department of Economic Development, and as a reward for his successes in that role Sheikh Muhammad gave him land. Alabbar began building and, as the saying goes, the rest is history. Alabbar has been a close advisor to Sheikh Muhammad, and a key force behind the administrative reforms that Dubai undertook in order to follow where Singapore had led.

In recent years Alabbar has led Emaar into a wider range of businesses. The company now has financial holdings that focus on mortgage markets, and is also a mover on the Islamic finance scene. Alabbar is vice-chairman of the Dubai Islamic Insurance and Reinsurance Company, and Emaar has turned to Islamic bonds to finance its projects. The brand most closely associated with Dubai's ambition and audacity, the builder of its new financial center, is also a brand that ties the glitz and glamour of the new Dubai to the Islamic sensibilities of the rising Muslim middle classes. Oil money and foreign investment money, coming out of Iran, Saudi Arabia, Russia, and Pakistan, finance Emaar's grand projects, but so do Islamic bonds that mobilize the savings of the religiously conscious. Alabbar and Emaar are superior examples of how a more robust capitalism can flourish in the Middle East. But the Dubai model is not without its limits and flaws.

One of the most pressing questions these days in the Arab world is whether Dubai is truly a good model for growth in the wider region. For one thing, Dubai's growth may have relied too much on construction—"build it and they will come" may become "we did but no one showed up." The financial crisis of 2008 hit Dubai's real estate market hard, with property prices dropping by as much as 30 percent while the costs of financing new projects and insuring that financing skyrocketed.[20] Many businesses have failed and many development projects have been scrapped or delayed.

The emirate's rapid growth caused worrying inflation, into double digits. That pushed up building expenses, property prices, and the cost of living, and made labor unrest a growing concern.[21] Dubai depends on cheap foreign labor mostly from India, Pakistan, and Bangladesh—young men who leave their families behind to live in cramped quarters on the outskirts of the city and work long hours for a few years before returning home. The government has talked of higher wages and labor-law reform, but resistance from businesses used to cheap and servile labor has stood in the way. Without reform, labor unrest may well come to plague Dubai's economy.

Dubai is also at risk due to the extremely high quotient of non-citizen foreigners of 202 nationalities who make up around 90 percent of its workforce, even after the global financial crisis has shrunk their numbers. Dubai is in no way a normal society. In 2008 out of 2 million residents only 180,000 were natives, and most of them worked for the government. Dubai may not have state-run factories, but it does have a public workforce of 70,000, and the natives hold the political power and benefit from government largesse. Education and health care are free for them, as are a host of other entitlements—ranging from handouts to newlyweds and new parents to job quotas and consumer subsidies—designed to nurture their loyalty to their government. The foreigners do all the work, and make plenty of money—even manual laborers make more money than they would back home—but have few political rights—no right to representation, organization, or protest, and few legal rights. Dubai is a place where many people do business but only the native few live as actual citizens. Dubai is also 75 percent male.[22] This is a model that works for Dubai, but cannot be replicated in larger states of the Middle East and South Asia.

Dubai is in a neighborhood that while advantageous in many ways, is also dangerous. Close to warring Afghanistan and imploding Pakistan, a stone's throw from al-Qaeda's lair, and only ninety miles from Iran, the emirate is vulnerable to collateral damage should war ever break out between America and Iran. War talk and fear of terrorism have benefited Dubai thus far, by impelling billions of investment dollars to flow there from Iran and Pakistan, but actual war or terror attacks will undermine the peace and security necessary for economic growth. Tourism and finance do not thrive amid war. A few stray Iranian Shehab rockets lobbed across the Strait of Hormuz will send tourists as well as banking and other businesses home.

All this may put a cap on Dubai's growth and could open the door to competitors. Dubai has the first-mover advantage, but staying ahead of the pack will become more difficult as time goes on. Already Abu Dhabi and Qatar are nipping at Dubai's heels, spending generously on infrastructure and construction in the course of their own drives to become transport, finance, tourism, and education hubs. These energy-rich competitors are also laying down new roads, putting up gleaming high-rises, building large airports served by world-class home-country airlines, and writing business-friendly laws and regulations to woo bankers and investment houses. How many entrepôts can thrive within driving distance of one another? The challenge for Dubai is to stay number one in this game, to remain the place where the global economy meets regional trade—the grand central station on the new Silk Road. But with the global financial crisis slowing its stride, it will be difficult to keep oil-rich challengers at bay. They have little need to worry about the vagaries of the market.

Dubai has its advantages, but lacks the deep pockets of Abu Dhabi and Qatar. Then again, the kind of oil wealth those emirates possess does not typically make for efficiency and nimbleness—the need to "try harder" that set Dubai on its course in the first place. So perhaps Dubai will be able to out-hustle and out-compete its richer neighbors. But even if Dubai turns out to be a long-term success, it has limits as a model for the rest of the region. There are no signs that Egypt, Syria, Iran, or Pakistan is about to embrace its model. After all, Dubai is small, and has no bloated public-enterprise sector born of decades of wrongheaded stabs at state-run industrialization. Also, its capitalist renaissance has relied crucially on enlightened leadership that has not seen itself as threatened by the growth of independent business power. The leadership of these larger powerhouses of the region is not similarly enlightened. And even Dubai's leadership has its limits regarding openness.

Dubai's media city, for example, was hugely popular with the new breed of independent Pakistani satellite TV channels that mushroomed during the early phase of General Pervez Musharraf's rule. The TV boom was widely touted as important to changing the cultural climate in Pakistan after 9/11. Independent outlets such as GEO or ARY (the TV arm of the Dubai-based Pakistani gold and real-estate conglomerate, ARY Holdings) chose Dubai because the facilities were state of the art and also fairly close to their home market and source of news. But in 2007 Dubai provided independent Pakistani TV with no protection when General Musharraf declared a state of emergency. Under pressure from Islamabad, Dubai authorities took all these stations off the air, casting a pall over the prospect of Dubai's becoming a regional media hub.

Critics argue that Dubai may well fail in the end, and that decades from now all of its building bonanza may amount to no more than white-elephant projects, nothing more than a pipedream.[23]

Nonetheless, even if other countries in the region cannot import the Dubai model in its totality, they are learning a good deal from it. One thing is sure. When the dust of the 2008 economic crisis settles, Dubai will have achieved two things: the infrastructure for doing world-class business will have proven invaluable to future development, and the emirate's boom will have done a great service in instilling capitalism in the Muslim mind-set. Dubai has shown that growth is possible if the right regulatory environment is created, administrative reform is undertaken, and a spirit of public-private partnership is fostered (rather than public-on-private predation). People in the region who visit Dubai return home wondering why their governments can't issue passports in a day or provide clean mosques and schools, better airports, airlines, and roads, and above all better government. That has created a "Dubai effect" around the region as governments seek to improve day-to-day performance at the small tasks of public administration, even if the leaders are not committed to an overall economic transformation. The effect can be seen in government bureaucracies across the Arab world, from passport offices to tourism boards. And you also run into it, happily, when you approach airline ticket counters, hotel desks, and bank lobbies, all of which in Arab lands are likely to be branches of the state.

These days, delegations of bureaucrats from around the region, and even beyond, travel to Dubai to learn about best business practices and how to develop and implement administrative reform. A favorite stop on their tour is the Dubai School of Government. Sheikh Muhammad's office set up the DSG in collaboration with Harvard's Kennedy School of Government in order to train Dubai's bureaucrats according to the global standards required of those who would oversee a global city. On one of the days I was visiting DSG, there was a group of Libyan government officials listening to lectures about the latest trends in public management. The Libyans were getting ready for more business as their country was coming out of isolation. They were not talking of becoming Dubai, but they did want to learn how to run their own shop more efficiently.

Indian and Pakistani doctors, engineers, businessmen, and financial-services workers have applied methods and technologies they encountered in Dubai to the Mumbai or Karachi stock exchanges and hospitals and factories in Chennai or Lahore. Even foremen and manual laborers go back to India and Pakistan knowledgeable in new construction techniques and systems of work planning. In time, lessons from Dubai may become the seeds of wider change.

Debating the longevity of what Dubai has achieved and how much farther it can go misses the larger point. Whether Dubai does or does not become Singapore, or is itself the ideal model for development in the region, Dubai has already proven something that is more important. It has shown that Muslims are ready to engage the world economy. They can be eager capitalists aiming to excel and prosper. Dubai shows that the enthusiasm for Islam need not mean opposition to thriving business. If trouble on Wall Street has robbed Dubai of some of its luster, the point should not be lost that this is because the little emirate bought

THE WORLD ACCORDING TO DUBAI

wholeheartedly into the promise of the global economy and so vigorously embraced capitalism. Dubai's economic pains are proof of how tightly tied its economy is to that of the rest of the world.

Another key way in which Dubai is instructive about the potential for wider capitalist growth and accompanying political liberalization in the region is the light it throws on Iran. A close look at the nature of extensive ties between Dubai and Iran, and the extent of Iranian money flowing into Dubai, speaks volumes about the inclinations of a vast community of Iranians to break free from the anticapitalist fetters of the Islamic regime, and the pressures the regime will inevitably face to allow them to do so.

————

There is an old joke in Dubai. One year there was drought. The emir asked all the residents to pray for wet weather, and it poured monsoon in India and Pakistan. So the government clarified its call, asking foreign residents not to pray, and emphasizing that it wished only "locals" to pray. Then the rain fell in Iran.

There are no hard estimates of how many Iranians are in Dubai, but you do not need to look far to conclude that there are many. A good portion—maybe as many as half—of Dubai's native population are of Iranian origin.[24] Rumor has it even the ruling al-Maktoum family has its origins in Iran's province of Baluchistan. When I travel to Dubai, it is not uncommon to hear government officials break into Persian in private. I have encountered ministry officials and equity-fund managers, all seemingly Arab, who wait till we are alone and then tell me, in Persian, of their Iranian roots. Estimates put the number of Iranian-passport holders in Dubai at 450,000; many more come and go as tourists and businessmen.[25] There are 11,500 Iranian students in UAE universities—the majority at the new American University of Dubai— and some 9,000 Iranian companies are registered at the Dubai Chamber of Commerce and Industry. The number is considerably higher if you count businesses that are not registered.[26] The financial downturn has reduced these numbers somewhat, and U.S. pressure combined with

Dubai's fear that Iranians may become too many has led the emirate
to try to trim their numbers and role in the economy. But Iranians in
terms of numbers and economic clout still loom large in Dubai.

Isolated as Iran is from the international economy, the Islamic
Republic has long looked to Dubai as its gateway to the world. Iranians
invest in Dubai, and trade with it, and through Dubai with the world.
They also visit Dubai for fun in droves, to shop and enjoy everyday plea-
sures not available in Iran. The Iranians in Dubai are of many kinds;
frontmen doing brisk business for the Revolutionary Guards; representatives of powerful state-run foundations and commercial interests; but
also merchants, traders, and professionals such as managers, doctors,
lawyers, and journalists. Some came to Dubai in the nineteenth century
to take advantage of lower taxes. Others left Iran in the early part of the
century when Reza Shah forced Iranian women to unveil. Still others
fled when drought and economic hardship made life difficult in southern Iran. A large exodus followed Khomeini's revolution, as professionals and businessmen escaped the tumult. Mahmoud Ahmadinejad's
election to the presidency in 2005 led to another surge as many Iranians bolted from his hard-line views at home and saber rattling, after a
decade of reformist politics and greater social freedoms.

Mehdi Amjad is perhaps the poster child for Iranian-born self-made
Dubai entrepreneurs. Only thirty years old and he was named 2008
Young Global Leader by the World Economic Forum. Born into a family of Iranian jewelers, Amjad charted a different course for himself. In
1995, barely out of his teens, he formed an IT company, al-Masa Holdings, which rapidly grew its market share across the Middle East, North
Africa, and Central Asia. With $450 million in annual sales in IT ser-
vices in 2004, Amjad turned to real estate, forming Omniyat (which
means "wishes" in Arabic). Since its formation, Omniyat has become a
real-estate giant, with $3 billion in projects under its belt in 2008.

Iranians like to say "Dubai is the best city in Iran." When the leg-
endary Iranian pop diva Googoosh—a singer who enjoys Elvis-like
popularity from the Persian Gulf to Central Asia—decided to break the
silence that living in Islamic Iran had demanded of her and sing for the

first time since the Revolution of 1979, she went to Dubai. Taking stock of the enthusiastic reception she received from large adoring crowds she said, "I feel as if I'm singing in my homeland to my own people."[27]

What the world denies Iran through economic sanctions finds its way into the Iranian market via Dubai and the other emirates. Around 80 percent of the UAE's imports are reexported, and since 1979, a good portion of that, now worth an estimated $3 to $5 billion dollars a year, has been going to Iran.[28] An Iranian IT manager once told me that when his company needs Internet routers, his buyer flies to Dubai with two empty suitcases first thing in the morning and the routers are installed the next day. Every night, picturesque wooden dhows set sail from loading docks in Dubai. They dart across the ninety-mile width of the Gulf not far inside the Strait of Hormuz, heading for hundreds of little piers—by some estimates there are more than seven hundred of them on the Iranian side.[29] The dhows carry everything from Carrier air conditioners to Dell computers, HP printers, Apple iPods and iPhones—quickly unlocked in Tehran by savvy technicians—to blue jeans, cosmetics, medicine, pirated DVDs, and construction materials.

Iran has also become a vital player in trade into Dubai. One night last year, I was strolling along the wharf in Deira, the old commercial center of Dubai. The area of the waterfront known as Port Saeed was chockablock with wooden dhows filled to the rim with boxes. Deira and its wooden dhows are a far cry from the state-of-the-art port at Jebel Ali with its seventy-one berths for large cargo ships and forest of gigantic modern cranes loading, unloading, and storing a sea of containers. But there was still ample business happening in Deira. A few shopkeepers were haggling with porters who were moving boxes on and off one of the dhows. I could hear Persian mixed with Arabic in their back and forth. I waited for a lull in the negotiations to ask one of the shopkeepers in Persian about how business got done at the old wharf. He told me that Deira was where all the shopkeepers got their wares, but there was not enough space on the wharf for all the dhows that import Dubai's needs. "I mean toothpaste and shaving cream, not big items," he said. So ships dock across the Persian Gulf in Iranian ports and wooden dhows haul their trade into Dubai.

"So is Iran now the offshore dock for Dubai?" I asked. "Exactly," he replied. "Without Iranian ports Dubai would choke." "What about Jebel Ali?" I asked. "The wait at Jebel Ali can be long, and plus it is suitable for large-ticket items, not for dried fruit or toothpaste." He explained that while Jebel Ali serves the whole region, importing goods that are then reexported; Deira still serves Dubai itself. "Shopkeepers like me don't have anything to do with Jebel Ali," he said "We get our supplies right here." Business had been so brisk, he added, that he had to "pay a premium to the dhow owner to get my supplies across the Gulf."

Dubai's non-oil trade with Iran was $8 billion in 2006, a 30 percent rise since 2004,[30] and these numbers do not capture all the dhow trade that goes on under the radar. And it is not only goods that come into Dubai from Iran, but also money. Billions of dollars leave Iran for Dubai every year, amounting, by some estimates, to the equivalent of a third of Iran's oil revenue. The estimated total of Iranian assets in Dubai is $300 billion.[31] Advertisements for Dubai real estate fill Tehran's billboards, and Iranians have bought plenty of apartments, buildings, and businesses in Dubai. Based on a survey of mortgages, banks estimate that some residential compounds in and around Dubai are mostly Iranian-owned.

Perhaps the most vital exchange from Iran to Dubai, though, is Dubai's voracious importing of Iran's rich natural-gas reserves. It takes a lot of energy to turn on the lights and run the cooling systems in Dubai's masses of new buildings. Water for the growing population and expanding golf courses depends on energy-intensive desalinization plants. Other sources are limited for Dubai. Much of the oil supply of oil-rich Abu Dhabi is committed to long-run contracts with Asian buyers. It is also cheaper to burn natural gas, and the largest gas reserves in the region are those of Qatar and Iran. That makes Iran crucial to Dubai's continued growth.

———

During the Bush administration America looked at Dubai as a "Riga listening post" for Iran; a modern-day equivalent to the Baltic city used for monitoring the Soviet Union. The American consulate in Dubai was staffed with Iran-watchers who sought to learn about Iran from the many Iranians who visit Dubai and, if opportunity arose, to help dissidents agitate against their government.[32] At the same time, the U.S. government saw little use for Iranian business activities in Dubai; they helped Iran work around international sanctions, the thinking went, so they had to be discouraged. And that was what the Treasury Department did, persuading many of Dubai's banks (local ones as well as branches of foreign ones) to sever ties with Iran.[33] But Iranian business in Dubai is not merely sanctions-busting by the Iranian government—far from it. The economic ties between Dubai and Iran are a vital means by which Dubai's capitalist fervor, liberal outlook, and openness to the world are being fostered in Iran.

Iranians in Dubai remain tied to their cities and hometowns in Iran, and small towns such as Lar and Lengeh in southern Iran have benefited from road construction, hospitals, and even airports paid for by native sons who have prospered in Dubai. The strong web of social and economic ties that binds Dubai to Iran is becoming thicker with time, and holds out great promise for building the momentum for loosening the Islamic regime's grip on the country. Dubai is a lifeline to the Iranians that the West must develop ties with. They are the force within their country who can bring about change. Dubai is where the Iranian private sector breathes and prospers. Dubai is not just where America can engage the emerging Muslim middle class; more important, it is where it can engage the all-important Iranian part of it.

CHAPTER 3

IRAN'S
PREDICAMENT

Iran is an enigma, a land of puzzling contradictions. It appears at once strong and weak. The ruling regime and many among its populace are exceedingly religious, yet secularism also has deep roots. Theocracy reigns supreme, yet tens of millions show up to vote and take to the streets and the internet to push for democracy. Iran is the one Middle Eastern country where fundamentalism actually rules, and yet the arts also flourish and serious political debate thrives. World-class scientists study space, split atoms, and clone, all under the watchful eyes of intolerant clerics who have imposed draconian laws on the society. Iran is simultaneously expanding its influence in the Middle East and isolating itself. The regime periodically flirts with rapprochement with the West, but then recoils, preferring to pull the mantle of fundamentalism around itself. The closer the West looks at Iran the more blurry its vision becomes. This is the one Muslim country that is at once closest to and yet most distant from the West.

Reporting about Iran in the West has focused almost exclusively on the country's efforts to gain nuclear capacity, its heavy-handed crushing of dissent, and the anti-American rhetoric of its president, Mahmoud Ahmadinejad, and the Islamic Republic's support of violent militias in Iraq and radical groups in Lebanon and the Palestinian territories. This focus has obscured vital aspects of the true story of Iran and the regime's hold on power. Behind Ahmadinejad's rise to power and re-election, and the regime's stepped-up anti-American ranting, lies a struggle over increasingly intense pressure from within the society, largely due to economic woes, for a loosening of the constraints imposed by the regime on the capitalist private sector. It was due to the perceived threat of mounting pressures for both economic and political reform that the clerical leadership first threw its support behind Ahmadinejad in the election of 2005, and again in 2009, considering him the perfect vehicle for stirring up the populist and revolutionary fervor of the lower classes and beating back a rising tide of reformist sentiment.

This is where the strong and growing economic ties between Dubai and Iran are so instructive, in revealing just how vibrant the capitalist energies of Iranian society are, despite so many years of autocratic smothering. And ties to Dubai are only one part of the story of how Iranian capitalists are forging ahead to extend their influence in the region, for the purposes of business growth rather than fostering terrorism or spreading the fundamentalist creed.

From the western edge of Herat, a bustling city (by local standards) in northwestern Afghanistan that has the distinction of having been sacked and razed by both Genghis Khan and Tamerlane, a two-lane highway darts across the desert plain toward the Iranian border. It is a good road, better than ones farther south, and it buzzes with traffic. Iranian money built the seventy-mile road in order to link Herat to Mashhad, the large metropolis that sits on Iran's borderlands with Afghanistan and Central Asia, and a former way station on what was once the Silk Road. Every day, hundreds of buses and trucks leave Mashhad for Herat, carrying people and goods to the bazaars of Afghanistan. The fall of the Taliban increased that traffic and that is why Herat has done so much better than the rest of Afghanistan in recent years (it is now the country's second-largest city after Kabul). But there was plenty of trade before America pushed the Taliban out.

When the Soviet Union invaded Afghanistan in 1979, two million Afghans took refuge in Iran, settling in camps in and around Mashhad and other Iranian towns and villages along the border. The refugees took menial construction or factory jobs, and whenever the fighting subsided they went back to their homeland, taking with them Iranian products to sell. The flow of people created commercial ties, integrating shops in Herat into the supply chain of Mashhad's bazaar and eventually tying western Afghanistan's economy to Iran and from there to new trade routes that opened into Central Asia following the fall of the Soviet Union. The highway from Herat to Mashhad now connects to another road that runs a short distance north to Ashgabat, the capital of Turkmenistan. Over the past two decades, a whole economic zone has emerged in this area where the borders of Iran, Afghanistan, and Central Asia meet. Iran is the linchpin—or, to change the metaphor, the straw that stirs the commercial drink—when it comes to these exchanges. Yet this role is not something that the Islamic Republic planned. Businesspeople, based in bazaars and eager to move goods, made it happen. They pushed the government to help with trade by building roads, railway lines, and electricity pylons. Business got the government involved, not the other way around. If Iran today is a force to contend with in Afghanistan, it is not because of its military support for warlords who fought the Taliban, but because of its economic footprint in that country.

The same is true in Iraq. I was driving around Basra, the country's second-largest city, on a hot summer day in 2008 in the company of Iraqi soldiers. They had recently taken control of the city after a grueling battle with Iranian-backed militias. The soldiers driving us around were full of bravado and did not miss an opportunity to criticize Iran for its support of thuggish militiamen whose criminal enterprises had plunged the city into violence. Finally, the tired and thirsty soldiers asked if we wanted to stop to enjoy some watermelons that had been piled into a little hill for sale along the road. I asked where the watermelons came from. "Iran, of course," came the answer. "The best watermelons of Mashhad." (There is only one Mashhad in Iran: The soldiers meant the same trading hub that is Iran's commercial window on Afghanistan and Central Asia.) Every time I asked about where newly opened shops in the central shopping district or local neighborhood bazaars got their wares, the answer seemed to be the same: "Iran, of course."

Basra, a Shia metropolis located a mere fifteen miles from the Iranian border, is not the only place in Iraq where Iran's economic presence is on full display. It is the same story across southern Iraq, and even in Baghdad or Irbil and Suleimaniyeh in the Kurdish north. Not just watermelons, but air conditioners, a host of consumer goods, and even new cars flood the Iraqi market. Iran also sells electricity and oil products to Iraq and has invested heavily in enterprises and infrastructure development in southern Iraq. Merchants start businesses with Iranian loans and Iranian businessmen invest in real estate and business across southern Iraq. No sooner had Iraqi forces cleared militiamen out of Basra than money from Iran began buying prime land in the city. In Najaf, Iranian money has gone into building hotels and businesses catering to the more than 1 million Iranians per year who visit the Shia shrine cities of southern Iraq.

In Iraq as in Afghanistan, Iranian influence has been most ominous and obvious in the guns and explosives that militiamen use to ply their trade. But as was evident in Basra on that summer day, Iraqi forces backed by American logistics, advice, and firepower had broken the hold of Iranian-backed militias on the city. Iranian watermelons, however, continued to sell briskly. It was a small but telling sign that Iran's enduring influence will rest not on political alliances of convenience or military pacts with gun-toting irregulars, but rather on economic ties and vested business interests. Political wheeling and dealing with trigger-pullers and their leaders is, if anything, the *weakest* link in Iran's effort to exert its power in Iraq. Business holds greater promise. When President Ahmadinejad went on an official visit to Iraq in March 2008 (the first by a Middle Eastern head of state since the start of the war) he asked Iraq to sign a "most-favored-nation" trade agreement with Iran (Iraq turned down the offer). The deal would increase the volume of trade between the two countries and more closely tie Iraq to Iran. The Iranian leader had gone to Baghdad on this historic visit not to ask for military bases or a defense pact, but for a trade alliance. Iranians understand that their influence next door can only be ensured by economic ties.

Consider also an overlooked irony of Iran's involvement in Lebanon. Attention in the West focuses on Tehran's support of Hezbollah, and with good reason. But the hard power that so impresses the outside world may well turn out to be a weakness. Lacking an economic foundation this most prominent of Iran's regional alliances may in time look a lot less steady.

South Lebanon is agricultural country, a stretch of valleys filled with farms and villages that separate Beirut in the north from the Israeli border in the south. This is Shia country, and has seen its share of war, occupation, destruction, and suffering as a frontline zone in the decades-long Arab-Israeli conflict. It was in south Lebanon that in 2006 Israel and Hezbollah fought a fierce seesaw battle that raged from village to village, wrecking roads, bridges, and farms and forcing residents to flee north or east into Syria.

South Lebanon is today a Hezbollah stronghold.[1] The party is the de facto government of a Hezbollah state within a state, and nothing happens there without its approval. Hezbollah subscribes to a fierce brand of fundamentalism inspired by Iran's revolution and its model of clerical rule. Hezbollah is a party at war. It has been fighting Israel in one way or another since the early 1980s, and has been at loggerheads with Christian, Sunni, and Druze rivals at home for almost as long. Everything about Hezbollah is about fighting; it sees itself as the defender of Lebanon, a war machine always on guard and ready to act.[2] Being on a war footing under fundamentalist rule makes south Lebanon an unlikely place for business to thrive. Yet that is exactly what has been happening over the past two decades. Fighting starts and stops, people leave and come back, and in the midst of it all south Lebanon prospers again with booming construction, small-scale manufacturing, services, and retail. There is something different about this Shia enclave and it does not have to do with war but with its uncanny ability to churn out entrepreneurs who generate wealth and sustain the rising local middle class.

For the past four decades, not only war but drought and other typical rural hardships have plagued south Lebanon. Not surprisingly, many young Lebanese, much like earlier immigrant generations from other parts of the semi-arid Mediterranean basin such as Greece and southern Italy, have left their country in search of work and prosperity. They have found their way to improbable places: Sierra Leone, Liberia, and the Republic of Congo in Africa; or Brazil, Argentina, Ecuador, and Venezuela in Latin America. In these faraway lands, some of which themselves have known chaos and the hard hand of war, these sons of Lebanon have opened shops and businesses, growing beyond their peasant roots to become merchants. In Africa, it was difficult to do business, but the migrants were veterans of wars and instability at home; they proved to be tenacious survivors, like lonely cypresses jutting out of barren rock. In Africa, the south Lebanese became the trading class, the shopkeepers, service providers, wholesalers, and traders. And they prospered. The money they made in Africa or Latin America went back to their towns and villages. New villas and mansions sprang up across south Lebanon. Roads improved and new businesses opened. The money coming in created local jobs in construction, retail, factories, and services, and that generated even more growth.

Despite war and destruction, south Lebanon has done well economically, and that is no thanks to Hezbollah, its fundamentalism or military vigilance. South Lebanon owes its wealth to businessmen and the provincial middle class that is riding on their coattails. It was these businessmen and the interest they served and represented that leaned heavily on Hezbollah to stay out of the Israel-Hamas war of 2008–09. The story is quite different in northern Lebanon. There has been little war in that region, nothing of the sort that has rattled the south time and again over recent decades, but there is plenty of rural poverty. The sons of the north have not taken to migration. Instead, they have stayed close to home, nursing resentment and frustration, and that has led a growing number of them into the ranks of extremist Sunni groups, some with close ties to al-Qaeda.

In the south there is a Shia fundamentalist party with a military agenda running the show, but on the ground it is business and moneymaking that is shaping lives. In the north the pro-Western Lebanese government is in control, but at the street level it is extremism that is gaining ground. Which part of Lebanon is more likely to turn in the right direction in the long run? If history is any guide, peace and progress, stability and democracy will have a better chance where commerce is vigorous and expanding.

Iran has long-standing ties to Hezbollah. It helped to create the organization, and continues to train its fighters, bankroll its growth, and arm its units.[3] There are personal, religious and military ties that bind Hezbollah to Iran.[4] Many Iranians see their own revolution reflected in Hezbollah, and they value the party as a rare case of successful export of the Iranian Revolutionary model to the Arab world. Hezbollah's leaders alone continue to pay homage to Iran's Supreme Leader as a source of religious emulation (although most Lebanese prefer more senior aya-tollahs, foremost among them the Grand Ayatollah Ali al-Sistani of Najaf, Iraq), and many among Iran's Revolutionary Guard command-ers have spent time in Lebanon and fought alongside Hezbollah. Iran's relations with Hezbollah are complicated to say the least, but they are overwhelmingly religious and political in nature, with virtually no eco-nomic component. Iran gives money to Hezbollah, but has little to do with the booming business life of south Lebanon. This means that Iran's influence in the one country where it is believed to have had its say the longest actually has little underpinning beyond the latest arms ship-ment or cash payout. Iran's presence in south Lebanon, in other words, has no economic legs of its own and could prove surprisingly fleeting.

Iran's support for radical groups and its leadership in fomenting fundamentalism and anti-Americanism should not obscure the truth of the increasingly difficult bind its clerical rulers find themselves in, faced with a growing demand from the populace for more robust economic growth—growth not wholly contingent on oil revenues, which have proven so volatile—while knowing that with the rise of those middle class merchants and business professionals who can deliver that growth will inevitably come demand for political reform as well. This is the true motivation of the clerical leadership's support of Ahmadinejad, and of his raging populism, regardless of dangers that are inherent in the presi-dent's wrong-headed policies and the passionate opposition they have generated.

A close look at the story of Iran's internal struggles since the 1979 revolution will reveal that the dominating feature of the regime's time in power has been the challenge it has faced to deliver economic good

fortune while also containing pressure for liberalization of both the economy and the political system. The degree of repression of open political debate, and organized activism, has ebbed and flowed in the years
since the revolution, but never approximated anything resembling openness. There have been times when the clerical regime has turned a blind
eye to women breaching dress codes and youth pushing for social freedoms, but invariably the heavy hand of the state has come down hard on
those who have pushed too hard for social and political freedoms. Most
recently confrontation between the U.S. and Iran over its nuclear program, and talk of war, sanctions and regime change have made it easier
for Iran's rulers to accuse their opponents of doing the bidding of foreign
enemies. Things have become more difficult for the many women's activists, political and religious dissenters, students, labor leaders, academics,
and journalists who have ended up in prison for challenging the Islamic
Republic's strictures.

But pressure on the population has hardly brought peace to the
Islamic Republic. Pressure is growing for the regime to relax its grip. The
more people the clerical regime has put in jail, the more have shown up
at rallies demanding rights and freedoms. No sooner had Iran's rulers
unleashed security forces to clamp down in 2006 than a group of women
activists founded the Campaign for One Million Signatures Demanding Changes to Discriminatory Laws, or the One Million Signatures
Campaign for short. It quickly became the most significant women's
rights effort in Iran and one of the most daring civil society-based challenges to the ruling theocracy since the revolution. The activists rallied
women of all classes and walks of life—and many men too—to improve
women's standings in divorce and custody cases and support equal pay
for women. They easily collected the one million signatures, and more
important, in doing so created a formidable web of civil society organizations and foot soldiers that was instrumental in mobilizing support
for reformist candidates in the 2009 presidential election and organizing the protests that followed. The pressure from below is, however,
only one element in Iran's politics, and for now not the decisive one.
In order to understand the true dynamics of power within the country,

we should start by examining the complicated nature of the blending of fundamentalism, populism, and statism that characterizes the Islamic Republic.

Iran is like no other Middle Eastern dictatorship or Muslim society. It is a theocracy ruled by the Supreme Leader who sits above the law but also relies on elections to choose its president, members of parliament, mayors, and city councilmen. The Supreme Leader—currently Ayatollah Seyyed Ali Khamenei—is elected by a handful of fellow clerics and rules for life. He controls the judiciary along with the largest economic institutions of the country and appoints the commanders of the military. He can veto legislation and overrule government officials, and it is he who gets the last word on all matters foreign and domestic. He will decide whether the Islamic Republic looks after the interests of Iran or those of Islam, whether it joins the world or stands against it. It is he who decides whether the regime embraces reform or hunkers down to enforce rigid laws; and it is he who has control over whether Iran will halt or surge ahead with its nuclear program. But under him the mix of "Islamic" and "republic"—openly at odds in the aftermath of the 2009 election—makes for a complex labyrinth of competing centers of power all of which rely on him for support and which he must work to constrain.

Iran's constitution is an unhappy mix of Islamic government and popular sovereignty—*vox dei* and *vox populi*—modern government and clerical authority as outlined by Khomeini's theory of *velayat-e faqih* or guardianship of the jurists, which, until the Hidden Imam (the Shia Messiah) returns, claims all political authority for the clergy as the proper guardians of the community in his absence.[5] The Iranian constitution gives the clergy extensive powers, but it also defines the Iranian state as a blend of modern institutions of government. All the power rests with the Supreme Leader, but the day to day work of government is the job of the president—who is elected every five years—and bureaucrats who work in government organizations. The legislature looks over the government's shoulders and also passes laws—not all that different from how executives and legislatures elsewhere in the world interact.

But what the legislature does must also meet with the approval of the Supreme Leader. The Supreme Leader's most powerful instrument is the Guardian Council. He appoints its members and relies on them to vet all candidates for public office and review all decisions of the government and laws passed by the parliament.

Khamenei is also commander-in-chief, the boss of Iran's army and Revolutionary Guards. The Guards do more than just protect the regime; it is also an important political institution. It has forged strong ties with clerics and powerful councils that oversee government actions, and Guard members are found in every branch of government. It was once customary for clerical families to forge alliances through intermarriage; now children of Guardsmen have been added to the mix.

Iran does not have one government, it has layers of government. There is not just the presidency, the parliament, and the Guardian Council, but also the judiciary, the Revolutionary Guards, the regular military, the police, the intelligence agencies, the clerical elite, the Friday prayer leaders, much of the media, and a constellation of formal and informal foundations, organizations, councils, seminaries, and business associations. Behind it all is an intricate network of family ties and intermarriages that decides the pecking order and who gets access to what. These power centers overlap and compete, bicker over policy and ideology, and all seek to curry favor with the Supreme Leader. All roads in Iran lead to him, but none is straight.

In recent years Ahmadinejad has hogged all the attention. That is because he has played a rabble-rousing role as president, but his support is more precarious than it may seem. Supreme Leader Khamenei has shown favor to Ahmadinejad and his hard-line brand of politics not so much because of sympathy he feels for that populism—which he likely does—but more important because he fears reformists who want to abolish his office, ambitious clerics who have set their sights on grabbing power, and Revolutionary Guards commanders who are exercising more and more control over not only the political system, but the economy as well. Khamenei encouraged the conservatives to rally behind Ahmadinejad in the presidential elections of 2005—his son worked diligently to whip up support for him among senior clerics—and nodded approvingly at Revolutionary Guards' underhanded financial support for the little-known presidential candidate. The Supreme Leader's favor was out for all to see once Ahmadinejad assumed power. It mattered little if he offended world opinion with his over-the-top rhetoric or shocked senior clerics in Qom with his religious opinions; the Supreme Leader kept showering praise on his government. Even gross mismanagement of the economy did not shake Khamenei's public trust in his populist president. Ahmadinejad's credentials as a man of the oppressed peoples outweighed these liabilities. So it was that Khamenei thought little of handing him the presidency in 2009 after it became clear that he was in trouble with the voters.

Ahmadinejad was not born into the clerical aristocracy and was not a member of the business networks that have pocketed so much of the country's wealth.[6] He came from those below that Khomeini had called to action in 1979. Everything about him is anti-elitist. He was born in a town called Aradan, in the midst of the desert plain southeast of Tehran, which virtually no one in Iran had heard of or been to before its favorite son became president.[7] Ahmadinejad was a small child when his father moved the family to Tehran, into one of the city's poorer working class neighborhoods, and opened his own business as an ironsmith. Working alongside his father as a child, he learned the tricks of the trade, as well as the ways of the street. He studied engineering in college in the late seventies and fell in with the revolution, imbibing both its populist idealism and fundamentalist worldview. He was typical of the young urban poor who formed Khomeini's revolutionary phalanx.

At that time he was more a religious zealot than a class warrior. Many have claimed that he was one of the hostage-takers in 1979, but confirmed hostage takers say that he was not one of them—they swam on the left side of the revolutionary tide, and he was on its right. He joined the Revolutionary Guards and fought in the war with Iraq, and then joined the thuggish Baseej vigilante force, which the clerical rulers unleash from time to time to intimidate their opponents. While rabble-rousing with the Baseej, he felt the need to finish his university education, and went on to get a doctorate in traffic management. He was not driven back to the classroom by the love of learning, but rather to obtain the title of "doctor" if he was to rise above his station. He joined the government administration and was appointed to several provincial posts, and during the reformist period, 1997 to 2005, his career took off. The clerical rulers were looking for fresh blood to stand up to surging reformists, and he was at the right place at the right time. He also proved adept at finding his way through the maze of Iran's politics, and soon the conservatives saw him as the answer to their prayers, the wunderkind who would vanquish the reformists. They made sure money flowed to his administration after he became the mayor of Tehran in 2003. He gave raises to bus drivers and street sweepers, and with the Revolutionary Guards eager to help, he built roads through military zones to relieve traffic congestion. Having thus crafted a "can do" image, he was well positioned to challenge the reformists for the presidency.

To the power elite, though, he is still merely a foot soldier of the revolution. They look down on his plebeian roots and cringe at his bombastic rhetoric. They also fear his populism—unleashing the anger of the poor against their business interests and laying waste to state institutions. Many among the high clergy are annoyed with his talk of messianism and his meddling in religious issues. For a long time after he became president, senior clerics in Qom refused to give him an audience or receive his emissaries, and when he went to Iraq on a state visit in March of 2008, Ayatollah Sistani turned down requests to either meet with him or speak with him on the telephone. Senior ayatollahs all lined up behind presidential candidates who challenged Ahmadinejad in the 2009 election, and several protested the outcome. But to many of his countrymen it is precisely his provincial roots and mannerisms that make him so attractive. Watching him speak, cutting the air vertically with his hands as he makes his points, every Iranian sees that Ahmadinejad is not simply a representative of that class. He is himself of it.

Ahmadinejad understands very well the power of being a man of the people; taunting wealthy clerics and corrupt politicians—fat cats who have betrayed the revolution's ideals and showed weakness before the West. He promises to break their hold on the country. Making a great show of living in his family's humble house, he refuses the luxuries normally afforded a national leader. He shocked Syria's President Bashar al-Assad, in Iran for a state visit in February 2007, by taking him directly from the airport to his modest home for a simple lunch on the floor. This sort of boldness has confounded his opponents.

His way to the presidency was paved by his attacks against reformists right after the 1997 election, when most conservatives had pretty much thrown in the towel. He became a force to contend with in the conservative camp, and a cult of personality formed around him, which he has been only too happy to cultivate. One of his acolytes wrote a book about him entitled *The Miracle of the Third Millennium*.[8]

Nothing endears him to the masses more than the way he brazenly expounds on issues of all kinds, large and small, generously sharing his opinions on world history, global politics, and international economics. He once lectured the Iranian national soccer team on the importance of passing the ball. "Does a ball move faster or a player?" he asked them, and when the players meekly responded "the ball," he played the all-knowing teacher and instructed them that they should therefore pass more often.

His frequent speeches before large crowds all across the country are full of obtuse circular arguments about good and evil, and in interviews and small gatherings, like ones he has held for academics and journalists when he visits the United Nations in New York, he answers questions with questions, ending with a joyous smile that reads as a distinct putdown. His logic is seldom convincing, but then he cares little about what elites and experts think of him. He knows that the poor masses like his folksy style. Though he may seem comical, to many in Iran he comes across as daring and confident. They like his audacity, and especially the way he stands up to the elites, belittling their education, their wealth and their blue blood.

The blessings conferred on Ahmadinejad by Khamenei were fundamentally about clamping down on a reformist movement that had been gaining momentum since 1997. The leaders of that movement—pro-democracy students, young clerics interested in Islamic modernism, as well as women's rights activists, journalists, business leaders, academics, lawyers, and many more among the general population and even the regime's true and trusted government agencies and military forces—had hoped that the 2005 presidential election would be the focal point of widespread protest against political repression, economic stagnation, and lack of social freedoms (although not all agreed on which mattered most). The hope was that the election would set the stage for real change in Iran by putting in office a pragmatic and reform-minded president. The informed coalition of the reform-minded rallied behind candidates who addressed their concerns, and when the first round of the voting failed to produce a clear winner, they turned to the former president Ayatollah Ali Akbar Hashemi Rafsanjani as their candidate.[9] Rafsanjani promised more openness in politics and greater prosperity, but he lost the second round of the election. Instead, due to Khamenei's support for Ahmadinejad, the election turned into a rout of moderate voices, confirming the hold on power of the ruling clerics and empowering a new breed of neoconservatives led by Ahmadinejad. Reformists made a concerted effort in 2009 to take back the presidency, but Khamenei again stood behind Ahmadinejad to frustrate renewed hopes of reform.

This turn of events was all the more perverse in light of the fact that in the wake of 9/11, the regime seemed ready for a time to mend fences with the United States. It acquiesced in the war against the Taliban in Afghanistan, and once the fighting was over Iranian diplomats sat down with their American counterparts—despite the lack of formal relations—to plan a new Afghan constitution and government.[10] The two countries worked together to solve a common problem, and the result was evident in how quickly and painlessly Afghanistan adopted the constitution, held elections, and inaugurated a president. The role of the Bush administration's stance toward the Islamic regime in the stanching of this hopeful progress in relations must not be underestimated. The United States and Iran had come close to thawing their decades-old frosty relationship during the Clinton administration (Iran's reformist President Khatami almost shook hands with Clinton at the UN), but a final breakthrough had eluded them. Cooperation over Afghanistan after the fall of the Taliban provided a new opportunity for putting their relations on a better course. But when Bush unexpectedly identified Iran as one of "Axis of Evil" powers in his State of the Union address before the Congress in January 2002, hopes were dashed. Those in Tehran who had been pushing for the mending of relations had their fingers burned.

Even so, they persisted with one more effort. In 2003 the regime reached out to the United States to propose talks on all issues outstanding between Iran and America, in the form of an unsigned letter handed to the Swiss embassy in Tehran, which represents American interests in the country. There was some debate within the U.S. administration about who in Tehran had sent the letter and whether it carried any weight. Some dismissed it as a hoax, while others thought the fact that it lacked a signature showed it was not a serious overture—no one on the inside seems to have been excited about the letter or to have argued for responding to it. In the end Washington decided not to test Iranian seriousness with a reply; what may have been a small opening slammed shut.[11]

The allure of the new role the Iranian leadership could envision for the country in the wake of the invasion of Iraq also played a part in the repudiation of Western accommodation. For the reigning clerics, a key calculation was whether what the regime might gain from shaking hands with America—assuming the United States could eventually be convinced to engage in talks—would be worth what it would lose by way of revolutionary image and popular accolade in the Muslim world, especially in light of al-Qaeda's rising prestige after 9/11. The Iraq War and soaring oil prices combined to present the regime with what looked like a golden opportunity to flex its muscles in the region. The toppling of Saddam had cleared the way for the emergence of what Jordan's King Abdullah called a "Shia crescent" of power stretching from the oil-rich Persian Gulf littoral across to southern Lebanon, and the Iranian regime was intent to be the dominating force in that ascent.

The strenuous objections in so many parts of the region to this rise of Shia power also played a role in the regime's support for Ahmadinejad's rabble rousing. Arab governments greeted Iran's expanding role with alarm.[12] The first thing American officials heard when they arrived in Arab capitals in the wake of the Iraq invasion was sure to be a litany of complaints about Iran and its influence in Iraq, Lebanon, and the Palestinian Territories. So intense was Sunni fear of Iran's growing power that in May 2008 Ayman al-Zawahiri, the al-Qaeda number two, lambasted Iran and Shiism and said he would like to see both destroyed, possibly at America's hands: "The dispute between America and Iran is a genuine struggle, and the possibility of the US striking Iran is real. . . . We hope that war 'saps' both Washington and Tehran."[13] Sunni-extremist websites began featuring rants about "Sassanid" and "Safavid" [read "Iranian"] plots against Arabs, with Iran seeming to replace Israel as the main focus of fear and loathing. A country aspiring to lead the entire Muslim world could hardly afford to have its reach limited by Arab-versus-Persian or Sunni-versus-Shia tensions. Ahmadinejad and his ranting anti-Americanism and threats to annihilate Israel were helpful in diverting attention from the Sunni-Shia issue and rallying the Muslim world behind Iran's leadership.

But we will miss the essential lesson of the closing of the door on reform that started in 2005—and hence of the impetus still alive within the country for economic and political opening—if we only look to these external factors for explanation. The Supreme Leader and his inner circle felt the need to fuel Ahmadinejad's populism and reignite anti-Americanism most of all due to internal pressures from long-simmering capitalist energies that the Islamic regime has alternately tried to control and contain since the 1979 revolution.

Much of the story in Iran, especially for the past decade, has been that of the clerical elite's effort to hold back the growing power of the same middle class that is rising in pockets all around the region.

———

The revolution that toppled the Shah mixed theocratic Shia fundamentalism with a strong dose of class warfare and hatred for capitalism.[14] Indeed, rage against inequalities in income and opportunity fueled the revolution a good deal more than did religious fervor. After the Islamic regime seized power, industries were nationalized, banks were turned into government holdings, and vast numbers of private businesses were closed. The state simply devoured large parts of the private sector. The only players in the sector left free to operate were small, bazaar-based merchants, who were hardly worth bothering with, and anyway for the most part ardently supported the revolution. The state and its payroll ballooned, with the number of public employees nearly tripling by 1982, and the private sector grew feeble.[15]

Before long, these actions began taking a terrible toll on the Iranian economy. Making matters worse were the sanctions the international community imposed on the country to punish it for its revolutionary excesses, most glaringly the taking of U.S. embassy hostages in 1979. Saddam Hussein's invasion in 1980 and the bloody eight-year war with Iraq that followed did considerable further damage to Iran's economy, crippling the industry, straining its industrial infrastructure, and depopulating large parts of its fertile southwest. In response, the government tightened its grip on the economy still further by enacting price controls and food rationing, diverting investments and resources from activities that would grow the economy to subsidizing the poor and funding entitlement programs, and bloating the bureaucracy even further. By the time the Iran-Iraq war ended in a stalemate, in 1988, Iran's economy was in dire straits, and the leadership knew a change of course was desperately required.

When Ayatollah Khomeini died in June 1989, Seyyed Ali Khamenei, who had been president during the war, was elected Supreme Leader, and the speaker of the parliament, Ali Akbar Hashemi Rafsanjani, became president. Khamenei was a devoted revolutionary and one of Khomeini's chief lieutenants. A mid-ranking cleric who had spent more time on the barricades and in prison than at the seminary, he had quickly risen through the ranks during the first decade of the revolution, mostly because he did well in running different programs in the government. But his new job was less about day-to-day affairs of government and more about protecting the religious and ideological foundations of the Islamic Republic. Khamenei lacked Khomeini's credentials or scholarly gravitas to impress senior ayatollahs. He had to grow in the job and that would take time and patient consensus-building—and that to a good extent explains why Iran's government is today such a maze of competing power centers.

Rafsanjani was a wily politician who came from a well-to-do family of pistachio farmers in southeastern Iran. A pragmatist, he grasped the urgency of getting the economy back on its feet, and he pressed for a redirection of priorities to economic development, and the reform of the institutions of the government and economy in order to facilitate that. Dyed-in-the-wool revolutionaries were pushed out of government offices in droves, in favor of business professionals who got busy devising five-year plans and new industrial polices, reforming the banking system, overhauling the energy sector, and plotting ways to jump-start growth, including even asking the World Bank for advice about creating a stock market.

The government also began privatizing—or more accurately, reprivatizing—businesses. Almost 3,300 square miles—or about 2.1 million acres—of confiscated land were distributed to farmers and several factories were returned to their original owners.[16] In 1991 alone, four-hundred companies were privatized.[17] In that year Iran's finance minister and its central bank chief went to New York to ask exiled Iranian businessmen, forced to flee the revolution, to return home and pick up where they had left off. More than a few did so and negotiated the buyback of their factories and businesses. The need to unleash capitalist energies had been granted, but that didn't mean that the system became truly capitalist. What resulted, instead, was a hybrid of state control and capitalism, with plenty of corruption worked in.

One friend of mine, whose industrial-scale family-owned bakery had been nationalized in 1979, told me that he got his plant back, but that privatization was a raw deal. The government sold him the bakery at a reasonable price and helped with the financing. He got all the supplies he needed and the government even guaranteed him a certain volume of sales, but he was not allowed to fire any workers, and would have to agree to take more on whether he needed them or not. Iran has pretty tough labor laws that provide employees with a wide array of entitlement and virtual job guarantee, which apply to every business with more than five employees. A common saying in the country is, "It is easier to divorce one's wife than to fire an employee." My friend commented wryly, "I have a feeling that my factory was the first stop for anyone let out of prison. Even after I took over, people still showed up with notes from officials to give them jobs."

Another method Rafsanjani used to privatize was a particular form of outsourcing of much of the work government agencies had been doing. His approach worked this way: A senior bureaucrat would step out of government, form a company (often in partnership with a well-connected cleric or politician), and then bid for a contract to do what he had been doing when he was in the government—accounting, information technology, personnel management, or some other project-management or service activity, depending on the government agency involved. The larger among such companies would then subcontract some of their work to smaller companies formed similarly. An executive who was a veteran of many such ventures once tried to explain the intricacies of the contracting and subcontracting processes to me by drawing an impromptu chart showing the welter of interconnected private-sector companies that have grown up around the oil ministry. He kept drawing bubbles with names in them and arrows connecting them to other bubbles. He went on and on, filling the paper. Finally he stopped and said, "I think that is most of it. Many of these companies also do work with other ministries and then have connections to other companies in those sectors. I don't have room here to draw all that and then there is how each company relates to different political factions and foundations."

One of the most distinctive, and limiting, features of Iranian capitalism is those "foundations" that my friend mentioned. Known in Persian as *bonyads*, they are vast conglomerates with tens of billions of dollars' worth of assets, which were set up after the revolution by putting together the many nationalized industries and to serve the Islamic Republic's supporters, war veterans, and the poor.[18] In time they grew in size and economic influence. They report only to the Supreme Leader, and are free from other government oversight. Neither truly public or properly private, their hybrid character and control by the Supreme Leader allows them great advantage in forming ventures to bid for government contracts, and then using those ventures to corner markets and create monopolies.

More overt corruption has plagued Iranian capitalism as well. Contracts go hand in hand with bribes and kickbacks, and higher-ups able to steer the flow of contracts have amassed vast fortunes.[19] No one has benefited more from this than Rafsanjani himself. With his backing, and with singular determination to make money, his family and close allies have gained control over large parts of the Iranian economy, virtually dominating business in oil, construction, and telecommunications. The House of Rafsanjani is a conglomerate worth billions, with holdings in manufacturing, real estate, farming, services, hotels, air travel, and numerous investments both inside and outside Iran.

Rafsanjani's use of political clout to build a personal business empire is a familiar story in the developing world, bringing to mind Suharto's Indonesia or Benazir Bhutto's Pakistan. Indeed, after years of Rafsanjani's reforms, Iran looked less like the puritanical Islamic Republic that Khomeini had fashioned and more like a typical predatory Third World state, and it had growing popular disgruntlement to show for it.[20]

But Iran was different in one important regard. Unlike other countries of its kind, it refused to open up to the world and was steadfast in its anti-Western stance and support for revolutionary causes abroad and its suppression of all political dissidents—reform-seeking insiders as well as those who rejected the Islamic Republic *in toto*—and those who violated its rules and regulations, often brutally.

Hostility to the West and suppression of agitators for more substantial economic and political reforms were vital to sustaining the power of the corrupted elite. Keeping the country closed protected their newfound economic interests.

Nonetheless, the Rafsanjani years ignited the engine of the private sector middle class that the revolution had all but shut down. And despite the often brutal crackdown on dissenters, the vitality of that class began to reassert itself in the realm of culture and the arts, especially in the flourishing movie industry that is now well known to the West.

Civil society activism took flight, and taking advantage of the cultural renaissance, it helped produce serious discussions about politics. Gradually talk of reforming laws, improving government, bettering quality of life, and even loosening the government's grip on power found its way into intellectual discussions and from there into public consciousness.

Women novelists such as Moniru Ravanipour and Shahrnoush Parsipour raised awareness of women's rights and questioned many claims of the revolution. Translation of western philosophical tomes encouraged a flurry of philosophical and political debates at home. Lectures, books, and magazines covered these debates at length, leaving little doubt that Iranians were interested in probing the boundaries of new thinking. Most unsettling to the ruling regime were religious thinkers—most prominent among them, Abdul-Karim Soroush—who took to questioning theocracy and the prerogatives of the clergy. *Goftogu* (Dialogue) magazine, a platform for Soroush's followers, quickly became the voice of forward religious and political thinking in the Islamic Republic. The magazine's editors and contributors would move on in the years to follow to produce many more publications championing reform. Political debate went hand-in-hand with the cultural pluralism celebrated in movies and the arts. The revival of the middle class began to add color and texture to the bleak picture of life in revolutionary Iran.

All of this intellectual ferment found greater meaning once grass roots organizations took flight to spur social activism. At first this took the form of social services. Many volunteers joined the Kahrizak charitable organization to help orphans and the poor, and the effort grew quickly into something of a national crusade, mobilizing people of all walks of life. Such activism would not remain limited to charitable work for long. Soon those who had learned how to organize and push for the eradication of poverty put their skills, and their networks, to use in forming political organizations that became the bedrock of the reform movement.

Intellectuals, academics, and journalists were the trailblazers—providing the ideas. But it was budding civil society associations, backed by the growing economic clout of the rising middle class, that allowed Iranians to dream of a serious movement for the reform of laws and political institutions along more liberal and democratic lines. The middle class was prospering—doing much better than it had during the first decade of the revolution—and with wealth came the dream of social and cultural freedoms, and even more, of political clout. The middle class was the principal consumer of new ideas that the intellectuals and artists were propounding. Neglected and shunned by the revolution, the middle class had learned to take care of its own needs and protect its own culture, but now it felt it could come out of the shadows and claim its place in the sun.

Before long, the government perceived how powerful the movement was becoming and tried to clamped down. Several intellectuals were murdered at the end of Rafsanjani's presidency in 1996–97, and the government dispatched thugs into the streets to intimidate activists. But what economic change had fueled political repression could not easily halt.

These hopeful developments were given a significant further boost when Rafsanjani was replaced in 1997 by Muhammad Khatami, who won the 1997 presidential elections by promising greater cultural openness at home along with a willingness to bury the hatchet with the West. Oil prices were low during these years, and Khatami and his supporters knew the country needed foreign investments to keep economic growth going. Economic realities put pressure on the ruling clerics to approve investor-friendly changes. Prospering ayatollahs and well-to-do businessmen supported the necessary reforms along with the middle class of business professionals and merchants that was pressing for them. Khatami shrank the government further, and parliament put a slate of new laws governing business practices, banking, arbitration, and ownership rights on the books (implementing them proved to be another story). Labor laws came in for review, as did limits on foreign ownership of business enterprises.

Heartened by these changes, and by the evidence of civil society activism and democratic stirrings, the West began warming toward Iran. Economic ties were forged as global brands such as Royal Dutch Shell, BP, Alcatel, Siemens, Nokia, HSBC, Deutsche Bank, Peugeot, Mitsubishi,

and Samsung all began doing business in the country. Foreign companies formed joint ventures with local partners to open the Iranian market
to foreign goods and provide services to key sectors of the economy such
as energy and telecommunications. Infrastructure boomed: Tehran got a
new metro and airport and the government poured billions into building a new port on the Persian Gulf. Imports too rose. Korean electronics
and European merchandise flooded the Iranian market as advertisements
pushing them changed the look and feel of Tehran. Billboards with
Hollywood stars and European models peddling the latest watches and
mobile phones started to compete in earnest for eyeballs with Tehran's
famous revolutionary murals. All this activity spurred economic growth;
GDP grew at an average of 4.7 percent a year during Khatami's ten years
in office, and at the much faster rate of 6.5 percent a year during his
second term between 2001 and 2005, much of it owing to growth in
manufacturing, which surged ahead at a robust 10.1 percent a year.[21]

For a time it looked like Khamenei and the clerical leadership would
support this trend. He specifically considered adopting the so-called
China model, keeping the government authoritarian while opening
the economy to global market forces.[22] A committee was dispatched to
study the issue and report back to the Supreme Leader. The issue was
debated for a while in the press and among top bureaucrats but in the
end it became clear that Khamenei was not convinced it was a good idea
to copy China. There were powerful economic interests who would lose
were Iran to drastically change course, and they lobbied aggressively to
dissuade the Supreme Leader. These naysayers were supported by some
of the powerful clerics at the top and their hard-line foot soldiers below.
They put the word on the street in small towns, villages, and poor city
neighborhoods where many depend on government jobs and handouts
that their economic security was at risk. There was also seething resentment toward the newly moneyed and the ubiquitous culture of corruption and conspicuous consumption, not to mention shock that the
middle class was back in play so soon and ready to make a mockery of
Khomeini's revolution and its Islamic values.

But there were other reasons as well. It was true enough that China had prospered without the government easing its grip on politics, but China's leaders had nevertheless abandoned their communist ideology and had embraced relations with the West. Khamenei was not ready to take that step. He knew that the Islamic Republic was too brittle to survive that sort of change.

Khamenei understood that opening to the world economy would strengthen oligarchs like Rafsanjani, but also a host of social institutions and civil society organizations that catered to their political and cultural needs. The more these economic actors grew in strength and developed ties with the outside world the more difficult it would become to resist their demands for more change. Khamenei clearly understood that behind the financial promise of the private sector lay something bigger: a new and rising middle class which if allowed to keep growing bigger and richer, would soon begin demanding serious changes in society and government. There was no such thing as economic reform without yielding on the political front as well. This prospect of a freer Iran was what he and his allies were desperate to forestall.

In the end the Supreme Leader decided he did not wish to go down the path of aggressive reform so he dismissed all talk of the China model and threw his weight behind those who opposed change.[23] Editorials in newspapers close to Khamenei along with official media and Friday Prayer sermons, and pronouncements by officials all made it clear that the mood had changed.

The opponents of reform were prepared for the angry reaction of the middle class and private sector—and the many associations and organizations tied to them—who were expecting good things to come from reform. The reformist media criticized the trend and there was some protest on the streets. But the regime was quick to use its security forces and militias to break up demonstrations, intimidate and harass democracy activists, and beat up and jail students and intellectuals. At any sign of unrest, large numbers of police and vigilante thugs would pour into the streets, preventing anti-government protestors from gathering. On numerous occasions scores of students and would-be demonstrators were beaten up and their leaders led to jail.

Reformist newspapers such as *Sharq* (East) were closed down, while women protesting for rights were harassed and their leaders arrested, and vigilantes were sent onto campuses to beat up student demonstrators. There is no telling how many went to jail and for how long, but the crackdown was severe enough to discourage any serious thoughts of continuing to confront the regime on the streets. The judiciary blocked legal reforms while various ayatollahs, acting through the powerful, unelected clerical councils that the Islamic Republic uses to cabin in democracy, interfered in elections, vetoed legislation, and generally demoralized the reformists.

To tighten the screws the Supreme Leader turned to the Revolutionary Guards, the Islamic Republic's last line of defense. The Guards grew in size and strength during this period, and even extended their reach into the economy. The Guards was founded in the early 1980s as a fundamentalist militia, comprised of die-hard fighters sent on the most daunting missions against the Iraqi army and the clerics' leftist rivals on the streets of Tehran. Now receiving training and equipment sufficient to turn them into a highly capable elite force, they sit atop Iran's military structure.

The Guards had accrued ever more power, both military and economic, during Khatami's reformist era, developing a taste for business and its rewards that puts one in mind of Pakistan's grasping senior military establishment. As the Revolutionary Guards Corps expanded in size and influence in the 1990s, it became a source for new contracts for private-sector firms, and also started to bid for government projects itself. By 2005, the Guards had become the largest source and recipient of government contracts, a critical node in the economy, and they were particularly important to trade. Economic growth had increased the demand for imported goods, but Iran was under international sanctions. What came into Iran came through invisible piers on the Persian Gulf (mostly via Dubai), and those piers belonged to the Guards. The Guards came to dominate the telecommunications, construction, energy, and mining industries.

More and more Guards also stepped out of the barracks to assume political office, and today former Guards commanders sit in the parliament—a third of whose members, by conservative estimates, have ties to the Guards—while many others serve as heads of foundations, senior ministers, governors, mayors, and corporate leaders. The Guards were—and by all accounts continue to be—only too happy to do Khamenei's bidding given their strong interest in continued tight control of the economy.

The crackdown was also greatly assisted by the manner in which economic benefits had been so disproportionately heaped on the upper and middle classes. As Iran's economy underwent change, beginning in the Rafsanjani period, the purchasing power of the middle class grew. Those in the private sector made money—often plenty of it—and were quick to spend it. The conspicuous consumption of the new business class—including luxury cars and multimillion-dollar apartments— sowed resentments among the lower classes that fueled support for the hard-liners' backlash.

The poor were taught that the revolution was all about empowering them and ending differences in wealth and class. Kalashnikov-toting radical clerics had preached the gospel of populism at every Friday Prayer, and self-styled militants with fists clenched had promised a classless utopia at rallies or on public television. The Islamic Republic confirmed its commitment to the poor every day and at every turn. The poor were resentful that so soon after revolution the classes that were supposed to have been thrown onto the garbage heap of history were back, comfortably flaunting their wealth. The award-winning film director Jafar Panahi captures this resentment powerfully in the movie *Crimson Gold*, the story of a one-time revolutionary and war veteran who turns to a life of crime out of desperation and anger at witnessing the revolution he had fought for leave him behind to cater to the newly rich.

Khamenei was sympathetic to the lower class critics. He has deep appreciation for the anti-imperialist Third Worldism that was all the rage when he was coming up in the 1960s.[24] If he read anything of the West it was probably Frantz Fanon rather than Alexis de Tocqueville. In the years leading to the revolution he was an ardent follower of Ali Shariati, and had heard his leftist rhetoric up close. When Khomeini was in charge Khamenei fell into the populist "state must do all and provide all" camp. He is something of a policy wonk and has strong opinions on how the government and economy ought to work, and his sympathies did not lie with free-spending businessmen.

For these reasons, Khamenei made a shrewd calculation to back Ahmadinejad in the elections of 2005 and 2009, as a further means of firming up the Islamic regime's hold on power. That calculation is a tricky one, though, and is fraught with ironies that reveal the bind the regime finds itself in as it struggles to reignite economic growth now that oil prices have so dramatically slumped. Populist measures enacted since Ahmadinejad's election have also contributed to a severe economic slowdown, undermining support for him.

There is no question that Ahmadinejad has been the biggest individual beneficiary so far of the regime's crackdown on reform. The fuel behind his electoral victories, and the reason for his appeal to the Supreme Leader, was his raging populist anger that the benefits of the economic reforms had not made their way down to the lower classes. During the 2005 campaign, he said little about the thorny nuclear issue and even less about religion and cultural freedoms. Instead he railed against corruption and the suspect wealth of clerics (including most famously Rafsanjani, who was running against him). Ahmadinejad vowed to halt privatization while protecting the consumer subsidies, price controls, and labor laws that were popular with those on the lower rungs of the socioeconomic ladder.[25] Asked about his intentions regarding women's rights, the aspiring candidate said: "People think a return to revolutionary values is only a matter of wearing the headscarf. The country's true problem is employment and housing, not what to wear."[26]

When he became president, Ahmadinejad followed through with sound and fury in clamping down on the private sector. He shoved aside the normal economic-policy agencies and put monetary, budget, and fiscal matters under the president's office. He then used that control to print money with no regard for the inflationary consequences. Iran's money supply soon ballooned by a staggering 40 percent. His office also used its discretionary authority over planning and budgets to hand out contracts large and small to allies and favorites. A series of central bank governors resigned in protest—the last to go accused the president of mismanagement and plundering bank reserves.

To combat the growing problems Ahmadinejad proposed price controls as well as tightening the regulation of banking and credit markets. He even mused aloud about the benefits of abolishing interest (which despite all the talk of Islam's ban on usury has remained the foundation of banking in the Islamic Republic), in the end settling for rates a good 10 and 15 points below the rate of inflation. Those who could withdrew their savings and bought real estate at home or abroad; those who could not saw their money dwindle amid Ahmadinejad's flood of devalued currency.[27] Salaried workers and pensioners suffered most. Ahmadinejad cared little if he was scaring businessmen into sending billions out of the country. At one point, he said that Iran's economic problems would go away if a few people from the stock market could be stood up in front of a firing squad. The economic sanctions that his wild rhetoric helped to attract seemed to concern him even less. Capital investment, especially in manufacturing, dried up. Production fell, and by 2008 many factories were working at less than half their capacity. The money that was flowing into land speculation and property development was causing higher real-estate prices and construction costs—the latter dealing an especially heavy blow to a country that desperately needs to build up its basic infrastructure.

Ahmadinejad flaunted his lack of concern with economic planning and numbers; to him inflation and unemployment were alien concepts. He once told a reporter that he got his economic news from his neighborhood butcher (when that butcher too complained about inflation to a newspaper, Ahmadinejad closed the paper). Ahmadinejad's game was raw populism. Why not bribe the poor for their support when there are so many more of them than there are of those wealthy Iranians who live in prosperous enclaves and depend on the private sector? He almost tripled government spending from $15 billion to $40 billion.[28] Everywhere he traveled he promised public projects, and then decided to do more, to take wads of cash and checks to rallies and distribute them among well-wishers. Pensioners may have had a hard time making ends meet, businessmen may have faced a credit crunch, but all the poor needed to do to get a home loan was to write to the president's office.

The steady rise in oil prices between 2005 and the third quarter of 2008 made this populist spending spree affordable. With dollars from oil sales flooding in, Ahmadinejad could afford to focus on currying favor with the voting masses while putting off hard economic decisions, and the Supreme Leader could afford to stand by and watch as Iran's president shredded his country's economy. Ahmadinejad used government contracts funded by the oil windfall to bolster his favorite businessmen and grease the Revolutionary Guards, whose support was essential to his political survival.[29] The private sector changed shape, breaking down into the president's preferred insiders (who got the contracts, cheap loans, and government support), and everyone else. The high oil prices made it seem, to the undiscerning at least, as if Iran could afford a political strategy masquerading as an economic policy.

When oil prices were peaking in 2007–08, Iran brought in $250 billion in petroleum income. Yet by the time prices fell off the table as a credit crunch cooled the global economy drastically in the second half of 2008, there was no more than $25 billion (some estimates run as low as $9 billion) of this left in the country's cash reserves. Where did all that money go? Not to growth-promoting investments, but to populist causes near and dear to Ahmadinejad. As 2008 came to a close, Iranians found themselves staring into an economic abyss.[30] The official rate of inflation was 27 percent (the real rate is almost certainly higher). Unemployment ran far into double digits too, possibly as high as 35 percent (the government admits to 20 percent). Merchants and salaried workers complained, and labor unions took to protesting for higher wages. The poor began complaining that their government handouts were not going far enough, and wanted more. The exceptionally cold winter of 2007–08 and a drought the following summer had caused first a fuel shortage and then an electricity deficit (Iran relies on rivers and dams for a good portion of its electric power). The depth of unhappiness manifested itself in September 2008, when merchants shut down bazaars across Iran for three days to protest a new sales tax. Growing government spending under Ahmadinejad had made the country dependent on oil prices in the $90 range (Iran claims its budget assumes $37) to stay in the black, and no one could say when prices that high would return.[31]

Such a reversal in economic fortunes can be a powerful impetus for regime change. When a period of boom in Southeast Asia ended in the Asian financial crisis of 1997, many governments came under pressure. Anwar Ibrahim led a serious but unsuccessful challenge against Prime Minister Mahathir in Malaysia, and in next-door Indonesia, the Suharto dictatorship unraveled. The global financial crisis of 2008 and the massive drop in oil prices that it brought have buffeted Iran—which relies on oil for 80 percent of its government revenues—and could well have far-reaching political consequences beyond the summer of 2009 protests.

The last time Iran went through a boom-to-bust ride on the oil rollercoaster, there was a revolution. That will not likely happen again, but the downturn could end the current detour down the blind alley of populism and spark renewed interest in economic reform, privatization, and a viable private sector. Government spending (including subsidies that equal 25 percent of annual GDP) is a drag on the economy. Falling oil revenues and mounting government expenditure leave little room for complacency. The government will have to tighten its belt, shrink in size, and look to the private sector to create jobs, generate tax revenue, and grow the economy; and that will require private sector-friendly policies. During his run for the presidency in April 2009, the reformist candidate Mir-Hossein Moussavi admitted as much, saying, "We need the private sector to help resolve unemployment. There is no bright prospect to deal with such problems through government investments."[32] "The stomach of the government has gotten bigger, but there is now less money to feed it," added his reformist rival, Mehdi Karroubi. [33] The Iranian parliament has already taken the first step, putting into law that the government cannot start new ventures. All new economic and business activities must happen in the private sector.

Another promising sign that the Supreme Leader may support a new direction for the economy is that back in 2006, even as the populist spending spree was reaching fever pitch, Khamenei overruled Ahmadinejad and decreed that privatization would continue. With populism's failure and discouraging inflation and unemployment numbers, the parliament is contemplating revisiting business-friendly economic reforms: relaxing labor laws, loosening of restrictions on foreign direct investment, overhauling banking, and spurring privatization.

The resilience of the private sector in the face of the populist backlash should also give us hope. About a quarter of Iran's economy is in private hands (the majority are companies with fifty employees or less, but several are large scale enterprises). Small to medium-sized companies predominate. Despite the setbacks of the Ahmadinejad years, many of these companies are growing fast, even expanding into regional markets. Many have benefited from the president's mass expulsions of seasoned state officials, a fair number of whom are now private-sector managers. Others have taken advantage of untapped markets and innovative technology to grow new businesses. ADPDigital.com was set up in 2005 (right around when Ahmadinejad became president). More Iranians use mobile phones than they do the Internet, and that meant value-added messaging services had tremendous potential. ADPDigital provided the software and business plan to provide mobile services for businesses through targeted alerts and text messages to their customers. Banks and insurance companies were among the first to adopt the new technology to create customer loyalty as well as new value-adding services. ADPDigital's business grew rapidly over the past four years as the number of mobile users in Iran grew and more businesses looked to communicate with their customers through mobile phones. ADPDigital is the kind of entrepreneurial software company and e-commerce initiative that one expects to find in Silicon Valley, or maybe Bangalore in India, but not in Tehran. Yet, there it is; and there are many more such companies in Iran, entrepreneurial and tech-savvy. They are a big part of the private sector scene.

Private sector businesses are now organized around business associations such as the Society of Producers (Jamiat-e Tolidgaran) or Confederation of Iranian Industry (Majma-e Sanaat). These associations bring together diverse private sector businesses to create networks, address common issues, and lobby government. There are leading companies in different sectors. Karafarin and Saman in banking, Alidad Group or Rouzaneh in food processing, and Pars Online in IT and telecommunications are attracting favorable notice among investors, including foreign investors. The Alidad family were industrialists before the revolution; much like my friend, they came back during the Rafsanjani period to reclaim many of their factories. They have since built a commanding position in the food industry, creating new brands that are now also popular outside Iran (the group also represents the Red Bull brand in Iran).

The private sector has also been expanding from the top down. Energy and petrochemical concerns, Iran's national airline, and a variety of manufacturing companies have gone up for sale. Russia's steel giant MMK has entered into discussions to buy Isfahan Steel Works (which Iran bought from the Soviet Union in the 1960s). Even exceptionally hard-hit parts of the private sector have been growing. Private banking, a target of both domestic populists and international sanctions,[34] has expanded of late—an unlikely development that speaks volumes about the tenacity and potential of the private sector in Iran.

Laws allowing private credit institutions were put on the books in the 1990s, and by 2001 full-fledged private banks were allowed. Among the best known of these is the Karafarin Bank. Started by veteran bankers and seasoned businessmen with private seed capital of $25 million in 2001, Karafarin now enjoys a market capitalization of $125 million on the Tehran stock exchange. It has $2 billion in assets, and employs 1,300 people at fifty-five nationwide branches.[35] It offers not only retail banking services but also investment banking, trade financing, and insurance products.

While the bank's founders had to work hard to overcome bureaucratic resistance and inertia in 2001, that was nothing compared to what they faced under Ahmadinejad. The intense pressure that he exerted to keep interest rates down made Karafarin's business hard, but the bank still thrived—in part by capitalizing on the banking-sector chaos that Ahmadinejad created in order to build a distinct brand and lure new customers. Karafarin, in short, sold reliability and competence, and offered customers the kind of quality banking experience that they had come to value based on their dealings in places such as Dubai.

It was a winning strategy. Karafarin could not compete with government banks when it came to number of branches, so it beat them on quality and variety of services offered. As with all successful innovations, imitators followed suit. Karafarin's competition was increasingly not the big government-owned banks but private ventures such as Saman Bank, which followed the same model. The World Bank's International Finance Corporation, which monitors financial institutions in developing countries, soon took notice. Impressed with Karafarin's positive impact on the Iranian banking scene, the IFC tapped the Iranian bank as a collaborator. A major early step in setting a developing country's economy on the right path is often fixing its financial sector. The task grows far easier if there is a bank that can lead the pack, a winner to bet on. In Iran, Karafarin looked to be best suited for playing that part.

Parviz Aghili is Karafarin's founder and head. A maverick businessman with a doctorate in finance from the University of Wisconsin, Aghili has become something of a legend in the private sector, a high flyer who has changed the way Iran does its banking. Aghili's father was a banker during the Shah's time, but the son like many other professionals left Iran once the revolution swept to power. He learned the banking trade working for the global giant HSBC and its various subsidiaries in Dubai, Canada, and Nigeria. It was in those faraway places that he learned how to manage a bank, grow its business, and structure its services and investments. He learned about the latest and greatest in international banking, but also how to navigate the requirements of Islamic finance, how to work around potentially crippling government regulations, and how to deal with predatory bureaucrats.

Aghili was one among many expatriate businessmen, like my bakery-owning friend, who had returned to Iran once Rafsanjani started to grow the private sector. He ran an investment firm, turned around a food-processing company, set up a brokerage house, and launched a business magazine. Then, when opportunity knocked, he went after his dream, opening his own private bank. Today, Karafarin is the leader among Iran's ten private banks (it and three others are fully private). Firms like it will have to grow and expand their reach if Iran's economy is to recover, and were that to happen, more important social and political changes would follow, much as they did in South Korea and Taiwan.

America may take comfort from the pressure that international sanctions and financial restrictions keep up on Iran's rulers, but it is this resilient private sector and the social classes associated with it that are hurt worst by economic isolation—and those are precisely the forces that must gain strength if Iran and the Middle East are ever to have a hope of becoming capitalist and liberal-democratic. When in June 2009 Iranians went to the polls to choose between Ahmadinejad and his challengers for the presidency, the campaign was bitterly fought, exposing the divide between the middle class and those below. Ahmadinejad's chief rival, reformist Hossein Moussavi, promised more tolerance in politics and greater private sector activity, and he mounted a serious challenge. The massive protests following his defeat, in which incredulous crowds took to the streets in anger that the election had been rigged to give Ahmadinejad a landslide victory, leave little room for doubt about their potential to force change. But that momentum for reform will become unstoppable only if the private sector and the middle class grow bigger and stronger. Sanctions are not the way to help this process along. An Iranian-American investment banker in Dubai explained the folly of sanctions to the author Robin Wright this way:

> Yes, [sanctions] can stop a guy in the Spice Market from getting a letter of credit, [but] that's not fomenting opposition. The guys who are hurting are in the business community. Yes, they hate Ahmadinejad, but they hated him from the beginning. The basic flaw is [the idea] that people who are unhappy with the govern-

ment can do anything. If the goal is to stop Iran from developing a nuclear capability, nothing that has happened here will achieve that objective.[36]

Sanctions, in other words, run the terrible risk of weakening the very forces upon which hopes for change—so vividly captured by the Green Movement of summer 2009—must depend.

There is no denying that the forces of fundamentalist rage and populist resentment that Ahmadinejad represents are powerful and represent a potent threat to the West. They also have the bully pulpit at the moment, and with so much of the coverage of Iran focusing on Ahmadinejad's rants, and the regime's tenacity in pursuit of nuclear capability, the failure to engage more effectively with the forces for change within Iran is understandable. The idea that the West could ever do business, or negotiate, with such a regime may well seem beyond the pale, but in order to become convinced of the value of doing so—even if that means sitting down for direct talks with Ahmadinejad—we must develop a deeper understanding of why there is still so much support within Iran for his breed of politics.

The power of his populism is not by any means primarily contingent on the support of the Supreme Leader and his inner circle. That populist fervor in the lower classes, who in the estimation of the economist Djavad Salehi-Isfahani make up around 20 percent of Iranian society, has been bred by a long and tortured history of failure, and corruption, on the part of prior reformers who promised to bring Iran—and so many other countries of the Muslim world—into prosperity. But it will not be too difficult to persuade these have-nots that government handouts will not give them what they expect for themselves and their families, and that unless the economy really grows there is no light at the end of the tunnel for them. Understanding how to engage this crucial populace, not only in Iran, but around the wider Muslim world, requires a deeper dive into the region's history of subjugation and bedazzlement by Western economic and political might.

CHAPTER 4

THE TRAGIC FAILURES
OF SECULARISM

The hard truth about the appeal of fundamentalism and anti-Americanism in the Middle East lies in the resentment all around the region of the perverse effects of a harsh, authoritarian imposition of so-called Western style modernity on the region's populations in the twentieth century. But this was no sinister plot. It began with the best of intentions, first and most aggressively in Turkey and Iran, and then in much of the rest of the region. After the First World War two powerful reformers, Mustafa Kemal Ataturk and Reza Shah Pahlavi, propelled their countries to modernity, and they brought great advances. But the state-driven style of development they pioneered also led to great problems. For one, an overreliance on top-down economic decision making led to patronage states, rather than robust capitalist economies, and also to a great deal of mismanagement and corruption. Those on top got wealthy but few economic benefits accrued to the teeming masses below.

Another crucial problem was the failure of a true bourgeoisie to develop, a middle class of merchants and professionals with their own bases of economic power, independent from state sponsorship, which is vital to the push for capitalism and democracy. A third tragic flaw in the model of development that would come to be known as Kemalism was that the reformers insisted that secularism was vital to achieving modernity, which led to intense resentment of the suppression of Islam. The fundamental reason that so much anger about this failed version of modernity has been directed at the United States is that the U.S.

government has provided so much support through the years to these authoritarian, and so often corrupted, states, and has been so enamored of secularist leaders, even in the face of their incompetence, as in the recent support of Pervez Musharraf in Pakistan.

The West recoils at the fury and violence of that resentment, seeing it not as a consequence of the failings of secular leaders but as the result of blind adherence to a rigid faith. Why does the Muslim world not move forward, they ask; why does it not embrace modernity? The knee-jerk answer to the question of why the Islamic world has not made better progress toward modernity is that it is Islam's fault. The faith is said to be at odds with modernity, frustrated with the world, and is currently going through a tortuous soul-searching with myriad destructive implications.[1] There is little doubt that the Muslim world is today going through troubling times and has difficulty adapting to the realities of the rapidly changing global environment, and that has led it to reject—at times violently—what the West preaches to it and demands of it. The knee-jerk answer, however, is not the right answer.

The right answer is that the region is stuck in the middle of an experiment that has gone terribly wrong. The Muslim world did embrace modernity, but it was of the wrong kind, and it was pursued in the wrong way, through a forced, top-down process of state-building that it was hoped would catapult the region to prosperity, making up for centuries of humiliating defeats to the West and the ravages of colonialism. It is the legacy of that authoritarian approach to reform that we are contending with in the appeal of fundamentalism and its vehement anti-Americanism. The story of the region's twisted path to modernity starts many centuries back, with the shocking realizations that followed a series of military defeats by Western armies beginning in the eighteenth century. Nothing in Islamic history had prepared Muslims for these encounters and the loss of both military and economic might that followed. They had never known sustained inferiority—quite the contrary. Muslims had come to expect power and to bask in its glory. Within a mere hundred years after the Prophet Muhammad began proclaiming the word of God, Islam had become a world religion.[2] Its mounted tribal warriors, led by caliphs who succeeded the Prophet, burst out of the Arabian Peninsula, and with shocking speed overran mighty empires, claiming a vast territory from the Atlas Mountains to the Indus Valley. Within another two hundred years the Muslim sphere of power had expanded to the south and east into Sub-Saharan Africa and India and on to Southeast Asia. Arts and architecture, sciences and mathematics, philosophy and literature flourished.

Periodic setbacks were suffered. The grand Umayyad and Abbasid caliphates, which ruled the heartland of this Islamic empire between the seventh and thirteenth centuries, fell victim to the decline and decay that is the fate of empires everywhere. From 1095 to 1104 Christian Crusader armies launched repeated attacks in their attempt to gain control of Jerusalem, and in a short four decades, from 1219 to 1258, the Muslim heartland was penetrated by Mongol hordes pouring in from the north and east and many of its cities were laid to waste. But throughout, the Muslim world remained intact; it retained its intellectual vitality, and after each setback recovered its potency.

By the thirteenth century, Muslim armies were on the march again, this time under the rule of the Ottoman Turks. They swept westward, claiming territories of the once mighty Byzantine Empire, and in 1299 Turkish tribes formed a new imperial force, the Ottoman Empire. The Ottomans conquered their way through Anatolia, extending their power to the Balkans and lower Danube by the late fourteenth century. The Greek territory of Thessaloniki fell to them in 1387 and Serbian power was shattered at the Battle of Kosovo in 1389. The Byzantine capital, Constantinople, fell in 1453, and the Turks went on to subjugate the Greeks, the Croats, the Hungarians, and the Bulgarians.

The Ottomans reached their limits, however, when they laid siege to Vienna in 1529. Rebuffed, they would return in 1683, to be turned back again, and this last defeat would prove a decisive turning point. Thereafter Ottoman power began to unravel, while Europe, having survived wave after wave of Turkish assault, grew stronger. Imperial overreach did in the Ottomans at the exact moment when technological advancement gave Europe new powers. Western armies began to win battle after battle against the Turks, and one after the other, the lands that had been won by sultans were lost: Hungary, Serbia, Crimea, and Greece.

There were no more Muslim comebacks; their forces were losing consistently and decisively. Western militaries were clearly qualitatively superior, both in the technology of weaponry and in the discipline and strategic sophistication of their training. The Muslim world had to contend with the rise of the West.

European colonialism began in the early fifteenth century. Traders, backed by well-armed armadas, opened vast areas of Asia and Africa to commerce. The more lucrative the trade became, the more European powers felt compelled to protect it, first against resistance by the natives, and then competition from other European contenders. So it was that a scramble for Asia and Africa ensued as European powers—led by Britain and France—carved up much of the world among them. The Muslim empire of India fell victim to British designs, and from Sub-Saharan Africa to Southeast Asia, sultanates large and small surrendered their kingdoms to British, French, Dutch, or Russian overlords. Colonial powers drew boundaries at will, at times lumping people of different cultures into one administrative unit, at others dividing up people who had lived as one. They conjured up new countries to serve their interests; Afghanistan was created to separate Russia from India, and Kuwait to serve British oil interests.

There were few holdouts. The Ottoman Empire and Iranian monarchy remained nominally independent—largely because Britain did not wish to have common borders with Russia in the Middle East. Their rivalry made it impossible to satisfactorily divide these Muslim lands. But even the Ottomans and Iranians did not escape the grip of European influence, which restricted their power and dominated their economies. By the end of the nineteenth century it was clear that Muslims were no longer a force on the world stage.

Colonialism's economic and cultural impact has been so pervasive and its legacy so dominant that the Muslim world has never moved out of its shadow. Islam shaped the Muslim past, giving Muslims their identity, but it is Europe's far more recent impact that accounts for the reality they live in today and the future they look to.

———

When Napoleon invaded the Ottoman province of Egypt in 1798 even though he commanded a much smaller force than the Ottomans, their power was no match for his well-trained army. The same would be true decades later when Britain assumed control of Egypt. The story was also the same in Iran, home to the mighty Safavid Empire. From 1501 to 1722 the Safavids and their successors ruled a vast expanse of the Asian landmass, from the Caucasus and Central Asia through Afghanistan and Iran into the Persian Gulf and southern Iraq. After two calamitous wars with Russia, though, by 1828 Iranian forces found themselves pushed out of the Caucasus and Central Asia. Then, in 1856 a voracious imperialist Britain forced Iran to abandon a long-standing effort to gain control of Afghanistan. The British also encroached on Iran's power in the Persian Gulf by taking control of the island-emirate of Bahrain from Iran in 1868. This change in military fortunes ushered in a long era of European domination. The eighteenth and nineteenth centuries witnessed the incursion of European commercial interests virtually across the Muslim world. In the Middle East British, French, and Russian commercial interests first penetrated agriculture then dominated mining, trade, and even banking. They decided what the local economy produced and consumed.

Economic exploitation was followed by imperial control across far-flung Muslim territories in Asia, North Africa, and Sub-Saharan Africa. In and around the Middle East the British took over India and Egypt, the French colonized Algeria, and the Russians devoured Crimea, the Caucasus, and Central Asia. Eventually Arab territories of the Ottoman Empire too would fall to European control, with Britain claiming Palestine and Iraq, and France Syria.

The dominant lesson learned from these humiliations by the figures in the Middle East who would be most instrumental in determining its course in the nineteenth and twentieth centuries was that the Muslim world must adopt the modern military and governmental administrative tools that were perceived to have given the Western nations their overwhelming power. The European state, distinguished by its modern administration, laws, and the efficiency of its practices—but most especially by its military capabilities—captivated the Muslim imagination. Influential Muslims in positions of power whether in royal courts or intellectual circles, were convinced that modernity was essentially brought about by the institutions of the modern state; the state *was* modernity. Therein lay the root of the problems to follow.

At the outset, the Muslim fascination with Western style modernity did not take adequate account of its full nature, giving little to no credence to the importance of liberal democracy and the capitalist market economy in bringing about the progress the Muslim world craved. This stunted view of what it meant to be modern led the Middle East down a path of dictatorship and stilted modernization. In addition, the change to Western styles of state administration would displace the role Islamic law—the shariah—had played throughout Islamic history in defining the nature of justice and good government and setting the boundaries of political authority.

A repetition of Europe's many centuries long historical journey to modernity, though, was not a generally appealing prospect; change was needed faster. Many among the ruling political classes, clergy, landed elite, and tribal chiefs disliked the whole push for Western-style reforms. Clerics in particular objected. They dismissed modernization as godless and heathen—a betrayal of religion and history before a foreign invasion—and some even provided fodder for concerted resistance, on occasion leading to intense clashes. This conflict between the pursuit of Western-style modernity and Islamic tradition became a chronic struggle in the region, leading to periodic Islamic rebellion.

But change also had its supporters among these very groups. In Istanbul or Tehran there were intellectuals and statesmen who were informed about the evolution of capitalism and popular sovereignty in the West. They understood the significance of the industrial revolution and the adoption of constitutions across Europe and in the United

States that recognized the rights of citizens and limited the power of kings. They argued that the problems facing their governments could not be resolved without such changes. In the Ottoman Empire they even persuaded the Sultan to start reforms, whereas in Iran supporters of change managed to successfully ignite a social movement in support of a constitution.

Between 1839 and 1876, the Ottoman Empire introduced the Tanzimat, a series of constitutional measures that were designed to improve administration but also to cultivate liberalism in the empire. The Tanzimat called for tax reforms, disbanded the Janissary Corps (once the terror of Europe) to make way for a modern army, and gave religious minorities more rights. In Iran, a constitutional revolution in 1905–1906 was spearheaded by secular intellectuals and conservative clerics who were joining together to demand parliamentary representation and the rule of law. They blamed the monarchy for Iran's poverty and backwardness and the country's inability to protect itself from colonial encroachment. Successful in forcing the adoption of a constitution that placed law above the prerogatives of kings, they turned Iran into a constitutional monarchy with a sovereign parliament, and elevated Iranians from subjects into citizens, while limiting the power of the king.

But those pushing for change weren't looking first and foremost for liberalism; they were intent on liberation from European control, and the way to break free from that seemed to be through improving militaries, government administration, and educational institutions. When it came to these goals, liberalism seemed to have little to offer in the near term; a strong state was what was needed to provide them.

Ottoman sultans followed the Tanzimat over the decades with more legal reforms, but also went further to modernize their militaries, societies, and economies. They built roads, schools, and hospitals, and promoted national self-consciousness. They also instituted changes in dress, with militaries adopting European style uniforms, and civilian men first donning the fez and leather shoes in place of turbans and sandals, and then adopting Western-style brimmed hats and suits. All along, these reforms met with a good deal of resistance, especially from clerics and those political elite who saw value in protecting the empire's traditions. But the naysayers looked to be fighting a losing battle; more change was coming and along with it more Western-style brimmed hats and suits.

It would have been a quick and straight path to modernization in Istanbul or Tehran were it not for the fact that reforms were not really paying off. The Ottoman Empire and Iran remained weak and if anything the gap separating them from European powers was widening further. Reforms did not produce economic revolutions—in Iran's case the economy began to sag further after constitutional reforms. After all those reforms the Middle East was still pretty much where it was in the world economy.

Shortly thereafter, World War I had a calamitous impact on the Middle East. The Great War saw England and Russia on the same side, and with their rivalry at an end, they talked of dividing up the Ottoman Empire and Iran. Were it not for the Russian Revolution of 1917 putting an end to the Anglo-Russian honeymoon, Iran would have ceased to exist in its current form—it would have been divided horizontally into Russian and British colonies.

The Ottoman Empire was even more threatened. It joined the war on Germany and Austria's side, and at the war's end lost its Arab territories, which the British had encouraged into rebellion. The Turkish heartland of the empire survived intact but the Arab territories of the empire were divided up between Britain and France. The Arabs had joined the fight expecting to emerge with a single Arab state, stretching from Syria in the north to the Arabian Peninsula in the south, under the leadership of Sharif Husayn of Mecca—the great-grandfather of King Abdullah of Jordan. At the time Sharif Husayn was the venerated ruler of the Hejaz province of Ottoman Empire. But the single Arab state was not to be. Syria went to France, and Britain took Iraq and Palestine. France carved Lebanon out of Syria, and Britain similarly separated Kuwait from Iraq and then Jordan from Palestine. Winston Churchill famously conjured up Jordan on the back of a cocktail napkin and said, "Here is six months and thirty thousand pounds, let us see if the idea works." It did.

Colonialism came to these Arab lands late, and was past its prime.

The European powers no longer had the means to impose their will at all costs. Rather than rule directly, therefore, the British set up new monarchies in Iraq and Jordan, and both Britain and France looked to local elites—those whom the historian Albert Hourani calls the "notables," the so-called *a'yan*—to play key roles in governing. These were the traditional magnates who sat atop society and mediated between the rulers and the ruled, a Middle Eastern equivalent of Europe's traditional nobility.[3] They might be aristocrats, landlords, tribal leaders, wealthy merchants, or men of the cloth, such as clerics or Sufi leaders. Distinguished by their hereditary social rank, the standing of their kinship networks, their ties to royal courts, their numbers of followers, and their general influence, they went by the names *pashas, beys, khans, shaykhs, zaims, muftis,* and *mojtaheds* in the Middle East; *nawabs, zamindars, pirs,* and *sajjadanishins* farther east, in India.[4] At times it even looked as if more money was going in to patronize these elites than was flowing to the imperial powers.

Colonialism was authoritarian by nature, with little patience for dissent or desire to represent those it ruled over. The colonial regimes had but one aim: to protect and perpetuate economic imperialism. That required military forces to suppress opposition, and since there were not enough young men in Europe for colonialism's many militaries, local boys had to be recruited and trained to do the job. The European overlords concluded that this task would be easier if they exploited religious and ethnic divisions within societies. They used minorities to suppress majorities, and put up majorities against minorities, to famously divide and conquer. Colonialism left a bitter legacy, which sullied all that Europe went on to introduce to the Middle East by way of modernization. Cultural, social, and economic changes that had served European interests became forever associated with colonialism's oppression.

In Lebanon, Syria, Jordan, Egypt, Iraq, and across the Persian Gulf, the British and French were able to solicit the cooperation and the influence of notables. Iran and Turkey, however, were past that stage. Elites there were intent on self-rule and they called for radical modernization—abandoning all fealties to the past to leapfrog into a

Westernized future. Seyyed Hasan Taqizadeh, the eminent Iranian constitutional activist and man of letters, typified the prevailing sentiment,
declaring that for Iran to be prosperous it must outwardly and inwardly,
in body and in spirit, become Europeanized, and unconditionally promote European-style civilization.[5] Ali Akbar Davar, who would lead
the charge to create a modern judiciary in Iran, similarly advocated the
adoption of Western technology to service a powerful state that would
impose reforms from above. "If you want one day to enjoy the freedom
which has embraced Europe," wrote the Iranian intellectual Moshfeq
Kazemi, "produce a knowledgeable dictator . . . an ideal despot who
could take the path of evolution many years with each of his steps."[6]

Two military men, the Turkish Mustafa Kemal Ataturk and the Iranian Reza Khan, later known as Reza Shah Pahlavi, would most forcefully take up this challenge, and in the process they wrenched their
suffering societies into nationhood in the Western mode. The model of
modernization-by-command that they favored, which became known
as Kemalism, after its Turkish version, scored remarkable successes, and
under the guise of both pro- and anti-Western ideologies, it would be
replicated all around the Arab world, as well as in Pakistan.[7] Kemalism
endures as a model for change across the Middle East, but now it is
playing a key role in holding the region back from more robust capitalist growth and liberalization.

The states that emerged in the Arab world and Pakistan, first after
World War I and later, World War II, looked very much like indi-
genized versions of colonialism. The leadership relied on some of the
same elites as had the imperialists, but also cultivated a new breed of
elite: lawyers, doctors, bureaucrats, writers, academics, journalists, and
businessmen, many of them with Western or Western-style training,
who rose from the lower class due to new educational opportunities the
state provided. These elites would sit securely at the center of power in
the society, working on behalf of the state to impose secularism, push
cultural change, and force the hand of development. Everything that
has happened in the Middle East—political and economic modernization, social, cultural, and religious change—for close to a century is a

product of what happened in Turkey and Iran in the two decades following World War I, for good and for bad.

Ataturk and Reza Shah saved their countries. But for them Turkey and Iran might not have survived as nation-states, but only as broken fragments ruled by foreigners. Both might have collapsed into low-grade local anarchy, as we see in today's Afghanistan. Neither man had much if any outside support for all the building that he did; no international community to rely on, no UN or NATO troops or generous foreign aid. In fact, much of what these maverick soldiers-turned-statesmen achieved was in defiance of the will of European powers.

These days, with so much hanging in the balance as state-building efforts go on around the world, we may look with envy at the Turkey and Iran of the 1920s. Iraq, Afghanistan, Sierra Leone, Somalia, Congo— they might all do worse (and indeed have at times done much worse by collapsing into anarchy and civil war) than Ataturk or Reza Shah. If reconstruction and development of infrastructure is a measure, it is useful to consider that in 1900 there were no more than 800 miles of roads in Iran, a country nearly the size of Alaska. In just the fifteen years between 1923 and 1938, Reza Shah built 14,000 miles of new roads.[8] By contrast, the Republic of Congo boasted 90,000 miles of roads on independence in 1960, but could account for only 6,000 twenty years later.[9]

The Iran of Reza Shah was closely modeled after Kemalist Turkey. On a tree-shaded stone wall facing Istanbul's picturesque Çiragan Palace—now a luxury hotel—on the banks of the Bosporus, a large photo of Reza Shah and Ataturk is displayed, showing the two old soldiers deep in discussion. The picture is from the summer of 1934, when Reza Shah made a state visit to Turkey to survey firsthand the Kemalist achievement. Duly impressed, he returned home freshly determined to push ahead with his reforms.

The direction of the visit made a certain sense, for Turkey was better endowed than Iran. Ataturk inherited a modern army—trained by Germans—as well as an elaborate system of public administration, and far more in the way of roads, hospitals, ports, and railways than Iran enjoyed. That is in no way meant to downplay his achievement; the success with which Ataturk thrust his nation forward is one of the great stories of political leadership in world history.

––––––

General Mustafa Kemal commanded the Turkish army brilliantly in the epic battle of Gallipoli in 1915. Four years later, he was sent by the defeated Ottoman government to the town of Samsun, on the Black Sea, and put in charge of disbanding what remained of the Turkish forces. Defeated and occupied by British, French, and Greek forces, the Ottoman Empire would soon be officially carved up, but the general who had thwarted British designs at Gallipoli was not one to acquiesce in surrender. He rallied first the dejected Turkish troops he found at Samsun and then much of the rest of the Ottoman army, and over the following three years they defeated the British, French, and Greek occupying forces in battle after battle. In 1923, the European powers and Greece were forced to recognize the independent Republic of Turkey in the Treaty of Lausanne.[10] Turkey had never existed before as a political entity. Turks had sat the heart of a far larger Islamic empire; now they had to imagine themselves differently, as a nation-state.

Ataturk was born in 1881 to a middle class family in Salonika, named Thessaloniki by the Greeks. He was a gifted student, especially in mathematics, earning him the nickname *kemal*, which means perfection. Shunning the religious education customary for young men then, he joined the military in 1905. At that time, the Young Turks movement was gaining momentum, agitating for Turkish nationalism and the adoption of secularism. Kemal joined in 1906, shortly before they staged a successful coup marginalizing the Ottoman sultan, ruling the empire from then through the end of the Great War. Critical of Islam and enamored of European nationalism and scientific and social progress, the movement championed Western ideals of scientific positivism and enlightened leadership by educated elite, and their ideas had a strong influence on Kemal.

Kemal rose to power as a national hero, the man who had defeated

European armies to save the Turkish heartland from division and occupation and create a Turkish nation-state. By 1923 there was no more popular and powerful man in Turkey than Kemal, and without him it would not be possible for Turkey to forge ahead, building on what he had achieved. Kemal had a vision for the future, one that saw Turkey as a prosperous and modern European country. He had little interest in the glories of the past and the empire's Islamic legacy. What he wanted was a modern republic. A new constitution saw to that, and he was quickly elected president. The empire was no more and the sultan had no place in Turkey's future, and the new republic also abolished the caliphate in 1924.

Turkey had no more than a toehold in Europe, with barely 5 percent of its territory stretching from the Asian land mass into the European mainland beyond the Dardanelles to the borders of Greece and Bulgaria. Yet in Ataturk's mind, the country was European, and development required not merely emulating Europe, but actually becoming Europe. That meant outright claiming to be in Europe and embracing European values, secularism, nationalism, and attire. Turks must learn to do things the European way, from administration of government affairs to personal behavior, and it was the job of the state to make sure they did so.

This effort to forge Turks into Europeans proved contentious, requiring, as it did, changing customs, values, and attitudes toward life and work, women and foreigners, and most provocative of all, changing the role of religion. Kemalism identified Islam as the most un-European thing about Turkey, a superstitious and unscientific belief system, whose legal and educational institutions and intricate network of mosques, religious associations, and seminaries were shackles around Turkey's ankles.

Turks could not have two masters and could not subscribe to two worldviews; religion had to yield to Kemalism. Islam had to be reformed into an enlightened faith, which was referred to as *çagdaş Islam*, and then excluded from public life, relegated to the private sphere.[11] Turkey must become secular.

Ataturk swiftly went about loosening the grip of the ancient Islamic network of clerics, judges, Sufi orders, seminaries, and trade and guild associations. Many were disbanded—at times violently—and those that remained had to go underground, but were nevertheless weakened by the appropriation of their finances and their operations were put under the authority of the public administration. This was not secularism American style but a strident version, far beyond the separation of church and state, enacting not only domination of religious institutions, but the effort to eradicate religion from society.

Understandably, these measures generated heated protest and seething resentment among many Muslims, both in Turkey and around the region. The Kemalist assault had begun with the highly symbolic, and offensive, formal abolition of the Islamic Caliphate in March 1924. In Muslim belief the caliphs were the rightful spiritual and political successors of the Prophet Muhammad himself, and a succession of Ottoman sultans had claimed the title of Caliph starting in 1517. Turkey's role as the seat of the Caliphate was cherished by many Turks, a hallmark of Turkish identity. In renouncing the Caliphate, Ataturk was severing the country's ties with its illustrious past and forfeiting its leadership of the Muslim world. The move was seen by many Muslims as a repudiation of Islamic civilization, and was felt as a heavy psychological blow. Protests and agitations broke out in India—whose large Muslim population was then embroiled in nationalist politics and saw the abolition as a bad omen for things to come—and conferences and debates were held across the Arab world. Though ultimately the decree was met with resignation, the insult would forever blemish Kemalism in the eyes of many Muslims.

Ataturk also abolished the office of Shaykh al-Islam, chief cleric in the Ottoman Empire, along with the religious courts and seminaries, and the Ministry of Religious Affairs. Numerous mosques were closed. The most magnificent of all, the Ayasofia Mosque in Istanbul, once the greatest of all Byzantine churches, was turned into a museum in 1934. Religious endowments were placed under government administration, and the judicial system was freed from religious control. Government ministries took over religious education (changing its curriculum and social function) as well as the management of mosques.

The clerics, long used to relying on power conferred by the sultan, were ill-prepared to resist the assault, but the independent mystical Sufi orders were a different story. Not aligned with the Ottoman court—a result of centuries of deliberate secrecy to avoid the scrutiny of disapproving clerics—they had their own power base and in March 1925 they launched an armed rebellion that rallied ten thousand peasant warriors and called for the restoration of the Caliphate. The rebellion was quickly quashed and its leader, Shaykh Said and some fifty of his followers were executed. Sufi orders were thereafter banned and the state redoubled its efforts to promote secularism.

———

Soon after the establishment of the Turkish Republic, Ataturk traveled to a conservative Muslim corner of Anatolia to introduce the local population to the new emblem of male modernity. Appearing before a crowd he donned a Panama hat, to which he pointed, saying, "Gentlemen, the name of this is *şapka* [hat]!"[12] Turbans and the traditional red fez were pronounced relics of the past. In today's Turkey, images of Ataturk are everywhere, and he always looks as if he has just stepped out of a Savile Row tailor's shop. He believed that European-style dress symbolized European power, and as Turks had always mused, "Behind the hat, there are warships."[13]

Taking his transformation of Turkish life still further, in 1928, Ataturk declared that the Turkish alphabet would be changed from its traditional Ottoman script, based on Arabic with Persian influences, to one of Latin letters. Words from modern Western tongues were programmatically injected into Turkish through a literacy campaign; as part of this, concerted effort was made to "purify" Turkish of Arabic and Persian terms.[14] A Turk today goes to see exotic fish at the *akvaryum* and may brave the Istanbul *trafik* in a *taksi*. To read Turkish writings that predate Ataturk, a college-level course in "Ottoman" is required, as English literature majors often learn to read *Beowulf* in the original

Anglo-Saxon. This radical cultural transformation ensured that much of the Turkish past would be unintelligible to the rising generation and its heirs. As Ataturk intended, Turks' mental compasses would gravitate toward Europe every time they so much as looked at a street sign.

So profound was the transformation Ataturk put in motion in his own country that it rippled through much of the Muslim world, and nowhere as rapidly and emphatically as in Iran.

A favorite picture of Reza Shah during the years of his reign showed the gruff-looking, white-mustachioed king dressed in his uniform and leaning out the open window of a railway car while peering down at the pocket watch in his hand. It was as if he was Iran's chief conductor, making sure not only the train but the whole country was running on time. The image is an ironically fitting one. Reza Shah came from a humble, unschooled background; with another set of breaks he might have had a career on the rails. But he was all about getting things done, as improbable as that was in a backwater of a country with few resources and no international support. In his eyes, politics and government had but two missions: to build and to change.

Reza Shah's rise to power began in 1921. Then known as Reza Khan (an honorific title for a commoner), he was an obscure forty-something soldier who had risen from the rank of private to command a battalion in the Cossack Brigade, a ragtag militia outfit that the Russians had trained to defend Iran's shaky Qajar dynasty. He had fought with the Cossacks against separatist forces in northern Iran, and that experience had heightened his anxiety about the disintegration of his homeland in the wake of World War I, as well as his dismay at the ineptitude of the Qajar monarchy in Tehran.

Persia (what Iran was called then) was a collapsed state, with the government in Tehran weak and divided. The economy was in ruins and the parliament could not break its gridlock to produce a strong government or help it with effective governance. Prime ministers rose and fell, nothing got done, and on all fronts Iran began to walk backward. Iran's political elite—shia clergy who had helped draw up the constitution and even sat in the parliament included—were at an impasse. They could not agree on a way forward and how to strengthen the government and keep the country together.

Meanwhile, European powers were no help. Britain was now a friend of Russia (and that would continue until the Bolshevik Revolution of 1917) and no longer deemed it necessary to shore up the government in Tehran as the bulwark against Russian encroachment. In fact, Britain and Russia agreed to divide Iran (that is until Lenin took over in Moscow), and that gave London and Moscow no reason to wish for a strong Iran.

With government at the center disintegrating, anarchy ruled nationwide as tribal leaders, brigands, and warlords carved out power bases, and some even made arrangements directly with European powers, exchanging their loyalty and services for handsome wages. Marauding pro-Soviet militias controlled the north while British-backed tribal forces ran wild in the south. Despairing Iranians yearned for effective government.

A wide circle of dissidents and political activists decided to take action, and joining league with the Cossacks, they plotted a coup, with Reza Khan, who was a popular and maverick leader in his regiment, put in charge.[15] At midnight on a wintry day in early 1921, he led six hundred men on a one hundred mile march to the capital. Tehran was barely out of its slumber when the coup-makers arrived at the city gates, meeting no resistance.

The coup did not undo the constitution or disband the parliament. It did not even topple the government. The coup-makers rather forced their way into the government, and then climbed to the top on the ladder of the constitution. With Cossacks controlling the streets the sitting prime minister had no choice but to invite Reza Khan into his cabinet. He first assumed the role of minister of war, but then maneuvered the parliament to choose him as prime minister in 1923. Preaching statebuilding on the Kemalist model, he had gained a strong following, and with the aim of controlling all power—those vested in the monarchy as well those of the prime minister—in 1925 he persuaded parliament to abrogate the Qajar monarchy. Recognizing that the conservative Shia clergy would almost certainly not accept a republic, as they had seen what Ataturk's republic was doing to religion, he assumed the throne as king, or as Iranians called him, *shah*.

Reformers who two decades earlier had fought for constitutional rights flocked to his support, putting aside their democratic hopes out of the conviction that he would save the country. Among his first acts as monarch was to abolish hereditary aristocratic titles; his was a monarchy of a distinctly republican cast. A humble villager himself, he trusted the lower and middle class people more than the notables, whom he assumed if given a chance would sell the country out by making the same arrangements with European powers as they had done during the colonial era.

Over the next twenty years, Reza Shah created a modern army and police force, established a central bank, built a national university along with a modern education system, modernized the judiciary—adopting European legal principles and copying Europeans in how courts work and dispense justice—built factories—the first modern industry in the country—and constructed a transportation system that connected the country's far-flung corners for the first time. The army subdued rebellious warlords and tribesmen, and Reza Shah promoted Iranian nationalism through a mantra of unity and progress.

In the matter of religion, Reza Shah was somewhat less ardently secular than his Turkish counterpart. Ataturk embraced secularism with a loving bear hug and backed it with an entrenched bureaucratic and military establishment that is a major force in Turkish life to this day. Reza Shah too saw religion as backward, superstitious, and a stumbling block to progress, but in clamping down on Islam he faced more formidable opposition than Ataturk. The Shia clergy who held sway in Iran had always been more independent of rulers than their Turkish counterparts—in fact, many Shia holy men lived in shrine cities in the southern part of the new kingdom to the west called Iraq, which had been part of Ottoman Empire and then a British mandate, and hence were beyond Iranian control. The Shia clergy were also enormously popular with the masses, in part because they had traditionally stood up for nationalism when the monarchs had forged cozy relationships with Britain or Russia or made deals with France or Belgium, granting them concessions that extracted much from Iran for little in return. But Reza Shah had developed a strong following for his reforms, and as long as large numbers of Iranians backed change and gave him their support, he could clip the clerics' wings.

He established a secular educational system, and pushed to marginalize religious education—deciding on its curriculum and who could take advantage of it. He also did away with religious endowments—vast estates and financial holdings that were placed in trusts to pay for religious charities, care of the poor, or education of seminarians. He also secularized the judiciary. Banished from courts, offices, and schools and restricted to their seminaries, many clerics soon saw their sons abandon the ancestral calling and opt instead for secular careers. The powerful clerical dynasties became better represented in the halls of power in Tehran than in the seats of Shia learning at Qom, the great seminary city a hundred miles southwest of the capital.

Looking to the pre-Islamic traditions of ancient Persian civilization, Reza Shah also worked to craft a new nationalism. He was enamored of the glories of Iran's pre-Islamic past. As a soldier he had spent many nights during long marches listening to his superiors telling stories of the Achaemenid and Sassanid empires that ruled Persia between 550 B.C.E. and 651 C.E., and of the magnificent splendor of the ancient ruins of Ctesiphon and Persepolis—once Persian imperial capitals.[16] He chose "Pahlavi" as his surname because it was the name of the language of ancient Sassanid Empire that ruled Persia before the arrival of Islam. Identifying Iran with its ancient Aryan past, when an Indo-European civilization ruled over the territory, was Reza Shah's way of casting Iranians as Europeans.

He sought to purge Arabic words from Persian speech, and he abandoned Islam's lunar calendar for a solar one that starts the year with the first day of spring and uses ancient Iranian names for the months.[17] He also forced men to adopt the "Pahlavi cap," which resembled a tall baseball cap, along with a longish upper-body garment that resembled the frock coat once in vogue in the West.[18] The devout resented the new attire, which was binding when one tried to sit on the floor in the traditional style, and the cap's bill was also clearly intended as an obstacle to touching the ground with one's forehead during prayers. Failure to wear the new clothes incurred fines, and though the clergy were officially exempt, the police often harassed them anyway.[19]

Matters of female attire proved even more contentious. In 1935, when Reza Shah decided that Iranian women must immediately shed the veil, the police began forcibly removing headscarves and the *chador*, the long semicircular cloth that Iranian women draped over their heads and shoulders. Many in the public were shocked and angry, but resistance met with brutal repression.

In summer of 1935 a group of angry demonstrators gathered in the courtyard of the magnificent Goharshad Mosque, a fifteenth century architectural marvel in the far-northeastern city of Mashhad, to protest the Pahlavi cap.[20] Reza Shah's army reacted viscerally and brutally. Violating the sanctity of the mosque, troops stormed the sanctuary, killing some demonstrators and injuring many more. The incident became an infamous symbol of the brutality of state secularism, whose memory would die hard. In 1979, shortly after revolution swept Khomeini to power, Islamic forces exacted revenge. A revolutionary court tried and executed the octogenarian, General Iraj Matbooie, who had commanded the assault force that day, and Khomeini's mausoleum in south Tehran stands on land seized from the general's family.

All of the turmoil was not without its tension for Reza Shah himself. Unlike his Turkish counterpart, he seems to have approached the imitation of European and secular ways more as a perceived necessity than out of personal conviction.[21] To support unveiling, Reza Shah decided that he would have to appear in public with his wife and daughters, all the women to be dressed in Western garb with heads bare, and his daughter Princess Ashraf would later recall the anguish that this caused her father.[22] Deeply traditional at his core, this son of a small upland village near the Caspian Sea paced his palace halls the night before, agonizing over the loss of honor and standing as a Muslim man that such a display would mean. In the end he did what he thought he had to. His womenfolk publicly dispensed with the veil. Reza Shah was not a man to shrink from his convictions. A popular urban myth holds that upon hearing that a cleric had questioned the royal honor from a pulpit in Qom, the furious king rushed to confront his accuser, interrupting the hapless preacher in mid-sermon and beating him before his stunned congregation.

He would never win the kind of admiration that Ataturk enjoyed from his countrymen. The Turks had lined up behind Ataturk to fight to the knife against occupation forces and save Turkey from extinction, and Reza Shah could not claim quite the same sort of glorious feat. Because he contended with more resistance from tribal leaders, land lords, and clerics in Iran, he also resorted to brute force to silence his detractors, and he paid a price for that in alienating many among his people. But the impressive extent of his accomplishments in holding Iran together and propelling its economy were also widely acknowledged, not only in Iran but around the region.

Reza Shah's end came with WWII. As Nazi Germany squared off against the Allied powers, the Middle East grew uneasy. Reza Shah quickly declared Iran neutral, but his efforts to keep his country out of the war could not last long. The Allies, desperate to shore up Stalin's army before advancing German forces, needed the railway line Reza Shah had built (an accomplishment that he was particularly proud of) to connect the Persian Gulf to the Caspian and thereby both unite his country and jump start its economy. Britain was suspicious of Reza Shah. He had been a thorn in their side ever since he had assumed the throne, pushing them for more royalties from the sale of the country's oil, but more important he was a fierce nationalist who would not easily bow to the Allies' wishes. He raised the ire of the Allies when he rebuffed their demand that he expel all German nationals residing in Iran, raising suspicion that he was inclined to support Hitler. Then, in August 1941, when he refused to allow Allied forces passage through Iran to transport badly needed war material to the Soviet Union, British and Soviet forces invaded. Reza Shah was compelled to abdicate,

on September 16, and the Allies installed his son, Muhammad Reza
Shah Pahlavi (the shah who would rule Iran until 1979), on the throne,
though firmly under the control of the occupying powers. They then
signed a treaty with Iran guaranteeing they would depart the country by
six months after the war's end and requiring in return that Iran support
the Allied cause. His Kemalist project interrupted and his country once
again in shambles, Reza Shah was exiled, dying in Johannesburg, South
Africa, a broken man, in 1944.

———

Ataturk and Reza Shah achieved astonishing feats of progress, and their
example was emulated all around the region, with variations on the
theme, and with variable success. When Colonel Gamal Abd al-Nasser
took over power in Egypt in a coup in 1952, he instituted reforms
much along the lines of Kemalism. Indeed, Nasser's new Egypt bore
an uncanny resemblance to Ataturk's Turkey: a formidable leviathan,
backed by a modern army, pressing rapid reforms, industrialization,
and wide-scale social change. Nasser invested heavily in infrastructure
and industrialization, reformed education and government administration, and promoted nationalism—in his case more Arab than Egyptian,
appealing to the yearning for Arab unity above and beyond national
boundaries. Nasser's vision was also of a secular state and society, and he
cracked down on the firm hold that Islam and its clerics had exercised
on Egyptian society for millennia. His government took over the management of religious endowments, reduced the role of religion in the
judiciary and national education, and even restricted the clerics' control
of mosques and seminaries.

In Pakistan, another military reformer adopted Kemalism, but with
more mixed results. When the new state of Pakistan was drawn onto
the map of the world on a fitful August midnight in 1947, it was no
more than a leap of imagination, with nothing resembling a functioning state. Pakistan owes its existence to Muhammad Ali Jinnah, and his
indefatigable campaign to convince Indian Muslims that they would be
no more than second class citizens in a Hindu-dominated India.

Pakistan was pieced together from the scraps broken off the edges of India—Muslim bits and pieces far from the British imperial capital—and the country inherited none of the well-oiled machinery of colonial government the Indian republic took over. What was worse, the country's two wings—one of which would become Bangladesh in 1971—were separated by twelve-hundred miles of hostile Indian territory. The people of the five provinces that were sliced away from British India to form the country spoke different languages and each had its own distinct cultural identity.

Pakistan desperately needed effective leadership, but for its first nine fitful years, the country suffered under a divided and bickering government hastily put together by Jinnah and his lieutenants. Rather than immediately adopting its own constitution, Pakistan followed Britain's colonial constitution, the India Act of 1935, until 1956, and squabbles over how the government should be structured would drag on for years. Making matters worse, the country's founding hero and most important political leader, Jinnah, died in 1948. The partition caused economic crisis and the country suffered droughts and food shortages, facing millions of refugees to care for. Prior to the partition, little other than religious identity bound the territories that became Pakistan. Each had its own ties with the heartland of Indian power and its economy.

State building was an uphill battle, with no agreement reached on power sharing between provinces, which delayed ratification of a constitution. Pakistan had been championed by secular men with secular ambitions for Indian Muslims as a country of their own where they would be free from Hindu repression. The formation of the country had received no support from clerics and religious activists, and none was represented in the leadership of the Pakistan movement. But with the secular leadership failing to form an effective government, Islamic forces took advantage of the power vacuum. They claimed it was their duty to speak up for the masses and look after their interests, and they blamed secularism for the leadership's failings. Pakistan must become a truly Islamic country, they argued. Fundamentalist voices were most prominent in articulating these sentiments, and it was they who forced the debate by organizing riots and rallies, demanding that the constitution establish an Islamic state. For this reason, when the government finally produced a constitution in 1956, although it called for a British-style parliamentary democracy, it also pronounced Pakistan an Islamic state. Though the designation of the government as Islamic was largely symbolic—shariah, for example, was not instituted as the law of the land—it did support future arguments demanding the implementation of Islamic law in the country and the imposition of Islamic values in legislation and policy making. What the adoption of the constitution did not do was lead to better government.

In 1958, a military coup overthrew the government and its leader, General Muhammad Ayub Khan, turned to Kemalism. Promoting himself first to field marshal, he later assumed the presidency, and rapid development, built on the back of a strong administration, became his mantra.

Pakistan prospered under Ayub Khan, with industrialization beginning in earnest, bringing economic progress and allowing the nation to gain its footing on the world stage. Ayub Khan hoped to reform Islam as well, turning it into a more liberal faith, and he sought to weaken Islamic institutions in Pakistan, ordering his subordinates in 1959 to draft a plan for secularizing the country along the lines of the steps Ataturk had taken. He gathered clerics from across the country to tell them to leave politics alone and instead to interpret Islam in ways that would support his vision. He created reform-advocating think tanks and met with the handful of intellectuals who were promoting a modernist form of Islam, throwing his favor behind their mission. He also nationalized religious endowments and placed many mosques and Sufi shrines under government control. In 1961, he changed family law to make marriage, divorce, and domestic disputes of various matters for secular rather than religious adjudication. A year later, he forced through a new constitution that removed the identification of the state as Islamic.

Islamic modernism never gained much traction in Pakistan, however, and Ayub's steps to weaken Islam's hold on the country set in motion a dynamic of conflict over the place of Islam in the government and society that has consistently plagued the country. Three decades after Ayub Khan left office, another general would try to pick up where Ayub Khan left off in the push for secularism, but Pervez Musharraf's efforts fared no better than Ayub's. Islam proved a powerfully resilient force in Pakistani life.

All across the region, Kemalism would prove both a success and a scourge; its legacy fraught with contradictions. For much of the twentieth century kings and presidents of the region, some leaning to the right others socialist in their creed, adopted the Kemalist model, setting up command economies and top-down reforms. They viewed secularism as an essential cultural change, and they not only restricted clerics, but, as Ataturk and Reza Shah had done, sought to mandate a new way of life.

Looking back over the decades since Ataturk and Reza Shah ruled we can see that much in way of economic development and social change has been achieved in the Middle East. Kemalist presidents, kings, and generals unified countries, and built roads, modern school systems, and hospitals. But those authoritarian regimes also often lost their way, succumbing to the temptation of despotism, and in the process growing corrupt. The leviathans they created also stifled market forces and hindered true economic change. Top-down modernization had its limits. States can do things faster and more efficiently than markets, but only to get things moving; they are notoriously bad at managing economies once they are out of the gate. Kemalist states did not know when and how to stop growing, and that was their undoing. Unchecked by parliaments and unaccountable to the people, the Kemalist states have lived up to the saying: "Power tends to corrupt, and absolute power corrupts absolutely."

Kemalism never had a problem garnering support in the West. Defenders of Kemalism, such as the historian Bernard Lewis, had hoped that by promoting secularism and modernity the state would serve as handmaiden of democracy, believing that modernity must come before democracy, especially given Islam's strong hold on the structures of power, and the hearts and minds of the populace.[23] Democracy would have to follow dictatorship.

But by the 1970s, Kemalism was running aground everywhere. The state remained imposing, but its modernizing edge was gone. The juggernaut of swift reform, secularism, and rapid change had ground to a halt. Accolades for the state and trust in its ability to transform society and economy had given place to widespread cynicism and doubt among the populace. In the Arab world modernizing states became platforms for the dynastic machinations of strongman presidents; their best-functioning institutions—impressive in their efficiency—became their dreaded *mukhabarat*, intelligence and security services.

One of Kemalism's legacies is pent-up rage among the lower classes, to whom so few of the economic benefits flowed, and who greatly resented the assault on Islam. This pent-up rage has in time inflicted much travail on the region—as well as on the West. It was the driving force that tipped the balance of power toward fundamentalism in the Iranian Revolution, and it has been the fuel driving the support around the region for Islamic extremism. Crucial to Kemalism's failure to generate more robust economic growth, and to distribute economic benefits more equitably, was the manner in which it bred a highly dependent, rather than entrepreneurial, middle class.

———

On a chilly afternoon in fall of 1928, three dozen students, dressed in dark suits and Pahlavi caps, filed into the grand reception hall of the Saadabad Palace in north Tehran for an audience with Reza Shah. He wanted to wish them well in person before they left for Europe to pursue their studies. Reza Shah's Iran needed educated professionals, and sending students to Europe on government scholarships was the fastest way of supplying modernization with its foot soldiers.

The students stood nervously in a single line as the towering figure of Reza Shah paced before them, sizing them up. Fixing his gaze on the students, he reminded them of their duties to their country: Iran was poor, and was sacrificing much to fund their educations in hopes that they would give back. They were Iran's ambassadors but also its eyes and ears. The king encouraged them to learn from Europeans about science and technology, culture and arts, but above all about patriotism.[24] He wanted to educate Iranians to put loyalty to their nation above all others. A few years later he would send his own adolescent son on the same journey; Iran's future leader too had to become modern before he could take the helm of power.

My grandfather, a cleric's son from a small town in eastern Iran, was among those boys, and for the rest of his life he worked to live up to Reza Shah's charge. He never ceased to feel the weight of the duty to change Iran for the better, and to do so by imparting to it the wisdom and ways of the West.

My grandfather studied medicine in Paris and he traded his provincial Iranian mores for the sensibilities of a Parisian gentleman, always dressing like one. He developed an appreciation for the arts, French cuisine, and the ideals of social democracy, and upon his return to Iran displayed the etiquette he had learned abroad. He also worked tirelessly to improve health care, in particular to eradicate tuberculosis—the fearsome "white plague" that was the scourge of a growing economy in need of able-bodied labor. The poverty and backwardness he was battling distressed him, but he was a builder, not a revolutionary. He spent many years raising funds and securing government support to build a convalescent clinic for tuberculosis patients in the dry air of the foothills that overlook Tehran. It was a labor of love; the trees in the garden that he laid out for his patients to enjoy were planted with his own hands.

My grandfather belonged to the new middle class created to carry out the mandate of Kemalism, from Turkey through the Arab world, Iran, and India. Western in orientation, patriotic and committed to the vision of a secular and prosperous Middle East, they were a new breed in the history of the region, and they had to find their way into a social structure still so much dominated by an aristocracy of royalty, land lords, high clerics, and tribal leaders. They stood between the elites and the masses, most of whom were serfs and peasants, and they were distinguished not only by their careers, as doctors, lawyers, and civil servants but also by how they dressed and spoke. They did a great deal to lift their countries and change their societies, and yet today their presence in the Middle East is spectral.

In this, the Middle East appears oddly unique, a global exception. In China and India—together the home of every third person on the planet—in Latin America and Eastern Europe, and across the rest of East Asia, the secular, modern middle class has been at the forefront of transitions to capitalism, and in many cases also to democracy. Only in the Middle East, it seems, did a sizeable middle class, friendly to Western values and desirous of political freedom, fail to put down roots deep enough to grow. Only there did it fail to gain dominance, and only there did it leave its modernizing task incomplete. The riddle of the Middle East in those eight decades since Reza Shah gave my grandfather and his mates their marching orders is: What happened to that middle class? Why did it never live up to its promise and play the same role as the burgers of sixteenth-century Europe or its more recent counterparts in East or South Asia? Why did it fail to command history, and fall victim instead to history's vagaries? The rise and precipitous fall of this class tells us much about why the Middle East remains mired in dictatorship and retrograde tendencies. And yet the middle class whose moment never came is a sorely neglected topic, even among experts of the region.

Those studying the rise of the West place great emphasis on the role of the bourgeoisie. The eminent Harvard sociologist Barrington Moore Jr. famously wrote: "No bourgeois, no democracy."[25] Capitalism, and eventually democracy, were, he argued, the result of a process by which Europe's urban middle class gained prominence, the governments becoming increasingly dependent on revenues from their economic prosperity and in turn increasingly subject to their will. In the Middle East, by contrast, after a promising start in the early twentieth century, the middle class was largely the product of the state, and it forfeited its role as the vehicle of liberalization, opting instead for state patronage. This was a tragic legacy of Kemalism.

The middle class did at first flourish with the rise of new states after World War I, its imprint clearly recognizable in the Istanbul and Tehran of the 1920s, and by the 1930s, in cities on the Eastern Mediterranean, and in the urban centers of India. This cadre of new social pioneers painted a stark contrast to the traditional lifestyles and mind-set of the notables, stressing education, service, and secularism, and more often than not, self-reliance. These young men joined government service, taught in schools or universities, and practiced law and medicine. Many spoke out for cultural, social, and political reforms, and they were early adopters of nationalism across the region. From their tastes in architecture, clothing, and furniture, preferring chairs over floor cushions, for instance, to their use of language and mannerisms, and beliefs in individual rights and less rigid gender inequality, they left a definite cultural imprint on the region. The power struggle between the notables and this new professional class explains the obsession that one still finds in the Middle East with titles such as "doctor" and "engineer," a leftover of the middle class's determined assertion that they could have titles too, but theirs would derive from acquired knowledge rather than bloodlines and wealth.

But in the years from Nasser's rise in Egypt to the turning point of the Iranian Revolution, it became apparent that the fate of this new middle class was ineluctably bound up with that of the state. Because the vehicle of modernity in the Middle East was the state, the middle class became unduly beholden to the state, a dependent class rather than an independently powerful bourgeoisie as described by Barrington Moore. They made a fool's bargain.

Like a moth flying too close to the flame, the middle class would find itself consumed by its proximity to the state, supporting not capitalism and democracy but political autocracies sitting atop command economies and preaching rigid ideologies of uniformity. When grandiose state-building projects began to fail, and state-engendered modernization was revealed as stillborn, the middle class began to pay for its too-close affiliation.

In Western Europe, the middle class thrived on business and operated through social networks it created rather than relying on patronage. Independent of state support the middle class was free to follow its own interests, and those led to demands for political freedom, and the wealthier the middle class became, the more it craved those freedoms. In the Middle East, the middle class was not independently generating wealth so it did not develop the leverage—or even really the will—to demand the rights and freedoms of Western liberalism. A telling example of the cozy relationship so many in this class made with the region's authoritarian regimes is that on the eve of the Iranian Revolution, the Shah's cabinet was dominated not by aristocrats but by Iranians hailing from middle-class or lower origin.

Fueling this problem was the surge of oil revenue. The wealthier some states grew in the age of high oil revenues, the more the region's capitalists became junior partners, dependent on state largesse. Governments had no need of the job creation and tax receipts that independent businessmen could generate. So it was that the middle class—destined to lead the Middle East to modernity—lost its way, failing to show up at the tryst with history to play its part in nudging the region in the right direction.

The legacy of Kemalism is most decidedly mixed, and as the story of the revolution in Iran to be told in the next chapter shows all too vividly, the abdication of the responsibility to push for liberalism on the part of the state-sponsored middle class had many tragic consequences. But even so, there is a degree of reverence in the region for the accomplishments of Kemalism, and that has much to say about the pro-modernism, pro-capitalism mentality of the middle class that is rising around the region today in the more authentic, independent manner that Barrington Moore's analysis indicates is the key to successful political liberalization.

———

During a recent research visit to Iran, I asked a burly barber how to get to Vali-e Asr Avenue, a broad colonnaded thoroughfare in Tehran named after the Shia messiah. The barber looked me up and down and in a reproachful tone said, "Young man, that road was not built by the Hidden Imam; it was built by Reza Shah." I got my answer only after I rephrased my question and asked for the street by its original name,

"Pahlavi Avenue." Renamed after the Islamic Revolution, the street had in fact been laid out as Reza Shah's answer to the Champs Elysées."[26] Reza Shah's legacy is a complex business.[27] The monarch who was once abhorred by revolutionaries for his iron fist and authoritarian ways is now celebrated, quietly but surely, as the man who kept Iran whole and then built much of its early modern institutions and infrastructure despite greatest odds.

Things are more openly laudatory at the grave of Mustafa Kemal Ataturk. His massive mausoleum sits majestically overlooking Ankara, the capital that he located in the heart of the Anatolian Plateau, as far from the Ottoman legacy of Istanbul as from the threat of foreign warships. The surge that Islam is enjoying in Turkey these days may seem a repudiation of Kemalism, but visit this burial site, and you will come away with quite a different impression. It is teeming with visitors, as if a curious Turkey has decided it must meet its revered founder. An estimated ten million people visited Ataturk in 2007,[28] quite a groundswell of curiosity and homage in a country of some seventy million. Search through the crowd and you will spot more than an occasional headscarf. The founder of modern Turkey attracts not only grateful secularists but also reverent believers. In Turkey, too, the legacy of the great modernizer is more complicated than may at first meet the eye.

Kemalism was most successful in Turkey, and most fraught in its unintended consequences in Iran. By taking a close look at the course of the revolution that swept Iran starting in 1979, we can see more clearly how the bitter ironies of Kemalism's shortfalls accounted for the stealthy takeover of the state by the forces of Islamic radicalism, and what the true source of support of Ayatollah Khomeini's populist fire-breathing was. Doing so is essential to understanding why the West should be working to engage with the sons and daughters of those ardent peasants and urban lower-class workers who came out in droves to support the revolution, and to engage them not only in Iran but all around the region.

CHAPTER 5

THE GREAT
ISLAMIC REVOLUTION

Great revolutions are like perfect storms: rare and monumental occurrences. They defy expectations and turn history in directions no one imagined, unleashing new ideas that capture imaginations and touching off unanticipated struggles. Those who come out on top of such upheavals often thrive on challenging the existing world order, acting as spoilers for years to come. So it has been with the Iranian Revolution of 1979.

Looking back on that cold February 9 day in 1979, three decades ago, when the revolutionary forces took control of Iran and swept the Pahlavi monarchy from power, we can see one era ending as another begins. Ayatollah Khomeini's rise ushered in an era of intense struggle over Islamic fundamentalism, both within the Middle East and between the region and the Western powers. Fueling a global movement spoiling for fights with the West, even as Soviet communism was imploding, the Iranian Revolution assured there would be no "end of history," in the words of political scientist Francis Fukuyama. Democracy and free market capitalism would not so inexorably prevail all over the world.[1]

The Islamic Republic of Iran has perfected the art of confrontation. Once the revolution triumphed, Khomeini and his inner circle saw themselves as the standard-bearers of a global Islamic cause, and the bulwark against Western cultural imperialism and American hegemony.[2] They planned to export their breed of Islam and sow the seeds of many more rebellions to come—producing a "fundamentalist international" in the mold of Lenin's Communist International. Right from the start, the ruling clerics supported fundamentalist activists in

the Arab world, Africa, and South and Southeast Asia. Though radical groups have caused much havoc since—most notably, assassinating
Egyptian president Anwar Sadat, leading riots and bloody uprisings in
Pakistan, Saudi Arabia, and Persian Gulf emirates, pushing conflicts in
Lebanon and between Arabs and Israelis in new and more violent directions, and carrying out bombing campaigns against Western targets
from the Marine Barracks in Beirut in 1983 to the 9/11 attacks—no
more major dominoes in the Middle East power structure fell into the
hands of fundamentalists. One can think of the Taliban's sweep over
war-torn Afghanistan in the 1990s, but then Afghanistan was not a state
but rubble left behind by war and the Taliban's fierce puritanical rule
was inspired not by fundamentalism about which they knew little but
by rigid Pashtoun tribal sensibilities.

Some thirty years on, Iran's hand is still firmly in support of the
myriad of radical forces in the Middle East, including not only Hezbollah but also Hamas in the Palestinian territories and the Sadrist militias
in Iraq. Radical Islam professes itself to be an unstoppable force. But
the truth is that it has risen to prominence, such that it has, only in
instances of the breakdown of state power—in places like Afghanistan,
Lebanon, the Palestinian territories, or Somalia. Fundamentalism has
gained footholds—and won in Iran—due to the failures of authoritarian leaders to execute on promises of economic progress for the masses,
and crucially, due to the abdication by the state-sponsored middle class
of a leadership role in bringing about robust economic growth and
political liberalization.

The Iranian Revolution ended in theocracy, but it did not begin
with widespread support for that outcome. Khomeini was always the
revolution's leader, but he shrewdly rode to power by keeping his plans
obscure. During the whirlwind years of 1978 and 1979, the revolution
did not take on a particularly Islamic cast. The protest against the Shah
regime was then a many-headed hydra of pro-democracy, socialist, communist, and Islamic activists. Its leaders and foot soldiers were not just
clerics and their followers, but more prominently, intellectuals, politicians, academics, students, lawyers, factory workers, and leftist guerrilla

fighters. There were no equivalents of Lenin's tracts or Mao's Little Red Book passing from hand to hand putting forth Khomeini's intentions, and there were no lectures or rallies dedicated to introducing his grand ambitions for an Islamic state or the fine points of his teachings on politics. Khomeini's was a revolution by stealth.[3]

So how to explain an Islamic revolution that began with little theocratic impetus? The revolution was in part an epic battle of Islam against secularism, and also a mass rebellion against dictatorship, but it did not turn on these things. The revolution happened in Iran, and has not happened since anywhere else, because Iran was unique among secular, modernizing states in a single crucial respect: Only in Iran did the Kemalist regime so totally and irretrievably lose the loyalty of its secular middle class. In large numbers, these educated professionals—lawyers, doctors, professors, government workers—shunned the Kemalist regime that had called them into being, and in their dissent, they became more enamored of socialism and communism than of Western-style capitalist democracy, though some among them did promote the latter. This helps to explain why the secular middle class so readily submitted to Khomeini's Leninist-style leadership. The revolution turned around a marriage of strange bedfellows: the educated and mostly secular middle class academics, lawyers, students and civil servants who wanted to depose the Shah but had vague and contradictory notions about the government that should replace him, and the devoutly religious lower class youth, labor, bazaar shop keepers, and clerics who rallied around Khomeini and the message of ridding Iran of a corrupt and oppressive monarchy that stood accused of plundering the country and brutalizing its citizens, and of serving only America's interests.

I was there, a teenage witness amid an awkward ceremony, to see the strands intertwining in their strange courtship dance. I vividly recall the morning of September 8, 1978, on the eve of the revolution. The occasion was Eid ul-Fitr—the feast that marks the close of Ramadan's holy month, when after a lunar cycle of dawn-to-dusk fasting Muslims gather for a special prayer. In a dusty vacant lot in affluent north Tehran, a large crowd had come together for an impromptu Eid prayer, as if to flaunt their rejection of Pahlavi secularism. A cleric led the prayer, and many pious men and women joined the crowd after a trek from poorer parts of town. Standing out in stark contrast were clean-shaven men and women whose Western-style appearance had been only thinly disguised by hastily donned headscarves and long skirts, clearly the fruit of last-minute raids on closets. These were not usual prayer attendees; they were there purely as a form of protest. I remember looking at writers, poets, and painters who I knew were not pious, or even particularly versed in Islam, lining the prayer rows and bending awkwardly in the direction of Mecca.

It was this alliance of the secular and the religious, the once Kemalist but now disaffected middle class and the pious lower-class masses, that made the revolution. The decisive factor was the willingness of so many of those in the middle class to put their hatred of the monarchy above the long-standing social divide that separated them from the religious lower class. The irony was that, although the Iranian Revolution could never have happened without the secular middle class, as it gained steam, the middle class could not retain control; in the end they stood no chance against the rising tide of Khomeini's lower class supporters, and they would pay a high price for their ill-conceived alliance. Blinded by their hatred of the Pahlavis, they acted against their own interests, and with the Pahlavis gone, Khomeini and his followers would make short work of their plans for themselves in the new government.

In the last months of the monarchy, scores of government employees went on strike, and before doing so threw the portraits of the Shah that the regime had required be so pervasively displayed in the country out of their office windows, to be burned on the streets below. The office cleaning was surreptitiously convenient. Little did the strikers know then that so many of them would not be returning to their offices; Khomeini's republic wanted no secular mandarins.

———

The roiling rage within the secular middle class against the Pahlavi dynasty that did so much to propel the revolution had been building for decades. The middle-class love affair with the monarchy—if it was ever truly such—was short-lived. As the population of educated professionals steadily expanded under Reza Shah's tutelage, they grew increasingly disdainful of monarchic rule. In the 1930s, the radical ideologies of the left, so popular then in Europe and even gaining ground in the United States, captured the imagination of more and more students and professors, and doctors, lawyers, and civil servants, as was true all around the Middle East, and especially in the Arab world. Many of those who became enamored of radical leftism in Iran had gone to college in Europe, particularly in France and Germany, and had become exposed to then popular arguments in support of socialism and communism, impressed by the glowing depictions of the great successes of Stalinism. In 1941 they formed the Tudeh Party, "tudeh" meaning masses, which became one of the most formidable communist parties in the Middle East. At the time there was no meaningful party politics in Iran and the parliament was weak and subservient to Reza Shah. Communists dismissed Reza Shah as a despot, and saw Iran as a backward feudal society ripe for revolution that could only imagine a future in communism.

Fearing Soviet encroachment, Reza Shah reacted with ruthless repression, famously killing Taqi Arani, the thirty-six-year old physics professor who was the communist ringleader, along with fifty-two other leading leftist and communist intellectuals and organizers making martyrs of them—"the band of 53" would for long after symbolize that act of infamy.[4] At his trial Arani dismissed the tribunal as a Nazi Kangaroo court and an example of medieval despotism that lay bare the hollowness of Reza Shah's claim to modernization. Arguing communism's case he said: "If you wish to adopt Western clothes, Western style, Western institutions, Western technology, and Western way of life, you must also adopt Western political philosophies."[5]

But Reza Shah fell victim himself that same year to the ravages that World War II would inflict on the Middle East. He had tried to distance his government and the Iranian economy from the clutches of imperialist exploitation, as Britain and Russia had vied for influence over the country. Britain had secured control over Iran's vast oil resources when it

founded the Anglo-Iranian Oil Company (AIOC) in 1907. The British
were at first happy to see Reza Shah rise to power, hoping that a strong
government in Tehran would make Iran less vulnerable to communist
penetration from the north. But once on the throne Reza Shah subju-
gated tribal chiefs loyal to the British and thwarted London's efforts to
create a sphere of influence in Iran's oil region in its southwest. As Reza
Shah gained in power he pushed Britain to give Iran a larger share of
the oil revenue. London resisted and in the process developed a dislike
of Reza Shah, seeing him as a brute and an upstart, who was too unruly
and headstrong to be properly managed—a threat to the colonial order
the British had set up all around Iran in the Middle East.

During World War II the Allies occupied Iran and removed Reza
Shah from power, laying waste to the state he had so painstakingly put
together. During the war Soviet troops occupied large areas of northern
and western Iran. Under their protection communist activists were free
to recruit followers, building up a substantial Iranian communist movement. The Tudeh Party formed student and labor committees, printed
newspapers and books, recruited large numbers of professionals and
government workers, and even penetrated the military. The party held
rally after rally, with hardly a day going by when thousands of wide-eyed
youth would not gather on city squares to hear passionate speeches by
communist intellectuals and party organizers about social justice and
workers rights, the evils of imperialism and the promise of liberation.
Their tales of the glories of Stalin's Soviet republic, and the magnificent
future that awaited the Iranian and wider Middle Eastern masses once
communist revolutions swept away oppressive and decadent capitalist
regimes proved enormously appealing. Stalin expected that after the war
Iran would fall into his hands like a ripe apple.

The United States and Britain feared the same, and also the loss of
Britain's control over Iran's oil fields, when at the end of the war, Stalin
made no move to withdraw his troops. Then, with Soviet instigation,
in December 1945, Azerbaijan and Kurdistan declared independence
from Iran as Soviet republics—the only time in history there has been
a formal Kurdish state. Washington and London placed intense diplo-

matic pressure on Moscow to withdraw from Iran. At the heart of the matter was the West's growing fear of Soviet expansionism, as well as Soviet aims on Iranian oil.

To provide the pretext for a Soviet withdrawal the Iranian government dispatched Prime Minister Ahmad Qavam to Moscow to sign an oil deal with Stalin. Stalin took the bait and no sooner had the Red Army left Iranian soil than the Shah's military marched into the separatist republics. The communist puppet regimes quickly folded and many of their leaders escaped to the Soviet Union. Meanwhile with the West's support the Iranian parliament voted down Qavam's oil deal with Stalin, denying Moscow a coveted foothold in Iran.

The Shah's mind-set about the relationship he would build with the West during the decades that followed was forged in this last-ditch effort to snatch Iranian sovereignty from the jaws of communism. He became convinced that the biggest threat to his country came from the Soviets, and that Iran would survive only if the West remained committed to protecting the country's territorial integrity. Ensuring that became his obsession from that point forward. The Iranian communists who had collaborated with Stalin had to be destroyed at all costs, and the regime cracked down, making mass arrests.

The monarchy lost the middle class for good after the two found themselves on opposing sides of the crisis over the nationalization of Iran's oil industry in 1953. Iranians had long been unhappy with their share of oil revenues. Reza Shah had constantly needled the AIOC over the issue, but all he got for his efforts was Britain's ill will. After World War II the issue came to a head. Iran needed the revenue to rebuild an economy shattered by the occupation, and fueling the fire was news that American oil companies had given far better terms to Mexico, Venezuela, and Saudi Arabia in exchange for exploration rights in those countries. A vast majority of Iranians deeply resented the colonialist sense of entitlement, and superiority, directed at them by AIOC; a sign at the entrance to its compound in the oil city of Abadan in southern Iran actually read, "No dogs or Iranians allowed."

In 1950 Prime Minister General Hajj Ali Razmara pushed for a

50–50 revenue-sharing deal, which AIOC refused. Then Razmara was assassinated by a fundamentalist fringe group (some of whose members would later surface as part of Khomeini's entourage during the revolution). In the wake of his killing, Mohammad Mossadegh rose to power. Mossadegh was an aristocrat, a scion of the Qajar dynasty, which Reza Shah had deposed. He was a French-educated lawyer with long experience in parliamentary politics and a checkered relationship with the Pahlavi Shahs. He had cast one of the four "no" votes when the Parliament voted Reza Shah king in 1925, and at one point Reza Shah banished him to a small provincial town. He was released from custody only after the crown prince (who later became the Shah) intervened on his behalf. Mossadegh was a champion of parliamentary democracy, but more important of complete nationalization of Iranian oil. His uncompromising rhetoric quickly captured popular imagination and he rode the wave of surging nationalism into the prime minister's office.

After Mossadegh's election, the long-simmering dispute over Iran's share of profits from AIOC boiled over.[6] In 1951 he led the parliament to nationalize the whole industry. It was a principled stance but one that ran head on into the immovable reality of Britain's formidable imperial power. Britain retaliated by lodging a complaint against Iran with the UN Security Council, but more ominously, cutting Iranian oil out of world markets. British oil technicians left the country, shutting down all production. At that time AIOC not only pumped and refined Iran's oil but also controlled the supply chain of tankers and oil terminals that took the oil to world markets. No other oil company or Western competitor showed a willingness to undermine AIOC—or risk legal action by the British government—by helping Iran with production, or by buying and shipping Iranian oil. American and British oil companies simply increased production elsewhere in the Middle East to compensate for the shortfall of Iranian oil. If that were not enough the British navy showed up in the Persian Gulf to enforce a crippling embargo against Iran, and warn Iranians that an invasion could be the next step.[7]

As the dispute raged on through 1952 and 1953, evolving into a full-blown crisis of government, Iran's economy collapsed due to the embargo, even as Mossadegh became a folk hero. When in 1952, it was time for the Shah to appoint a new cabinet, Mossadegh insisted he be given authority to appoint the minister of war and the chief of staff of the military, as the constitution stipulated, but had never been practiced by Reza Shah. The Shah refused, and Mossadegh resigned, which prompted five days of massive strikes and rioting all across the country. Troops were deployed to restore order. When the military pulled back from cracking down on the protests, the Shah reappointed Mossadegh prime minister. A constitutional crisis ensued as parliament granted Mossadegh sweeping emergency powers, after which he announced a series of reforms. These included land reform, improved labor and press laws, and increased funding for housing and education.[8]

History has charitably characterized the Mossadegh period as a democratic revolution in the making. But Iranian politics was not then truly moving in the direction of liberal democracy. Mossadegh talked of reducing the power of the Shah but was amassing power in his own hands and was quick to cross the constitution when it suited him— including dismissing the parliament in 1953. Far from liberal democracy, Iran seemed to heading for the familiar story of an elected Third World politician riding the wave of nationalism and transforming himself into an authoritarian ruler, leaving his country broken in the process.

As Mossadegh stepped up tensions with Britain, cutting off diplomatic relations in October 1952, the British government requested U.S. assistance, suggesting that the United States collaborate in overthrowing Mossadegh. The Truman administration refused to take direct military or diplomatic action against Iran, fearing that Mossadegh was naïve about the Soviet threat and too close to the communist Tudeh Party, which had backed Mossadegh's election. Cold war paranoia fueled fear that Iran would join the Soviet sphere of influence. Shortly after Dwight Eisenhower won the presidency in the 1952 election, he approved a plan for the CIA to sponsor a propaganda campaign to foment protest against Mossadegh, allocating $1 million in funding to the plan (of which not much more than $60,000 was eventually spent), which was dubbed Operation Ajax.[9]

The CIA urged the Shah to execute his constitutional authority to remove Mossadegh from office, but he resisted doing so, and in a preemptive move, Mossadegh, who had learned of the intentions against him, announced that he was dissolving parliament and he organized a national plebiscite to affirm his hold on power.

His extreme moves ignited further agitation against him, and the crisis came to a head when, in August 1953, the Shah finally did formally dismiss Mossadegh from power. When Mossadegh refused to step down, the Shah fled the country to Rome, appointing retired General Fazlullah Zahedi prime minister. With Mossadegh still in charge and the Shah gone, however, the Anglo-American plan failed and the crisis deepened. Massive protests erupted in the streets of Tehran and around the nation, with brutal fighting breaking out between pro-Shah and pro-Mossadegh factions. Four days later General Zahedi, widely popular in the royalist military, led troops to storm the capital in a second coup attempt. Mossadegh surrendered to Zahedi the next day, and the Shah was reinstalled in power. It has been common wisdom that the CIA did all the heavy lifting for the coup, but in reality it was General Zahedi, taking advantage of the growing popular apprehension with the worsening situation, who planned and led the second coup that won the day.

The Shah believed that the economic crisis and political turmoil would rally the middle class to his side. He was under the impression that they had joined the crowds in the streets to support the coup; but he was wrong. It was true that the middle class, scared by the chaos unfolding around it, had not come out in support of Mossadegh at the moment of crisis. But in the wake of his ouster, they increasingly demonized the Shah, turning their ire on the United States as well, for having fomented the coup.

The Shah moved quickly to consolidate his power, clamping down on the Tudeh Party, uprooting its organizational network, killing, jailing and exiling many of its leaders.[10] Many dejected communist activists would recant and even join the Shah's regime, but he would never stop fearing the subversive potential of the movement. Communists would be hounded throughout the Pahlavi period.

Nothing the Shah would do in the years to follow would restore his prestige in the eyes of the middle class. He aggressively took up the modernizing mantel of his father, with grand ambitions for Iran, stating that his goal was to make Iran a major industrial power by the end of the millennium.[11] Educated in Switzerland from a young age, he admired the West, and he was even more intent than his father that Iranians should emulate the West, though democracy would have to wait. To his mind, only those who truly developed their economy deserved democracy and could live by it.[12] He had little patience for the intricacies of politics, and even less for Islam and historical Iranian culture, which his father had so revered, and his unyielding pro-West perspective drove an ever wider wedge between him and the Iranian people.

During a visit to Pakistan in the 1970s Prime Minister Zulfiqar Ali Bhutto took the Shah hunting. Eager to strengthen ties between the two neighbors Bhutto used the occasion of a rustic dinner to lay out his vision of a united Third World standing up for international justice under Iran and Pakistan's leadership. The more Bhutto waxed poetic, the more visibly uneasy grew his guest. Sensing the trouble, the quick-thinking prime minister hastily concluded, "of course Iran only *happens to be* situated in the Third World."[13] That was exactly how the Shah felt; his country belonged to the West and he wanted nothing to do with the Third World, its pains, passions, and politics. But those pains and passions were exactly what had led to support for Mossadegh, and the Shah's attempts to further wrench Iran into modernization met with heated, and increasingly organized resistance.

Meanwhile the mantle of leadership in the region passed from the tainted Shah to the galvanizing Arab nationalist Nasser of Egypt. If Washington and London had hoped that Mossadegh's fall would put an end to nationalist politics in the Middle East they were sorely mistaken. The same coalition of nationalists, leftists, and religious activists that supported Mossadegh would time and again rear its head elsewhere in the Middle East to challenge Western policies and economic interests, and in the process set the region's politics on the path to radicalism. Nasser rose to power in 1952, in a military coup against British colonialist rule, casting the ineffectual King Farouk from his titular throne. Cairo had been called "The Paris of the Middle East" between the two world wars. Sitting at the crossroads of three continents and major trade routes, the thousand-year-old city was cosmopolitan and wealthy. Ornate palaces and majestic baroque mansions lined the city's broad, tree-shaded boulevards, and ancient mosques sat cheek-by-jowl with European architectural marvels, such as the grand opera house, where in 1871 Verdi's *Aida* had its premiere. But this was Britain's Egypt, a weak vassal that since 1882 had been run by a viceroy who imposed exploit-ative control over a weak king and a chaotic parliament. European financiers ran commerce—and pocketed most of the profits. Egyptians themselves were little more than spectators in their economy.[14]

When, in 1956, Nasser made the bold anticolonialist move of nationalizing the Suez Canal Company, he shocked the world, precipi-tating an international crisis. Britain and France, who stood to lose vast profits from their control of passage through the canal, hatched a plot to topple Nasser and take the canal back, persuading Israel to start a war with Egypt. Once Israeli forces got to the Suez Canal, the plan went, Britain and France would intervene on the pretext of wanting to keep the canal open. It all sounded good except that the plotters forgot to inform the U.S. government. So when the Soviet Union cried foul, call-ing out Britain and France's colonial ploy for what it was and threat-ening war—indicating that missiles would rain down on London and Paris if necessary—Washington declined to support Britain and France, and the British, French, and Israeli forces withdrew. Nasser, who had not done anything to turn the tide of the war, emerged as a hero not just to Egyptians but to all Arabs.[15] He had won a prize jewel from the West, doing what Mossadegh had failed to do, and Egypt assumed preemi-nence in leadership of the Arab world.

———

The rise of Islamic fundamentalism as its own challenge to the Shah's power was galvanized when, starting in 1963, the Shah instituted an ambitious set of reforms, in what he dubbed his White Revolution. This six-point program called for land reform, nationalization of the forests, the sale of state-owned enterprises to private interests, electoral changes to enfranchise women and allow non-Muslims to hold office, profit-sharing in industry, and a literacy campaign across the nation.

This was the beginning of the rise of the man who would become known as Ayatollah Khomeini. Khomeini was then a highly regarded up and coming cleric with a mercurial temper and steely resolve, who was respected especially for his mastery of philosophy and mysticism. Khomeini had come of age during the Reza Shah years, and like many other men of his profession nursed grudges against the Pahlavi monarchy and its Kemalist ways. He had had little involvement in politics until this point, but had come to the view that the Pahlavi monarchy was an enemy of Islam, and if religion in Iran was to avoid its fate in Turkey, then clerics had to fight back. After Reza Shah was dethroned religion had made a comeback, but the Shah's reforms promised to undo those gains, with the monarchy pushing for more secularism. Khomeini denounced the reforms of the White Revolution as un-Islamic and the monarchy as illegitimate, and he called on the clergy and their supporters to actively resist the government.

On January 22, 1963, Khomeini issued a strongly worded declaration denouncing the Shah and his plans, which provoked demonstrations. Two days later the Shah ordered an armored column to Qom, and delivered a speech harshly attacking the clergy as a dark force determined to hold Iran back. Khomeini continued his denunciation in fiery sermons in which he accused the Shah of violating the constitution, spreading of moral corruption in the country, and serving the interests of America and Israel. He even compared the Shah to the much-reviled Caliph Yazid who had killed the Shia Imam Husayn at Karbala in 680—an event that shaped Shiism and has since been commemorated by Shias every year. Demonstrations grew larger and more bloody. On June 5, 1963, after months of agitation, Khomeini was put under house arrest. This sparked three days of major riots throughout Iran and led to several hundred deaths. The Shah contemplated trying Khomeini for sedition, but after senior clerics cautioned him about the danger of doing so—especially if it meant executing Khomeini—in 1964 the ayatollah was sent into exile, first in Turkey and then in Iraq.

Many in the middle class, far from feeling alarmed by Khomeini's muscle flexing, began to idolize the clergy as champions of Iranian nationalism and partners in the struggle against the Shah. Khomeini emerged from his 1960s showdown with the monarchy as a hero not only to the religious lower-class masses, but also to many influential intellectuals, writers, journalists, and academics, and to much of the secular middle class.

So tainted was the Shah that reforms of a nature especially friendly to middle-class interests were alienating the very people whom they were calculated to help. Now even modernization, boosted by impressive growth rates for much of the 1960s and 1970s, led by wide-scale industrial development,[16] and resulting in the highest GDP per capita rates in Iran's history, became suspect because it was the monarchy's goal and served the Shah's power. There was nothing cosmopolitan or liberal here; the opposition was more in the spirit of communist "people's democratic republics" of the time than in that of Western liberal democracy. The ideas peddled by intellectuals, political leaders, and writers in speeches, manifestoes, and novels were a mishmash of voguish anti-imperialism, leftist ideologies, and the improbable embrace of Islamic fundamentalism. Many intellectuals who once advocated Westernizing progress took to lamenting "Westoxication"—a term popularized by the left-leaning writer Jalal Al-e Ahmad, who also did much to smooth relations between religious militants and his fellow secular leftists—what the Shah with loathing called the "red-black alliance.[17] Al-e Ahmad glorified clerical leadership as wise and brave—the true representatives of the people and the proper voice to articulate their demands—all in the hope of solidifying this alliance. He was dismissive of secular intellectuals and lionized the clergy's leadership in rejecting the Shah's modernization. He wrote, "When western-educated children of the aristocracy were busy passing a translation of the Belgian Constitution as the Iranian Constitution [referring to the 1906 Constitution], ordinary people were following the clergy and saw those Europeanized intellectuals as foreigners."[18] The fight against dictatorship in Iran thus became entangled with the clergy's drive to protect the role of religion in Iranian society. Iran's march to democracy was thus derailed into a revolutionary protest against modernity.[19]

As the 1960s gave way to the 1970s, the red and the black would twist themselves around each other more tightly, most famously in the speeches of the Marxist thinker of Islamic coloring, Ali Shariati.[20] Shariati was born into a religious family and studied sociology first at Tehran University and later in France. In Paris he joined leftist circles, hobnobbed with Algerian freedom fighters, and debated Marxism and existentialism with French intellectuals in Left Bank cafes. He grew fond of Frantz Fanon and his call to liberation of the Third World and increasingly saw the world through the lens of Marxism. But his ideas would also bear the mark of his religious upbringing. Back in Iran he taught sociology at the university, and soon gathered a following for his lectures that tightly wove Islam and Marxism into what became the main strand of power in the anti-Pahlavi revolution. Shariati believed Shiism had everything a Marxist revolution needed and even more, because it spoke the language of the masses. Shiism was Marxism in the garb of Islam. Of Shiism he wrote that it has a clear "worldview, ideology, philosophy of history, vision of the future, social base, leadership, and experience with organization and activism," going back to the early days of the faith, and preserved through the centuries by "high clerics, valiant warriors, orators, poets, and even petty preachers."[21]

By the middle of the 1970s the converging Islamic and leftist opposition posed a serious challenge to the Shah's regime. The Shah cracked down on dissent on campuses and in the streets, resorting to brutality and torture to stem the tide of resistance. He could not so easily suppress the writing and speeches of popular intellectuals, however, whose formidable moral authority came to shape the hearts and minds of much of the public in the same manner as Emile Zola or Jean-Paul Sartre swayed French opinion. The Shah's repression deepened anger against him, steadily fanning the flames of revolution.

The failure of the Shah's efforts to bring the middle class back

into his fold is all the more striking when one considers the patronage of the regime not just for education, health care, and generally
raising the standards of living for the middle class, but also for culture
and the arts. These were spearheaded by the Shah's French-educated
wife, Queen Farah. The Paris of her youth endowed her with a love of
the arts and cosmopolitan values, and she was intent to temper Iran's
Kemalist experiment by infusing it with appreciation for the arts, as
well as for mystical and philosophical traditions in Iranian culture. She
directed her attention and government funds to a variety of cultural
projects, including cinema, music, art festivals, and traditional crafts.
One impressive example is the acquisition of a major collection of modern art—probably the best outside of America and Europe—for the
new Museum of Modern Art that was built in Tehran. The collection
included masterpieces by Monet, Pissarro, Van Gogh, Kandinsky, Miró,
de Kooning, Rothko, Warhol, and possibly the best Jackson Pollock
outside the United States.[22]

Avant-garde movie directors, novelists, musicians, and artists too
benefited from her patronage. Abbas Kiarostami, whose *Taste of Cherry*
was the toast of the Cannes Film Festival in 1997, first made films
for children at the national child development center established by
the Queen. She founded an annual art festival in the southern city of
Shiraz—in the shadow of the magnificent ruins of Persepolis. The Shiraz
Art Festival gained world renown and attracted the best and brightest in
world music and theater. Tibetan chanting, Shia passion plays, and Pakistani Qawwali shared the stage with European orchestras, theater pro-
ductions from New York's Lower East Side, and Parisian modern ballet.
Leading lights of modern art, including Jerzy Grotowsky, Peter Brook,
Morris Bejar, Karlheinz Stockhausen, and Shuji Terayama all performed
in Shiraz.

Some of the performances at the festival sparked controversy. Not
everyone appreciated the shock therapy of Stockhausen's electronic
symphony, *Sternklang*, being blasted to the unsuspecting masses into
the ancient city bazaar in 1972; and the city was scandalized into a riot
by the public performance of a risqué play by a Hungarian-American

troop in 1977. But then such provocation is the hallmark of artistic freedom of expression. The festival was a cultural achievement of the kind that might have been embraced by an educated middle class, a unique experiment in the Muslim world at the time of mixing the old with the new and building bridges between cultures. But the Queen's efforts only infuriated many of those they were supposed to impress. The money spent on the arts was dismissed as waste, while clerics found the attention to the arts an affront. Her patronage was dismissed for the most part as excessively westernized, and her dabbling in religion was considered inauthentic, derided as "court Islam."[23]

The same derision met the Shah's efforts to tout Iran's ancient civilization and imperial ambitions. He was roundly criticized for the extravagant celebration of the 2,500th anniversary of the Iranian monarchy that gathered dozens of world leaders at Persepolis in 1971 for a week-long homage to Iranian history. The ceremonies were wasteful to be sure, and easy to dismiss as kitsch imperial pomp—an over-the-top Cecil B. DeMille production in the words of the journalist William Shawcross[24]—but it must be said that the celebrations were a great success in that everything ran like clockwork.[25] Much as the Chinese government construed its lavish Olympics opening ceremony in 2008 as a wake-up call to the world about China's sophistication and wealth, the Shah thought the anniversary ceremony would signal Iran's arrival as a world player, a country worthy at least of Western respect, if not membership in the West. His critics saw only pretentiousness and waste.

The momentum for revolution was checked for much of the 1970s as the price of oil shot up 400 percent (largely the work of the Shah) and easy money fueled an economic boom. The Shah launched a host of large industrial projects and ambitious development plans that included not just steelworks and petrochemicals but also a nuclear industry that would support some two dozen nuclear power plants purchased from the West. Small businessmen prospered as well, and the surging economy encouraged a mass migration of the rural poor to industrial centers, especially to Tehran. Yet the boom at best produced only grudging support for the monarchy. The lavish government spending on mega-projects was widely criticized as corrupt and wasteful, lining the pockets of the high and mighty but benefiting few among the population. The projects were seen as proof of the Shah's megalomania, and there was some truth to these allegations. But the Shah's opponents typically underestimated the potential of the investments for transforming Iranian economy and society. The critics were simply unwilling to see any value in what the Shah did.

The oil boom also fed the Shah's ambition to raise Iran's profile in the Middle East and on the world stage. He saw Iran as the preeminent leader of the Middle East, and self-styled *gendarme* of the Persian Gulf. In 1971 Britain left the Persian Gulf, and with Vietnam diminishing America's appetite for involvement in crises around the world, the Shah convinced the Nixon administration that Iran could ensure the security of the Gulf and the flow of oil to the West—that is if America agreed to arm Iran's military. He wished for Iran "Great Power" status, the same ambition that drives Iran's power play in the Persian Gulf today.

But power came at a price. In his last years the Shah became increasingly despotic. His picture was everywhere, and every project large or small bore his name. In the past, he had claimed to support a two party system and declared, "If I were a dictator rather than a constitutional monarch, then I might be tempted to sponsor a single dominant party such as Hitler organized."[26] But in 1975 he did just that, instituting a one-party system under the Rastakhiz (Resurrection) Party. He explained his decision, saying, "We must straighten out Iranians' ranks. To do so, we divide them into two categories: those who believe in Monarchy, the constitution and the Six Bahman Revolution [his 1963 reforms] and those who don't. . . . A person who does not enter the new political party and does not believe in the three cardinal principles will have only two choices. He is either an individual who belongs to an illegal organization, or is related to the outlawed Tudeh Party, or in other words a traitor. Such an individual belongs to an Iranian prison, or if he desires he can leave the country tomorrow, without even paying exit fees; he can go anywhere he likes, because he is not Iranian, he has no nation, and his activities are illegal and punishable according to the law."[27] In addition, the Shah decreed that all Iranian citizens and the few remaining political parties must become part of Rastakhiz. University campuses were wracked by riots and leftist guerrilla groups stepped up their attacks on the regime, while the population at large grew cynical and angry, increasingly unsympathetic to the Shah.

The chasm between the Shah and his people had become glaringly obvious. What was less clear, but equally important, was a chasm between the communist and socialist visions for the country of the secular intellectual elite and the middle-class professionals and the hopes of the ardent lower-class followers of Khomeini. At least the chasm was misunderstood by the secularists. Among the secular agitators against the monarchy, clerics and their followers were widely regarded as harmless hangers-on to the great bandwagon of revolution. The secularists failed to perceive both Khomeini's true intentions, and the surging momentum—and force in numbers—of the backing for him among the teeming urban and rural lower and working classes. The exploding numbers of urban factory workers had no infatuation with the ideologies that fascinated the middle class; Khomeini's populist call for freeing Iran of dictatorship and spreading the oil wealth among the population is what appealed to them.

Azar Salamat studied at Berkeley in the late 1960s, and there joined radical Iranian students agitating against the Shah. When she went back to Iran in the late 1970s she was determined to do Lenin's work, spreading the gospel of communism, organizing the working class, and setting Iran on the path to a communist revolution. With comrades in tow she would visit factories on the outskirts of Tehran looking for the proverbial proletarian laborers to convert to the cause. Workers on their lunch break listened politely to the Marxist harangue, humoring the young idealists, but understood little about dialectical materialism or capitalist exploitation. Communism was an alien tongue; so "when we turned to leave," remembers Salamat of one telling lunchtime encounter, "one of them called to us, waving his hand. 'Bye bye,' he said in English, grinning with amusement. Nothing seemed to express more clearly the foreignness of our contingent to those workers whom we thought our natural allies."[28]

It was as if years of thinking secular thoughts and following secular ideologies had blinded these secular activists to reality. They correctly perceived that their support for Khomeini was vital in building widespread support for a revolution. Leftist jargon did not percolate down into society very well, and the revolution needed the support of larger numbers—of the poor and traditional Iranians who looked to the clergy for moral and political leadership. But the secularists failed to appreciate the intensity of Khomeni's mission to establish an Islamic state, or to think through what would be in store for them if and when the clergy took power.

Secular revolutionaries stayed deliberately silent on the issues of Islamic government and Islamic law, hejab and women's rights, and engaged in little discussion of how individual liberties, economic aspirations, and democratic goals could be affected by clerical rule. This absence of serious discussion in speeches, rallies, meetings, manifestoes, media, and everyday conversations is astonishing on reflection. So strong were their opposition to the Shah and their trust in the clergy— their conviction that the only issue that mattered was ridding Iran of the Shah—that they forgot all about those other hard-earned cultural freedoms that were so vital to their lives and future. When they did finally wake up to the reality of the revolution, it was too late.

The spark that finally ignited the revolution was a precipitate drop in oil prices beginning in 1977 that led to an economic crisis. The bust coming on the heels of a boom raised tensions, and trouble was unleashed when a letter attacking Khomeini was published in the leading government-controlled newspaper. No one knows why the Shah had decided to pick a fight with the clergy at the time, or whether it was his overzealous lieutenants who were responsible, but the impact was immediate and decisive. Seminarians rioted in the religious city of Qom, and troops were dispatched to brutally suppress the uprising. This incident provoked a larger riot in Tabriz, and then more riots followed. Each time, some protesters were killed, and then their funerals and the

commemorations of the seventh and fortieth days after their deaths—
which Shias traditionally observe—provided occasions for more riots.
The revolution was afoot.

Events took a turn for the worse when troops opened fire on a
large crowd that had gathered at Jaleh Square in Tehran on September
8, 1978, killing scores. The Shah declared martial law but the demon-
stration grew even larger. Labor strikes followed; journalists, civil servants, and labor (most notably, oil workers) all joined in, paralyzing the
economy. The Shah yielded, relaxing press control and political pressure on the opposition, but that only emboldened his opponents. He
then promised wide-ranging reforms, reaching out in particular to secular pro-democracy forces, but his efforts were futile. Khomeini deftly
assessed the Shah's weakness, and sensing victory, he was uncompromising. He refused to accept anything short of the Shah's fall, and proved
surprisingly effective at focusing the opposition on that goal. As demonstrations grew in size and frequency Mossadegh's party, the National
Front, formally submitted to Khomeini's leadership in 1978. The revolution eventually just swept away the Shah's regime as it lost control first
of the streets and then every institution in the country.

With the streets in his opponents hands and his military stretched
thin the Shah appointed Shapur Bakhtiar, a secular French-educated
lawyer who had once served in Mossadegh's government, as prime minister, and on January 16, 1979, with tears in his eyes, the Shah left Iran.
He was suffering from cancer and died in Cairo on July 27, 1980.

Two weeks after the Shah left, on February 1, 1979, Khomeini
returned to Iran from exile. Millions poured into the streets to cheer his
motorcade. There was now no doubt that he was the undisputed leader
of the revolution—the one who commanded the streets and called the
shots. The military declared neutrality, Bakhtiar slipped into exile, and
crowds on the streets poured into government buildings and military
barracks.

With the revolution triumphant throngs of class warriors banded
together in revolutionary committees and militias, and backing Khomeini's cause, came out of slums and working-class neighborhoods,

bazaars, and poorer quarters of the city to claim their prize. They were quick learners. None knew what dialectics of history was about or what Marx had penned in his *Das Kapital*. Khomeini had taught them it was not necessary to convert to Marxism to be a revolutionary; it was more important to make the revolution Islamic.

The middle-class pro-communist and pro-democracy protestors were shocked by the numbers of Khomeini's forces and their zeal, and they quickly came to understand they were outgunned. The clergy drew large crowds to demonstrations day after day, and even larger numbers to voting booths for a national referendum and constituent assembly elections that were to decide the fate of the revolution. The middle class cringed at the takeover unfolding, and efforts were made to better orga-nize and resist. But leftist and pro-democracy rallies were disrupted by club-wielding thugs, who also stormed Tehran University to purge it of leftists.[29] When in March tens of thousands of middle-class women poured into the streets to demand freedom of dress, vigilante thugs attacked them. Pro-democracy forces formed a new party, the National Democratic Front, and at first large crowds showed up at its rallies. But after only a few confrontations with Khomeini's stone-throwing and club-wielding mobs, the Front melted away.

The U.S. embassy hostage crisis brought the final curtain down on the middle class. During those fateful 444 days, starting on November 4, 1979, Khomeini's forces made use of the crisis to build further sup-port for their cause. Claiming that America was hatching a plot to undo the revolution they whipped popular passions into a frenzy and brought large crowds into the streets day after day to vent their anger at Ameri-can policy, setting an increasingly radical tone for the revolution.

The hostage taking was prompted by the perception that the United States was once again working to reinstall the Shah in power. Exiled in Cuernavaca, Mexico, the Shah was dying of cancer, and when on October 22, 1979 his longtime friends David Rockefeller and Henry Kissinger brought him to Cornell Medical Center in New York for treat-ment, some revolutionaries thought that the U.S. government was busy hatching a plot to revisit 1953. Khomeini and his inner circle knew the Shah alone would not be the U.S. government's pick to install in power. Much more likely the plot would rely on moderate Prime Minister Mehdi Bazargan. Three days after Khomeini returned to Iran, he had picked Bazargan as provisional prime minister, to run the country while the revolutionaries decided on a new constitution and government. Bazargan was a veteran National Front politician who had served Mossadegh in the 1950s, and favored democracy.

When on November 1, 1979, shortly after the Shah was flown to New York, U.S. national security advisor Zbigniew Brzezinski met with Bazargan and his foreign and defense ministers in Algeria while they were all there for the funeral of the country's president, that suspicion mounted. But when the hostage takers invaded the American embassy, Bazargan had little choice but to resign. How could he stay on when the country's foreign policy was hijacked by a band of radical students and egged on by Bazargan's boss?

Bazargan's allies were then purged from the government, and Khomeini unleashed thugs to storm Tehran University and carry out a "cultural revolution," purging leftist and pro-democracy professors. Some Marxist guerrilla groups and Mojahedin-e Khalq (MEK)— a cultlike guerrilla group that was inspired by Shariati's mix of Islam and Marxism—picked up guns to combat Khomeini's forces, with the MEK assassinating several high-ranking clerics. Using suicide bombing for the very first time in the Muslim world, the MEK also killed the Khomeini-appointed president and prime minister and famously destroyed the headquarters of the Islamic Republic Party, killing over seventy of Khomeini's top lieutenants. But in intense fighting over the course of the next year, the fundamentalists won out. Tens of thousands of leftists were killed in bombings, assassinations, and pitched battles, and thousands of those fighting against Khomeini's forces were rounded up, jailed, tortured, and later executed.[30]

By the time the dust settled, at about the time the American hostages were being released, on January 20, 1981, the Iranian Revolution had been completely converted into the Islamic Revolution. The hostage crisis meant one thing to Americans, but something entirely different to Iran. There it was the period during which the revolution settled its internal power struggle. The hostage crisis had conveniently diverted international attention from what amounted to a fundamentalist coup.

———

Khomeini insisted that Iran would not be a "republic" or an "Islamic democratic republic," but simply an "Islamic republic." Turbaned guardians of the new order quickly consolidated power, carrying out bloody purges of the military and bureaucracy. Industries, banks, and businesses were nationalized, and businessmen and landowners, who were seen as close to the Shah's regime, as well as high-ranking government officials lost their property. Islamic laws and regulations were instituted covering criminal justice, family matters, commerce, and a mandatory dress code, as well as rules for media coverage.

The Nobel laureate Shirin Ebadi, a judge in the Shah's time, had hardly caught her breath from agitating clench-fisted against the Shah when she was told by her new turbaned bosses that she should consider a petty clerical job in the new judicial system. A little later, even that offer was withdrawn.[31] Even now, thinking back so many years later on what became of her life and career, Ebadi is nonetheless kinder to Khomeini than she is to the Shah. Her autobiography, *Iran Awakening*, makes it clear that for her and her generation the Shah had ruined his reputation forever in 1953. Regrets about the course of the revolution, though, were profound.

———

Bamdad-e Khomar (Drunkard's Dawn) was a hit the minute it appeared in the bookstores in Tehran in 1995. The publisher could not keep up with the demand. Hundreds of thousands of copies were sold and each was probably devoured by more than one rapt reader. This was a peculiar bestseller. It was not great literature; in fact, it is best described as a sappy romantic tale, the kind that would make a good Harlequin romance novel. In the story a young girl from a prosperous family falls in love with a poor servant boy. She willingly abandons her enchanted world to follow her heart. But then the story takes an unexpected turn. It is not that she finds poverty demanding but that she finds the poor narrow-minded and mean-spirited. She soon tires of their pettiness and longs for the civility and sophistication of the world she had left behind. The heroine finally finds redemption in her old world, regretting the folly of her choice; the youth she wasted is gone forever. This was not the soppy love story bridging class difference that is the stuff of Hollywood romances. What made this book a hit was the heartbreaking calamity that would befall the heroine for her fateful romantic choice— for believing that love bridges the cultural difference that separates classes.

The love story was of course a metaphor for the middle class's mistaken infatuation with the lower class a decade and a half earlier. The drunken dawn, much like the fog that follows a night of revelry, is fraught with regret and pain. This was a novel of remorse and redemption; it glorified the lost world of urbane middle-class Iranians, elaborately describing their lives, mores, and culture, and in equal measure ranting against the avarice and small-mindedness of the lower classes. If the novel described anything accurately, it was the regret that the middle class felt for choosing revolution over its own interests.

Though the heroine of the story would eventually find her way back to her world, the same would not be true of her readers. Many left Iran after the revolution for life in exile in the West, while inside Iran middle-class life, what was left of it, went underground. Social gatherings, intellectual discussions, displays of western clothes, and drinking all had to be confined to the privacy of homes.

The plight of the Iranian middle-class intellectuals and artists, writers and academics, businessmen and civil servants after the Islamic Revolution made an enormous impression on their counterparts elsewhere in the Muslim world. From Morocco to Malaysia, whatever the sins and failings of the state and its elite, the middle class perceived that it would be subjected to the same fate without the state's protection. The middle class would not be fooled again. All around the Middle East ever since, though the secular middle class has engaged in plenty of criticism of government, and when the opportunity has presented itself, has often expressed support for democracy—even spearheading massive protests in Iran and Pakistan recently—they have generally shunned alliances with Islamic forces. When push comes to shove, the middle class has lined up behind authoritarian, secular leaders as against fundamentalists. This dependence has been expedient, but it has also meant that the secular middle class has not, by and large, acted as a force for cultural, economic, and political liberalization. In the many battles between governments and fundamentalists that have raged in the region, the middle class has played a secondary role at best.

This has much to do with the failure of the Islamic Revolution to spread. At first, the Iranian Revolution created widespread expectations that a wave of fundamentalist victories was in the offing. Islamic groups around the region abandoned caution and embraced the Iranian model. To the west of Iran, fanatical young members of the Muslim Brotherhood assassinated Egyptian president Anwar Sadat in 1981, hoping that an Islamic republic would spring up amid the pyramids. Disturbances in Saudi Arabia, Pakistan, and Syria followed, and so potent did fundamentalism seem as a vehicle of revolution that leftists in Indonesia, Lebanon, and especially Turkey adopted Islamic rhetoric. After all if the goal was revolution, then fundamentalism had proven itself a more effective vehicle than Marxism-Leninism. And yet, after Iran, no more dominoes fell. By hook and by crook, secular states survived.

The power of the secular middle class, though, and the leading role it must have played around the region in promoting economic and political reform, was compromised. In country after country, once staunchly secular leaders began making concessions to Islam, and the promise of the secular middle class began to recede. Huge new mosques appeared—and are still appearing—on the skylines of Casablanca, Islamabad, and Kuala Lumpur; state television networks showed more religious programming, and government funding for religious causes increased. Many officials went on well-publicized pilgrimages to Mecca, known as the *hajj*.

When, decades earlier, in Egypt Nasser had faced the threat of an increasingly powerful Muslim Brotherhood—which had attempted to assassinate him in 1954—he had banned the Brotherhood and thousands of its members were rounded up and jailed. But over time even Nasser had made accommodation to Islam; he had understood that he must not veer too far from popular religious sentiments. So he too made the pilgrimage to Mecca, and he marketed his preferred style of government, socialism, as representing the true spirit of Islam, while Islam was painted as the ideal form of socialism.

In Pakistan, Sudan, Bangladesh, and Malaysia, rulers went even further and claimed that theirs were Islamic states, though they instituted none of the harsh measures imposed by Khomeini. They adopted some Islamic laws, but more prominently, peppered government pronouncements with Koranic verses and Islamic concepts and put more religion on television. There was none of Iran's class war at home and war with the world abroad.

In Malaysia, Prime Minister Mahathir Mohamad couched his aggressive pursuit of globalization in Islamic language, confidently declaring that if the Prophet were to appear in Malaysia, he would fully approve of what he saw.[32] These governments sought to emulate the growing piety of their societies, and their claims to be putting into practice the mandates of fundamentalists made Islamic parties redundant. They co-opted fundamentalism, and it was a feat of genius. Of course there were also some states that took a different approach, resisting the Islamic tide brutally.

Saddam Hussein reacted to the Iranian Revolution by suppressing his country's majority Shia community, enamored of fundamentalism, most notoriously by murdering its leader, Sayyid Muhammad Baqer al-Sadr, whose nephew, Mugtada al-Sadr, has been a leader of sectarian warfare in the Iraq war. But Saddam too would make concessions to Islam, after he was humbled in the first Gulf War and his iron grip began to slip under the pressure of sanctions. He allegedly had the Koran copied out in his own blood, built one mosque whose minarets were in the shape of missiles, and promised another and bigger one that would sit in the middle of a Baghdad lake, though owing to the sanctions he could not find the right construction material to support the football field–sized dome that he had in mind.[33]

In other countries, armed insurrections were decisively quashed. In 1982, the Syrian Muslim Brotherhood, emboldened by the Iranian example, revolted against the Baathist regime of the Alawite ex-general Hafez al-Assad. The Syrian dictator ordered tens of thousands of troops to ring the Brotherhood stronghold of Hama and began a siege that left his country's fourth-largest city looking like Stalingrad in 1943, with whole buildings pounded to rubble by merciless shelling. No one knows exactly how many died; some say thirty thousand, others eighty thousand. The message was clear: Hafez Assad was no Shah of Iran or Anwar Sadat, and would get fundamentalists before they could get him.

If the message had not sunk in, Algeria would drive it home a decade later. In late 1991, the Islamic Salvation Front (or FIS in its French acronym), a local offshoot of the Muslim Brotherhood, won nationwide municipal elections. The military replied with a coup. The FIS took up arms, and there ensued a brutal decade-long internal war that claimed the lives of as many as a hundred thousand people out of a total population of thirty million (about the same size as the United States at the time of the Civil War). In the end, the FIS lost. The war fragmented its ranks, and the growing radicalism and hyperviolence of the most militant fundamentalist fighters turned off the populace at large. When the dust settled, the military was holding all the power. Algeria erased the lesson of Iran. Khomeini's victory had led fundamentalists to conclude that secular regimes would fold before the power of committed activists armed with faith. But the secular regimes in Damascus and Algiers had fought back viciously and survived. In the words of the Tunisian fundamentalist leader Rachid al-Ghannouchi, "Khomeini died in Algeria." Islamic fundamentalism as an ideology of revolution, the effective means of toppling states, was discredited. There would be additional sporadic revolts in Egypt, Jordan, Nigeria, Indonesia, and Uzbekistan, but each time they were successfully contained.

———

Had Iran turned out differently, had its middle class not facilitated the rise of Islamic fundamentalism and paved the way to lower-class dominance, the Middle East might well be quite different today, and the sons and daughters of Kemalism might be playing a leading role in development and liberalization, as have the middle classes across Latin America, Eastern Europe, and East Asia. The lesson the West must take away from Iran's fate is that it matters less that the middle class is secular than that it is the right sort of middle class, one rooted in commerce and therefore focused on economic growth and on the loosening of state control, so that it will see past the false promises of radicals to protect its interests in robust, capitalist prosperity.

Khomeini's radical breed of fundamentalism is by no means ascendant in the region today. The great promise of the new pious middle class that is rising to prominence in so many pockets of the region is that it has rejected such extremism and is practicing a new blending of Islam and capitalist belief in entrepreneurship and self-reliance, which can pave the way for liberalization, and for accommodation with the West. Those championing this blending for the most part seek ever more integration for the region's national economies into the global capitalist system.

The violent fire breathing practiced by al-Qaeda and other radical groups has been on the wane in the region for many years, and even within the ranks of supporters of fundamentalism there is more support today for attending to the glaring needs of the poor in so many countries and war-torn regions than for the fomenting of terrorism, let alone revolution.

CHAPTER 6

THE TRUE COURSE
OF FUNDAMENTALISM

Choose any warm weekend afternoon in Istanbul for a stroll along the banks of the Bosporus, and you will find picnic blankets spread out over stretches of green as far as the eye can see. Women in headscarves tend to samovars as their children chase soccer balls. Many of those enjoying the breezes and sunshine by the majestic ramparts and grand mosques of the old city come from much farther east, on the Asian side of the Bosporus where the city's poor live cheek-by-jowl in congested neighborhoods and slums that extend for miles. The more debonair part of Istanbul's citizenry, the secular elite, cringe at this weekly conquest of the city's waterfront parks by "barbarians" flaunting their headscarves.

A Turkish friend who joined me for a stroll by the water chafed openly at the sight of these "village yokels" making themselves at home in her cherished European enclave. She was offended by their religiosity, which was doubly damning because it also betrayed their low birth. My friend was embarrassed, as if these picnickers were unwelcome reminders of how shallow Kemalism's roots ran and how hollow Turkey's pretense of being European may appear to an onlooker. Muslim Turkey, with all its Middle Eastern mores and sensibilities, harkens back to the country's roots. Closing on a century since Ataturk set Turkey on a secular course, the country is deeply divided over secularism. Even within the Middle East, the resurgence of Islamic piety can be quite unsettling. The fatal flaw in such concern over the rise of piety is to confuse the expression of conservative, devout Islam being practiced, by and large, by those picnicking in the park that day in Istanbul with the extremism of fundamentalism.

The conservative, devout Islam that has been gaining so much popularity in Turkey, as well as in Egypt, Pakistan, and the Persian Gulf, is not sympathetic to the violent extremism preached by Osama Bin Laden and his followers. Even within fundamentalism, there is a crucial—and growing—divide between extremists who support terrorism and a fundamentalism that wants a seat at the table and is focused on providing care and social services for the poor. The truth about fundamentalism that has not been appreciated fully enough in the West is that ever since the Iranian Revolution, the militant breed of Islam that draws its strength from attacking America and Western values and launching terrorism attacks has been forced to find footholds in countries, or regions of countries, where the government is weak if not in chaos. In countries with relatively strong governments, it has either been suppressed or it has been evolving into a less militant strain that has abandoned the call for violent revolution and opted to participate in electoral systems. Militant extremism definitely has footholds, and it is currently wreaking havoc in Pakistan, Afghanistan, and the Palestinian territories, but it is not on the rise around the region, and it is not the brand of Islam that appeals to the rising class of Muslims who are interested in being free to do vigorous business even while staying true to their Islamic faith.

Islam did not become a world religion claiming the following of one out every five human beings because of extremists who wage violence in its name, but by embracing cultural diversity and intellectual curiosity. This was an attitude that the Prophet encouraged in his Bedouin followers, telling them: "Seek knowledge even unto China." Islamic civilization flourished through the ages, not because of the faith's unbending rules or quick resort to the sword, but because of what it accomplished in philosophy, science, the arts, and architecture, producing the splendor of Andalusia, the Baghdad of the Abbasid caliphate, and the Mughul Empire in India. Islam spread more as a result of its scientists, artists, mystics, and philosophers than of its warriors. Even today the thirteenth-century Sufi poet Jalal al-Din Rumi—also a widely read source of spiritual inspiration in America—has sway over many more Muslim hearts and minds than Osama Bin Laden and his fanatical followers.

At Islam's core—as with so many religions, including Islam's Abrahamic cousins Judaism and Christianity—is a call for people to live lives of sincere personal holiness, to attain peace by submitting to the will of God. But it is also God's will that believers do more than live in accordance with Divine law or kneel in prayer and fast during Ramadan. They are tasked to share God's bounty with the needy and take care of those less fortunate: the orphans and the widows, the vagrant and the destitute. Muslims are taught to emulate the Prophet in how they practice their religion, and his message was that charity mattered more to God than even following his law. "A certain man in Medina came to the Prophet to confess a sin and to receive whatever punishment was due him," writes the scholar of Islam Charles Eaton. The Prophet asked if he could provide food to the poor as penance; he could not. "At this point someone came in with a large basket of dates as a gift for the Prophet, who then presented them to the waiting man and instructed him to give them as [a gift to the needy]. 'Am I to give them to someone poorer than myself, Messenger of Allah?' asked the man; 'I swear by Allah there is no poorer family than mine between the two lava plains of Medina!' The Prophet laughed . . . and told the sinner: 'Then give them to your family to eat.' "[1] That was his penance.

Islam strives for order in the world as both the embodiment of spirituality and the necessary foundation for it.[2] That order can come only through justice in every aspect of society, economy, and politics. Islam encourages charity to bring about equality and relies on Divine law for justice, but the rigor of that law is tempered by mercy, a virtue that is prominently featured in the Koran and closely associated with the Prophet.[3] This is not the face of Islam familiar to the West, where it is seen so much as a religion of violence.

The idea of war, holy or otherwise, was not central to the Prophet's teachings, and the meaning of the word *jihad* has been badly distorted over the past two centuries, first by those fighting against colonialism, and more recently by extremists. The historian Ayesha Jalal writes that "the root word [for jihad] appears forty-one times in eighteen chapters of the Quran—and not always in the sense of sacred war—while prohibitions against warring occur more than seventy times."[4]

The literal translation of jihad is "a struggle" or "a great effort" and its primary meaning for Muslims over the centuries has been that they have to strive vigilantly to be true to their faith. It is a daily struggle to live up to what God asks of the believers and that daily struggle Muslims have called the "greater *jihad*." That struggle—man's burden before God—thought the great nineteenth-century Indian Muslim poet Mirza Asadullah Khan Ghalib is not to overcome hardships of life but to be fit to be the greatest creation of God:

> *Alas, not all things in life are easy;*
> *Even man struggles to be human.*[5]

Islam demands of Muslims to be exemplary human beings, to strive to perfection in their thoughts and deeds; to cleanse their minds of want and greed, and to be kind and charitable to their fellow man.

Jihad was also used by Prophet Muhammad to describe military struggle, but not as in the waging of a war of aggression in the name of Islam; rather as in the waging of a war of necessity, to protect the Muslim community against aggression or oppression. Even where in the Koran the word jihad refers to armed struggle (*jihad fi sabil-Allah* or jihad in the path of God), writes Jalal, "verses employing the term are typically followed by exhortations to patience in adversity and leniency in strength."[6] Islamic law has been quite specific about rules governing military jihad, for instance, forbidding the targeting of noncombatants, especially women and children.

Islam is also in no way antimodern; not even extremist fundamentalism is against modernity. Fundamentalism is better understood as a peculiar call to modernity, one that wants to rely on bureaucratic and legal structures to bring about the fruits of modernity, but that wants modernity without secularism. Fundamentalism claims to be able to manage society and politics better than secular governments, but it in no way rejects the idea of bureaucracy. The Islamic Republic of Iran, the only state ever created from scratch by fundamentalists, has turned out to be a bureaucratic machine with all the modern trappings. It is even larger, albeit less efficient, than the secular state that it replaced. Neither do fundamentalists want to unplug their phones, televisions, and computers—they are not Amish. By contrast, they believe that they can engineer a better modernity.

In a sense, Islamic fundamentalism is an Annie Oakley ideology; it wants to be beating Kemalism at Kemalism's own game, and says, in effect, "Anything you can do, I can do better," which has been a large part of its appeal. Fundamentalists have tapped into the deep resentment of Kemalism's failures.

The Taliban would seem to contradict this characterization, as they have most emphatically rejected modernism. But the Taliban must be understood as a unique faction—puritanical rather than in line with the larger movement of fundamentalism. When they took power in Afghanistan, they established a Pashtun tribal political system akin to a medieval emirate, ruled by tribal code rather than the legal and bureaucratic structures that fundamentalism advocates. Speaking to how distant they are from the wider fundamentalist community is the fact that when in 1997, in order to make a show of their intense piety, the Taliban destroyed the ancient giant standing Buddhas of Bamiyan in Afghanistan, Iran's Supreme Leader Ali Khamenei declared his Afghan neighbors an embarrassment to Islam. To many in the West, this seemed like a moment of mordant comedy as the kettle called the pot black. But the distinction was real enough; what Khamenei meant was that the Taliban was a gang of "pre-moderns" and that by the same token the Islamic Republic of Iran stood within the ambit of modernity.

The appeal of fundamentalism cannot simply be attributed to irrational, unsophisticated thinking. The belief in the West that extremism arose in traditional Islamic seminaries, the so-called *madrasahs*, is in keeping with the idea that fundamentalism is a throwback that appeals most to those least exposed to modernity. Modernizing education, or

so a corollary argument goes, should breed moderation, if not secularism, by bringing these backward people into the twenty-first century.
Yet none of those who participated in the 9/11 attacks had received a
traditional Islamic education, and more than a few had studied science
and engineering. In fact, long before 9/11, fundamentalism was most
popular with science and engineering students—those most exposed to
modern rational and scientific thinking, many of whom had lived and
studied in the West. A generation earlier they would have been the pil-
lars of many a secular Middle Eastern state. Fundamentalism presents
rationalism as Islam and Islam as rationalism. As baffling as this may
seem to Western observers, it is a strong source of appeal to followers of
fundamentalism.

That does not mean that fundamentalism isn't fraught with contradictions, not only as regards modern life, but regarding Islam itself.
A primary point of departure from traditional Islam in the teachings
of fundamentalism is the argument that in order for Muslims to attain
their spiritual goals they must live in a strictly Islamic society, which
must be governed by an Islamic state. Fundamentalism, for most of its
relatively short life, has for this reason been focused largely on the political realm, rather than on the nurturing of individual souls, and in its
authoritarian orientation, it is ironically a mirror image of Kemalism.
Fundamentalists, too, would like to wield state power in order to bend
the populace to their will. Fundamentalists preach strict piety; they
promise paradise and threaten hell. But in the end, they are concerned
less with the fate of the individual than with their ambitions to build a
certain type of state and run a certain type of society.

That said, there is no unity of thinking about just how the ideal
Islamic state should be run; there is no one model for the Islamic state.
It is a state run in accordance with Islamic law to make sure society and
individuals remain true to the teachings of Islam. But beyond that lofty
goal there is little agreement on how to interpret and implement Islamic
law or run the government in the Islamic state, and there are few examples to go by. The only such state actually in existence is Iran—although
there are many more from Pakistan to Sudan claiming that status but

that are not actually run by clerics. Some fundamentalists have conceived of the Islamic state as a caliphate—which would be run as the Prophet's successors ruled during the early years of Islam, as both Pope and Caesar. Others have conceived of it merely as an Islamized version of a modern bureaucratic state, the Iranian model. For some it should cross national borders, unifying Muslims, while for others the focus has been on their own country. At any one time there are as many definitions as there are Islamic parties and factions.[7]

One thing common to all conceptions of an Islamic state is that it must be ruled by shariah law, and Islamic courts must be given authority to rule on all areas of law, from family affairs to commerce, criminal cases, and even on foreign affairs. And yet there is no one interpretation of just what the shariah stipulates. Noah Feldman, the scholar of Islamic law, argues:

> we are not all using [the term "shariah"] . . . to mean the same thing. Although it is commonplace to use the word "Shariah" and the phrase "Islamic law" interchangeably, this prosaic English translation does not capture the full set of associations that the term "Shariah" conjures for the believer. Shariah, properly understood, is not just a set of legal rules. To believing Muslims, it is something deeper and higher, infused with moral and metaphysical purpose. At its core, Shariah represents the idea that all human beings—and all human governments—are subject to justice under the law.[8]

That leaves much room for interpretation, and as a result there is little agreement over which should become canon.

Consistent throughout the many versions of fundamentalism, though, is an autocratic approach to compelling social conformity. Muslims have always modeled their lives on that of the Prophet, with his sayings and the records of his conduct studied as crucial guides for daily living. But fundamentalism has taken this practice to an extreme.

Like the early and most fervent Kemalists, fundamentalists have in many instances been quick to distinguish themselves by dress, gesture (especially when at prayer), and grooming (beards of a certain length and shape are a preoccupation). In Pakistan, fundamentalists took to wearing long beards but shaving their upper lips, while in Saudi Arabia, they began wearing the male robe known as a *thobe*, at ankle-length. Osama bin Laden was particularly zealous in the practice; he was at one time known for refusing ever to drink through a straw because the Prophet had not used one.[9]

In its strict demands about the smallest habits of daily living, fundamentalism is again much like Kemalism: attempting to shape individuals' beliefs and identities into a stifling uniformity. This is one of the reasons it has run up against quite formidable limits in its appeal to the majority of Muslims, and not only with the upper and middle classes, but with much of the lower class as well. Tracing the story of its rise, and its evolving fall, will expose the significant rifts within the ranks of its supporters, and the pragmatic move away from militant agitation, that characterize the true course of fundamentalism today.

———

Though it burst upon Western consciousness with the taking of the U.S. embassy hostages during the Iranian Revolution, Islamic fundamentalism was not a new idea in the 1970s. Its origins date to the 1920s and 1930s,[10] during which time much of the teaching that has formed the core of fundamentalism flowed from the pens of three men: the Pakistani Abul Ala Mawdudi, the Egyptian Hasan al-Banna, and later, his better-known countryman, Sayyid Qutb. Certainly many others throughout long centuries wrote of reviving Islam, and medieval clerics provided much of the inspiration behind fundamentalism, but these three Sunni Muslims gave a new vibrancy and force to a new approach to the religion. At the core of their teachings was vehement resentment of the ravages of colonialism, and later failures to win battles against Israel and India—in the Kashmir conflict—and anger over the suppression of Islam by the Kemalist governments in so many countries.

At the heart of fundamentalist teaching lies a simple line of reasoning: In the beginning of the faith, religion and politics were one and Muslims rapidly attained power and glory. They can therefore regain that power and glory if religion and politics become one again. Early Islamic history is presented as ideal, from the first generation of Islamic believers in the time of the prophet through the flourishing of the religion under the earliest four caliphs, who ruled between 632 and 661 C.E.[11] In the fundamentalists' telling, that golden age was a time of simple piety, justice, and above all, spectacular worldly success that vaulted Muslims to the rule of a vast empire. The first four caliphs, Abu Bakr, Umar, Uthman, and Ali, were close companions of the Prophet, who had fought alongside him in battles and heard his counsel in religion and government. Each was chosen caliph by the Muslim community as the most qualified in religion, charged to uphold Islamic law and manage affairs of government, and each was said to enjoy divine legitimacy, which was confirmed by the community's vote.

The fundamentalist founders argued that the decline of Islam began not, as popular wisdom held, with the decline of the Ottoman Empire, but much earlier, in 661 C.E., when the Umayyad dynasty rose to power and turned the caliphate into a monarchy. Muawiyah who founded the Umayyad caliphate was not a companion of the Prophet or respected for his religious standing. He was a general who strong-armed his way to the top to rule an empire that he then passed on to his son. From that time on, went the argument, clerics had betrayed the faith by submitting to the will of religiously unqualified rulers who in turn sustained them through patronage. They had allowed for religion to be separated from politics, which fundamentalists thought ran counter to the religion's intent. "The chief characteristic of Islam," wrote Pakistan's Mawdudi, "is that it makes no distinction between spiritual and secular life."[12]

Mawdudi was particularly effective in articulating this vision of history and politics. He taught that Islamic history after the seventh century was therefore "un-Islamic"[13] a shocking assertion, rejecting as it did centuries of impressive achievements of Islamic society in the sciences and arts, culture, and the building of powerful empires. Those achievements did not impress him, and he found fault with the manner in which, throughout history, as Islam spread to new regions of the world, it had found expression through local cultures. Such compromises he thought had altered the true meaning of Islam.[14] He also dismissed the moral efforts and spiritual accomplishments of the countless Muslims who had lived by and handed down their faith's teachings across all those centuries.

Mawdudi did not preach violence; on the contrary he argued that the goal of an Islamic state would be achieved by a steadfast process of proselytizing. To Mawdudi fundamentalism was all about a practice of educating; he would write and give speeches, argue and persuade, and his followers would do the same. The process would be slow and tedious, but by this means, more and more believers would be converted, until everyone was in the fold. The Islamic state would then follow naturally. He told his followers in 1941, "we desire no demonstrations or agitations, no flag waving, slogans, or the like . . . [for us] such display of uncontrolled emotions will prove deadly. . . . You do not need to capture your audience through impassioned speeches. . . . but you must kindle the light of Islam in your hearts, and change those around you."[15] There was more than a pinch of elitism here. Mawdudi wished first to convert the educated—professionals, bureaucrats, and intellectuals; the same class upon which Ataturk and Reza Shah had pinned their hopes. If the best and brightest converted to Mawdudi's cause, then an Islamic state could not help but follow, he argued, as the educated elite would be running the state.

His teaching was also not expressly antidemocratic. The Islamic state was not conceived of as a true democracy, but through tautological reasoning, Mawdudi and his followers did claim that their Islamic state would be democratic. If democracy is a cherished quality in a state, then the Islamic state must by definition have it too, so Mawdudi described his imaginary republic as a "theodemocracy" or a "democratic caliphate."[16] The state's duty was not however to enact the will of its citizens but to make sure that its citizens followed religious dictates in their daily lives. Mawdudi assumed that this in itself would win the state popular support.

After all, he argued, in a gemlike example of the closed-circuit rhetoric at which fundamentalists excel, if a state truly reflects God's will and its citizens are good Muslims, then how could they possibly want otherwise or disagree with their rulers? If you offered sovereignty to the people, they would give it right back, assuming they had been properly educated in what is expected of them. Fundamentalism is therefore not, in its own mind, antidemocratic; it merely thinks democracy is irrelevant.

Fundamentalists have generally not been shy about forming parties and organizations, though for the most part they have again not been truly democratic in spirit and intent. The tasks of these parties have been to gather followers and broadcast the message, as with the early communist parties, embodying the ideology and orchestrating Islamic activism rather than representing popular interests. Mawdudi started the Jamaat-e Islami—Islamic Assembly—party in 1941, which now has branches in England, India, and Bangladesh. There are other local Jamaat-e-Islamis in Southeast and Central Asia as well as Sub-Saharan Africa. But the best known fundamentalist organization is the Muslim Brotherhood, founded in 1928 in Cairo by Hasan al-Banna, a small-town teacher who had come of age in a religious household during a time of growing frustration with British colonialism.

As did Mawdudi, al-Banna believed that all social and political matters must be in accord with Islam's teachings, because, "the decisive factor [in history] . . . is the discovery by Islamic thinkers of the noble, honorable, moral, and perfect content of the principles and rules of [Islam], which is infinitely more accomplished, more pure, more glorious, more complete, and more beautiful than all that has been discovered up till now by social theorists and reformers. . . . For a long time, Muslims neglected all this. . . . Muslims could not but do justice to the spirit and history of their people, proclaiming the value of this heritage . . . to follow the sacred path that God had traced for them."[17] But now they must do just that, al-Banna argued, if they were to live up to their potential. He set out to make this happen, forming study circles that quickly proliferated across Egypt. By 1938, a decade after its formation, the Brotherhood claimed half a million followers.

Al-Banna injected a new militancy into fundamentalism. He charged his followers to actively work for an Islamic government that would use Islamic law to properly manage affairs of the state; he was proposing revolution by charging the citadel—toppling secular states. This was then a radical idea, and fearing persecution, the Brotherhood organized in small clandestine cells that then set out to recruit and train followers in preparation for confrontation with government forces. The Brotherhood also formed military units to fight in Palestine against Zionist forces in 1948, and when after the war the government tried to shut down the organization, its members resorted to violence, including the assassination of the prime minister.

While the Brotherhood helped topple the monarchy in 1952, its relations with the nationalist officers who took over the government were tense. Confrontation came with a vengeance after the Brotherhood attempted to assassinate Nasser in 1954. In response, Nasser cracked down mightily on the Brotherhood, determined to eradicate it altogether as a force in Egyptian life.[18] The Brotherhood was banned and some four thousand of its members were put in jail, including a rising star named Sayyid Qutb. Many members escaped to Jordan, Syria, and Saudi Arabia, where they would continue to foment for the cause.

Nasser's clamp-down further radicalized the organization, and no one would do more to advance the cause of revolution by violence than Qutb. A bright boy from a small village, Qutb benefited from a good education in the secular Egyptian educational system. He was primary in giving fundamentalism its sharp anti-American, anti-Western edge, and in advocating violent guerrilla warfare. Qutb's hard-line views took shape while he was in graduate school at Colorado State College of Education (now the University of Northern Colorado) where he studied education in the late 1940s and early 1950s. He was offended by American culture, particularly upset by racial prejudice that he encountered due to his dark complexion and the brazen outspokenness of American women. Some of what he felt was the awkwardness any foreign student may feel, but Qutb formed hardened views of American society as racist, morally corrupt, and licentious.[19]

Once back in Egypt he railed against America and denounced Nasser's secularism, arguing that the Koran itself should serve as the constitution of any true Islamic state. He focused the Brotherhood's ideology on challenging the state by violent means,[20] and the torture he was subjected to in prison only convinced him more of the wisdom of his teachings. He was prolific behind bars; what he wrote appeared in the form of tracts that were widely disseminated not just in Egypt but across the Muslim world, and soon became gospel to the generation of hardened fundamentalists and extremists that followed in his tracks. They were moved by his argument that "The establishing of the domain of God on earth . . . and the bringing of the enforcement of Divine Law (Shari'ah) . . . cannot be achieved through preaching." It was necessary to wage jihad "to establish God's authority in the earth; to arrange human affairs according to the true guidance provided by God; to abolish all Satanic forces and Satanic systems of life; to end lordship of one man over others."[21] Jihad, thought Qutb, was not spiritual but physical; it would unfold in the world to make Islam triumphant. So influential is Qutb that he can be seen as the godfather of modern-day violent Islamic extremism, the bridge between fundamentalism's political yearning and the cult of violence that now claims the mantle of its fight for power.[22]

Qutb drew on the writings of thirteenth-century Islamic jurist Ibn Taimiyah for inspiration in arguing forcefully for separating the righteous from the less vigilant, equating the latter with the age of *jahiliyah* (pagan ignorance) before the Prophet proclaimed his message. The most zealous fundamentalists follow this line of thinking, and are self-described Salafis—which means literally those who follow the example of the righteous forefathers, the first generation of Muslims who lived at the time of the Prophet. Qutb also drew on Ibn Taimiyah to justify violence in the cause. Ibn Taimiyah had little tolerance for apostates and had advocated a violent form of jihad—by which he meant putting heretics and even questionable Muslims to the sword.

Qutb read Mawdudi closely, but he rejected his call for nonviolent persuasion. Nasser was not permitting him or any other Brothers to persuade. In Egypt, revolution had to be revolution; preaching and educating mattered but could not take the place of brass knuckles and hand grenades.

The more radical among those who followed Qutb in Egypt went so far as to denounce the larger society as heretical for its support of the impious government and for that they came to be known as *takfiris* (extremists who denounce others as *kafirs* or unbelievers) and took to terrorism.[23] The most prominent among them, Ayman al-Zawahiri, would rise to global renown as al-Qaeda's second-in-command. Zawahiri grew up in an elite Egyptian family. He studied medicine and was destined for the enchanted life of Egypt's upper crust were it not for his falling in with the Brotherhood. That put him in jail where torture and suffering hardened his views. Once out of prison he broke with the Brotherhood, which he thought had gone soft, to wage war on the Egyptian government. He joined with other takfiris to form the violent Islamic Jihad group, which carried out a brutal terror campaign against government targets and foreign tourists. Eventually the government set Islamic Jihad on its heels, and Zawahiri and what remained of his fighters escaped to Afghanistan to join Osama bin Laden and his fledgling al-Qaeda.

Bin Laden too, had read Mawdudi, al-Banna, and Qutb; but his views on takfir and jihad had been strongly influenced by Wahhabism, the puritanical breed of Islam of his home country, Saudi Arabia, which also sees the world in terms of unending struggle between true believers and infidels. Bin Laden and many more Saudi youth had learned about fundamentalism from Brotherhood members in exile in Saudi Arabia, but in the 1970s of their youth, the Kingdom, and its distinct flavor of Islam, were also rising to new prominence in the Muslim world on the back of the oil boom of the 1970s.

———

In October of 1973, Arab oil producing countries, led by Saudi Arabia, proclaimed an oil embargo against the United States in protest of assistance given by that country to Israel in the war that had just broken out between Israel and a coalition of Arab nations. The embargo sent the U.S. economy into crisis and exposed the West's dependence on oil. This in turn led the Organization of Petroleum Exporting Countries (OPEC)—which had many non-Arab members—to raise the price of oil fourfold, bringing windfall profits to the oil-producing states. That massive injection of cash proved to be a gust of wind in fundamentalism's sails.

The Arab monarchies of the oil-rich Persian Gulf suddenly gained prestige, after sitting for centuries on the margins of Muslim history and Middle Eastern politics. Muslims all around the world were greatly impressed by the display of power against the United States and the new influence that oil wealth bought in Western capitals. Saudi Arabia's pious King Faysal, who was the architect of the oil embargo and a force behind OPEC's price-setting strategy, became an instant hero.

The Kingdom of Saudi Arabia, home to Islam's two most holy cities, Mecca and Medina, came into being in 1932 after Abdul-Aziz ibn Saud consolidated his hold over the Arabian Peninsula. Only a decade earlier his tribal army had burst out of the desert to conquer the urban settlements of the peninsula's Red Sea and Persian Gulf coasts. The al-Saud clan had formed an alliance with the powerful cleric Muhammad ibn Abd al-Wahhab in the late eighteenth century and embraced his puritanical form of Islam, referred to as Wahhabism. Abd al-Wahhab was a reformer, keen to purge Islam of cultural practices that he thought had polluted the faith. He too was influenced by the writings of Ibn Taymiyah that tolerate little other than strict adherence to Islamic law, and then narrowly interpreted. With the al-Saud clan in control, Wahhabism quickly became the dominant form of Islam on the Arabian Peninsula. Wahhabi clerics decided the country's legal system, counseled its rulers, and mandated how its citizens lived and practiced Islam.

The Saudi kingdom was also sympathetic to fundamentalists, who shared Wahhabism's puritanical streak, and who were fighting secular Arab regimes that at the time threatened Saudi Arabia. The kingdom offered exiled members of the Muslim Brotherhood and other fundamentalist activists a safe haven. Over the decades these fundamentalist exiles exchanged ideas with their Wahhabi hosts, and used their time in the kingdom to write, teach, and recruit.

Now that the Saudis were astonishingly wealthy, to many Muslims they made Islam look "cool." Muslims may have cringed at the nouveau riche tastes the Persian Gulf emirs and sheikhs would display, but they could not help being delighted by how the Saudi rulers lorded their power over Western contractors, bankers, lawyers, and envoys. They bought into what the kingdom promoted. Saudi Arabia in the 1970s stood apart from the Kemalist norm in the Middle East, and with plenty of money at hand was eager to spend lavishly on promoting Islamic observance, what Kemalism had fought so hard to do away with. In 1977, for instance, Saudi Arabia created a stir across the Muslim world by hosting the first international conference on Islamic education in Mecca. Counter-Kemalism had arrived with a splash.

The rise of Saudi Arabia and its spending on Islamic causes came hard on the heels of the decline of secular regimes in the Arab world. These regimes had already failed at delivering on their promise of development, but it was the devastating loss they suffered at Israel's hands in the 1967 war that took their shine off forever. In that war Israel demolished the combined armies of Egypt, Syria, and Jordan in a matter of days and took from them the Sinai Peninsula, Golan Heights, the West Bank of the Jordan River, and most important, the city of Jerusalem— the third holiest site for Muslims after Mecca and Medina. If the Suez Crisis of 1956 gave Arabs a momentary feeling of strength, their shattering defeat in 1967 put an end to that particular illusion. In the wake of that defeat at arms, people flocked to mosques, turning to God for comfort. The rulers whose secularism was shown to be but a paper tiger were compelled to follow suit. Secular Arab regimes never recovered from that loss, and not surprisingly, fundamentalism went from strength to strength as secular regimes continued to fail before Israel.

Islamic observance was already on the rise by this time in many places in the Muslim world. Egyptians and Pakistanis had turned increasingly pious, and would soon be followed by Iranians, Turks,

Nigerians, Malaysians, and many other nationalities. But Saudi Arabia also gave a substantial boost to this trend and pushed it in a more conservative and fundamentalist direction.

The Saudi rulers poured money into Mecca and Medina, upgrading the cities' accommodations so that vast new influxes of pilgrims could perform the hajj.[24] By the 1980s, an average of two million more pilgrims a year were arriving for the hajj, and many others were coming in the off-season.[25] Saudi Arabian Airlines began marketing travel packages to Europe via Jeddah (the gateway city to Mecca) to pious Asian Muslims with the marketing logo "Fly to Europe, Perform the Umra," referring to a visit to Mecca outside the hajj dates. Many visitors went home profoundly impressed by the displays of wealth and power they had seen in Saudi Arabia.

The booming Persian Gulf region also drew millions of migrant workers from all around the Muslim world—mostly manual laborers to work on the host of major construction projects oil money was bankrolling—but also plenty of middle-class and professional types. The puritanical Islam of the Arabian Peninsula began to spread to Yemen and Egypt, Jordan, Pakistan, and Bangladesh, and wherever else workers came from. Meanwhile at home in the kingdom, ultraconservative Wahhabi radicals began to foment against modernizing steps being taken by the House of Saud, such as reforming the legal and education systems, starting industrialization, and generally, opening the kingdom to the outside world. In 1975, King Faysal was assassinated by a young radical in the wake of protests by Wahhabi conservatives against the introduction of television into the kingdom. The shooting took place at a public reception, and, in an ironic twist, was captured by television cameras. Four years later, on November 20, 1979—the final day of that year's hajj—a band of extremists led by Juhaiman al-Utaibi laid siege to the Grand Mosque in Mecca and declared the arrival of the Islamic messiah, the Mahdi. These forerunners of al-Qaeda's brand of extremism held out for two weeks, and according to some reports were subdued only with the help of French commandos. Hundreds died and hundreds more were injured in the siege, which drove the monarchy to the brink of collapse. Putatively, Wahhabi clerics offered to support the crushing of the militants in exchange for a greater say in governing the kingdom's control over its subjects' lives.[26]

In an effort to deflect Wahhabi rage over modernization, the House of Saud also began lavishly bankrolling the proselytization of Wahhabism around the world, supporting its long-standing vision of dominating the Muslim practice of Islam. By diverting their Wahhabi subjects' energies and attention toward the export of their piety, the kingdom's rulers bought themselves a new lease on stability within the kingdom.

Money flowed into the building of hundreds of mosques across Africa, Asia, Europe, and America. Then cash went to Islamic causes, preachers, and organizations that followed the Saudi line, and to pay for seminaries and schools and eventually to support Islamic groups, social services, and charitable causes. In time, money would also support wars, not only in Bosnia, but in Afghanistan, the breakaway Russian republic of Chechnya, and the disputed province of Kashmir between India and Pakistan. All of this fueled the rise of extremism, not only as practiced by al-Qaeda and the Muslim Brotherhood, but also by winning over many in the Muslim mainstream to the cause of fundamentalism.

Money, as they say, talks. In 1986, I paid my first visit to a small mosque on the outskirts of Lahore in Pakistan whose imam was an amiable man, conservative but tolerant. When we talked of faith and piety, he espoused no rigid views. As I came back over the years his beard grew longer and his girth bigger, but so did the size of his mosque, the seminary that sprang up next door, and the scholarships and stipends that went to its students. As his religious empire grew, his tone became more strident, reflective of the puritanical views of his patrons in the Persian Gulf.

Extremism was given another boost when in the 1980s Islamic tribal warriors in Afghanistan rose up against the Soviet occupation of their country. Islamic fundamentalism had been popular with students at Kabul University in the 1970s,[27] where influential mujahideen commanders such as Gulbudin Hekmatyar and Shah Ahmad Masoud, were introduced to Mawdudi and Sayyid Qutb as students.[28] Their success in the war, which was a source of great pride around the wider Muslim world, had more to do with the American CIA's hidden hand, Saudi Arabia's generous funding, and Pakistan's military training and support. But all of that factored little in the prevailing Muslim wisdom of how the war was won. Those who told the story of the war to the Muslim masses, bin Laden included, emphasized the heroism of tribal warriors taking on Soviet tanks in Islam's name. Sermons at mosques, popular tracts, audiocassettes, and fireside chats by returning veterans all repeated that theme. In the Muslim world, Afghanistan was not *Charlie Wilson's War*; America hardly figured in the narrative. Khomeini had shown fundamentalism to be capable of bringing down a secular state, but the Afghan jihad showed that it could win freedom against a superpower.

The so-called Arab Afghans, legions of young men who had traveled to Afghanistan to take part in the fight, returned home to Yemen, Egypt, Algeria, and Jordan at the war's end intent to instigate rebellions.[29] Employing skills in bomb making and war fighting that they had learned in the mountains of Afghanistan, they hatched plots and introduced a new level of violence to fundamentalist causes in their home countries. Tensions rose as they escalated attacks and bombing campaigns and daring armed confrontation claimed the lives of thousands, including those of foreign tourists, but they ultimately failed in their aim. Violence provoked brutal and effective government reaction. Waves of arrests put large numbers of activists and their sympathizers behind bars. Those who escaped the dragnet went to the West or returned to Afghanistan where they would take part in bin Laden's movement. Violent resistance was no match for government repression, and when the dust settled the children of Afghan jihad were all but defeated in their homelands.

In Afghanistan they embraced a global view of jihad, divorced from the fight for any one country or territory,[30] and they changed their focus from toppling ruling regimes at home to waging war on America in the belief that it was the "far enemy" across the oceans that accounted for the staying power of Arab dictatorship. If they defeated America, they thought, Arab governments would fall into their hands.[31] In this too they were wrong. 9/11 only brought them calamity. They lost their base in Afghanistan and were hounded in Pakistan, Yemen, Jordan, Algeria, Morocco, and Saudi Arabia—and in Indonesia and Uzbekistan as well. With many of their leaders killed or captured the remaining fighters took refuge in the mountainous no-man's land that straddles the Afghanistan-Pakistan border to lick their wounds and live to fight another day.

Even as extremism was being cracked down on, however, the secular and ostensibly pro-Western states of the Middle East were also throwing it lifelines. In the 1990s many of these governments called on extremists to do their bidding. The Pakistani military would support the Taliban in Afghanistan and extremists in Kashmir, using groups like Lashkar-e Tayiba (Army of the Pure) to mount attacks against India, in order to further its foreign-policy interests in the region. Indonesian gener-als would flirt with Abu Bakr Bashir and his Jamaah Islamiya (Islamic group) followers—who would later be linked with al-Qaeda and held responsible for the gruesome 2002 Bali bombing—along with another shady extremist group, the Lashkar Jihad (Army of Jihad). Even the Turkish military is rumored to have followed suit, flirting with the Kurdish Hezbollah, an extremist outfit of no relation to its Lebanese namesake. The argument goes that Ankara hoped the organization would hunt down members of the secular–nationalist Kurdish Work-ers' Party (PKK) that has been agitating for creation of an independent Kurdish state in southeastern Turkey.[32]

Fundamentalism and extremism speak to the Muslim world's deep-seated yearning for change. Sentiments that decades ago supported left-ist ideologies across the Muslim world today fuel Islamic ideology and more so the extremist interpretations of it. Look and listen closely and you can see Lenin's ghost standing behind Khomeini, and an undertone of Che Guevara in bin Laden's bluster. Bin Laden is not quite as dash-ing as Che, and al-Qaeda is far too steeped in jihadism to have come up with a really good T-shirt, but still it has attained glory as the iconic flag-bearer of resistance in the postcommunist world. It appeals to those who, after the fall of the Berlin Wall, still yearn for revolution.

Until violent jihadism meets the same fate in the many pockets of the region where it is currently wreaking havoc that Islamic revolution met in Algeria, many Muslims will continue to see in the jihadi fighter a compelling representative of their hunger for success and respect. This is why the effort to quash radical groups is vitally important and must be sustained. But fundamentalism has also been changing from within, recognizing the limits of revolutionary violence and turning attention instead to participation in elections and to winning over converts by championing the cause of social justice and representing the interests of the poor in the political system, providing much-needed social services.

———

With the putting down of Islamic revolts in state after state—Egypt after 1981, Syria in 1982, Algeria after 1991, and most recently, Saudi Arabia after 9/11—many fundamentalists conceded that the creation of Islamic states was no longer in the cards. The call for an Islamic state was not entirely abandoned, but increasingly it was recognized as a distant prospect, and social activism took over as the work at hand.

Many popular clerics have also stepped up to denounce violence in the name of Islam, especially in the wake of 9/11. Even Shia fundamentalism, which was the force behind Khomeini's fashioning of the Islamic Republic as the domain of clerics and which sees politics as inseparable from Islam, has been moderating. Three decades after the Iranian Revolution, it is not Khomeini's heirs who are the most popular voices of Shia faith, but the quietist Ayatollah Sayyid Ali al-Sistani, who sees to the affairs of his community from his perch in the holy city of Najaf in southern Iraq. Sistani stands for the older Shia tradition, which holds that, absent the return of the messiah, the Mahdi, the ideal Islamic order is not within the realm of the possible. Clerics, he says, should merely see to it that the state does not repress Islam or violate major Islamic teachings, and should otherwise leave politics alone.

Since 2003, Sistani has gathered an impressive following and is today the most venerated and influential Shia cleric not only in Iraq, but far beyond. Shias from Detroit to Delhi embrace him as their "source of emulation." Even in Lebanon, where Shiism is usually associated with Hezbollah, most Shias follow Sistani. That is also now the case in Kuwait and Saudi Arabia. Even in Iran, observant Shias have turned to Sistani. A 2007 World Public Opinion Poll of Iranians found Sistani to have an approval rating of close to 70 percent, higher than any leader, religious or secular, Iranian or non-Iranian.[33]

Another popular fundamentalist voice speaking out against violent extremism is the Pakistani cleric Javed Ahmad al-Ghamidi. One afternoon in May 2004, I accompanied a Pakistani friend on his weekly visit with Ghamidi. I had first met Ghamidi back in 1989, when he had just left the Jamaat-e Islami over what he saw as the party's excessive attention to politics and willingness to compromise its principles to gain power. He was affable if a bit bookish, and impressive in his thoughtfulness and command of Islamic sources. He was then little known, the sort of fundamentalist that preferred the life of the mind to political action. In the years since our first meeting, he had evolved into a formidable Islamic thinker with an impressive following among thinking fundamentalists and Islamically oriented literati in Pakistan. When I visited him that May afternoon, he was holding court in a colonnaded mansion in an affluent suburb of Lahore—his residence and offices, paid for by wealthy patrons. The mostly young students who took in his talks on Islamic thought and Pakistani politics were, everyone in Lahore seemed to agree, among the best and brightest.

I had heard about Ghamidi's rising star and I was keen to hear what he had to say, particularly intrigued by his principled stand against Pakistan's jihadis. Since 9/11 he had taken to ridiculing their wayward religious ideas and fantastic theological assumptions in his journal. He faulted them for bad theology, and questioned the motives behind their reading of Islam. Ghamidi's arguments had caught on and were repeated and debated in Islamic circles. Jihadis were in no mood for intellectual sparring and had threatened to kill him, which only brought them condemnation from the broader community of Islamic thinkers and their followers. I asked Ghamidi why he had taken on the jihadis. He answered nonchalantly that he was simply stating the facts and setting the record straight; the jihadis had got their theology wrong.

Muslim governments have also made accommodation with these conservative but nonradical Islamic leaders, seeing them as bulwarks against jihadism. In Saudi Arabia, state-paid clerics and rehabilitated extremists are preaching against radicalism and for practice of faith that is personal and does not extend to politics. In Egypt, high-profile ex-jihadis imprisoned since the internal war of the 1990s or 9/11 have been publicly denouncing violent extremism—on Islamic grounds.[34] For secular regimes to take refuge behind Islamic conservatives is a smart move and it highlights just how weak the support for Kemalism has become in the region. States many years ago ceased pushing for uncompromising secularism, happy to rule over pious citizens as long as they do not use Islam as a weapon.

The turn away from violent radicalism to working within the political system has not been without controversy, splintering fundamentalism, both in terms of tactics and as regards those it targets for recruits. When in the late 1980s the leadership of the Muslim Brotherhood decided to join the political process and participate in elections in Egypt the ardently radical Ayman al-Zawahiri led a faction in revolt from the group, unleashing a string of violent attacks in Egypt and eventually joining league with Osama bin Laden and becoming the number two man in al-Qaeda. Increasingly those who have stayed committed to Islamic revolution have gravitated toward al-Qaeda and al-Qaeda-style terrorism, as in the adoption of suicide bombing by Afghan and Palestinian extremists. Their message has been most potent in recent years among the alienated youth and the most radicalized poor, with much less appeal for the lower middle class.

Those who joined in the creation of fundamentalist parties such as mainstream Muslim Brotherhood parties in the Arab world or Jamaat-e Islami in Pakistan, by contrast, have increasingly aimed their message at the lower and lower middle class, voicing the demands of these up-and-coming classes of shopkeepers, traders, petty bureaucrats, craftsmen, and laborers for jobs, security, poverty alleviation, and social justice.

The angrier fundamentalist voices in the Palestinian Territories, or Hezbollah in Lebanon, and the Sadrist movement in Iraq represent the revolutionary fundamentalism of the poor. The lower-middle-class fundamentalism of Malaysian, Bangladeshi, Pakistani, or Turkish Islamic parties, as well as various Arab world offshoots of the Muslim Brotherhood, is conservative and eager to impose Islamic values on society, but it is no longer pursuing violent rebellion.

In Algeria, key to turning the tide against the revolution was that shopkeepers who supported the fundamentalist cause grew tired of the chaos. A similar trend can be seen in Iraq today, where Shia shopkeepers, traders, and merchants—all men with vested interests in security and an orderly climate for business—have thrown their support behind Prime Minister Nouri al-Maliki's Dawaa Party or the Supreme Iraqi Islamic Council in their power struggle with the more radical Sadrist movement, whose origins lie in the slums of Baghdad and Basra. Where there is an interest in business, there is an impulse toward moderation and order over extremism and chaos. Here is an important lesson for American policy: The current battle line in many Muslim societies lies not between Islam and secularism but rather between types of Islam. The less commerce there is among the lower classes, and the poorer the society, the more appeal revolutionaries will exert. They will prove weakest, conversely, where commerce forges economic ties between the lower and middle classes and undergirds a yen for social stability. Commerce may not be guaranteed to breed secularism, but as David Hume and other thinkers of the European Enlightenment recognized centuries ago, it does reliably encourage moderation.

To see only undifferentiated fundamentalism in the region, where in fact there are various breeds, is to miss vital truths about opportunities as well as threats that these different fundamentalisms pose. It also serves to blind the West to the equally pressing issue of the abject failures of so many of the secular states to which we have lent our support.

———

In 1992, a major earthquake shook Cairo, killing hundreds and leaving thousands more homeless. When the tremors stopped, there was more damage to Egypt's government than to its ancient capital. Virtually all the immediate relief came from a network of mosques, many affiliated with the Muslim Brotherhood. The speed with which these non-state relief workers handed out food, blankets, and water stunned the bloated and ineffectual public bureaucracy. When the government had been most badly needed, it was nowhere to be found. The same was true when far more devastating earthquakes killed tens of thousands near Istanbul in 1999 and in the high mountains on Pakistan's Kashmiri frontier in 2005. While government relief efforts fell short, voluntary organizations—some of them Islamic groups—filled the void. In Pakistan, Lashkar-e Tayiba, which would gain world renown for its attack on Mumbai in 2008, took a break from causing mayhem in Kashmir to get food and medical relief to those without shelter in brutal winter cold in remote mountain villages.

These tales of superior private earthquake relief illustrate a troubling problem that the West has not truly begun to come to terms with in its dealings with the governments of the region. Across the Muslim world, governments are failing their citizens. Civil society groups and Islamic organizations get credit almost by default, for picking up whatever slack they can.[35] Buffeted by financial crises, and buckling under the combined weight of size, mismanagement, and corruption, since the end of the 1970s states from North Africa to the Levant and on to Asia have been doing less and less. They are providing fewer jobs, and offering less schooling, health care, sanitation, and housing. In Egypt, uncushioned by oil revenues, there is less for food, fuel, power, and transport subsidies, and even rent control is under threat. Some cuts in government spending have been mandated by the IMF, due to its rules for the restructuring of failing economies. Foreign investors that the governments have tried to woo have also insisted on less government spending. The shortfalls are likely to grow worse as these outside economic forces continue to exert influence.

The net result is falling standards of living for most people in these lands. The poor in slums circling large metropolises such as Algiers, Baghdad, Istanbul, Karachi, and Cairo are affected most, but many in the middle are unhappy too. Filling the vacuum are civil society and self-help initiatives. Some are Islamic, others not avowedly so, but the phenomenon has become closely associated with the growing Islamic consciousness that is sweeping the Muslim world.

In the Middle East, a maxim of politics might be summed up as "no welfare provision, no legitimacy." For the state to lose monopoly control over welfare threatens the loss of political control as well.

Take the case of Baghdad's Sadr City slum in the 1990s. The vast conurbation is home to some two million mostly poor Shias. Saddam Hussein had long treated these residents of his capital with suspicion and malign neglect; his regime was particularly hard on the Shia. What the state would not do for them their religious leaders were only too happy to do. The popular Shia cleric, Muhammad Sadeq al-Sadr (d. 1999) embraced Sadr City (then ironically known as Saddam City but later named after the do-gooder cleric). He organized social services for the poor, directing his followers to use religious taxes and charitable contributions to set up food banks and health clinics, and provide security, basic schooling, garbage collection, and even sewers. The vast slum is still poor, and it is still the Sadr movement rather than the U.S.-backed Iraqi government that provides whatever can be called social services.[36] The Sadr family owes its popularity in these quarters to what it has done and continues to do for those who live there.

The story of Sadr City is also true of south Beirut and the Gaza Strip, not to mention the poor neighborhoods of Cairo and Istanbul. Here too, social services are bad or nonexistent and an increasing share of the populace must fend for itself. What separates Gaza, south Beirut, and Sadr City from the plight of Cairo or Istanbul is that in the latter two places there is a functioning state. No single Islamic organization of the like of Hamas, Hezbollah, or the Sadr movement can step forward to provide all the social services and assume all the loyalty that goes with it.[37]

The danger is that the provision of services may prove a slippery slope, offering extremists a route to more power. Once an Islamic group establishes firm control in an area, it is in a position to begin imposing terms on the populace. Such has been the case with Hezbollah in south Beirut, where the social contract is no longer voluntary. Like it or not, residents have become "citizens" of "Hezbollahistan." Hezbollah is better armed and stronger than the Lebanese army and poses as defender of Lebanon's sovereignty against Israel, while the Mahdi army has acted as the neighborhood police and sectarian army of the Shia in Baghdad and southern Iraq. Their appeal has not come primarily from the power of their preaching; it is the failures of the secular states meant to be governing the countries in which they've found their foothold that have opened the door to these Islamic nemeses.

Other regions and governments may fall prey to similar incursions before long if they don't dramatically improve their provision of good governance. The poor neighborhoods of Cairo are potentially vulnerable. Some charitable outfits have no religious mission, but often they are run by staffers who have been affiliated with Islamic fundamentalism at some juncture, as students or even as professionals. These activists know how to organize. They are effective because they are close to those they serve and do not have to go through government red tape to get things done. Religious language gains the trust of locals, mobilizes donations, and makes it clear that this is not the corruption-riddled secular state that people are dealing with. By the late 1980s, such Islamic groups accounted for half of all welfare associations in Egypt. Some four thousand *zakat* (Islamic religious tax) committees now operate out of Egyptian mosques, serving an estimated 15 million people (Egypt's population is 81 million), up from 4.5 million in 1980.[38]

Similarly, in the Pashtun areas that straddle the border of Afghanistan and Pakistan there is a robust jihadi "state within a state," a Taliban tribal confederacy at war in Afghanistan and Pakistan. Decades of fighting, first against Soviet occupation, then between various mujahideen factions and the Taliban over control of Afghanistan, and then against American enterprise in Afghanistan has produced a jihad economy that in turn supports those who wield power in its name. A whole generation has grown up defined by jihad and depending on it for their livelihood. The lords of jihad provide social services and government to those who live in this economy and they in turn demand allegiance, taxes, and young men to fight. In this way, extremist organizations may increasingly become rulers of "states within states," and it may become increasingly difficult to check their influence as they ramp up their military capabilities. In 2009 they even got the government to recognize their Taliban emirate in Pakistan's scenic Swat Valley for a time, and hand over the administration of justice to their shariah courts. In the end it took a war to dislodge them.

The route from poverty to extremism is surely not inevitable. The militia gunmen and suicide bombers carrying out extremist attacks are usually poor, but their leaders often come from a higher class, as was true with Ayatollah Khomeini, who was born into a family of landowners. Osama bin Laden and Ayman al-Zawahiri both grew up in affluence. A recent Gallup poll of the Muslim world found that extremists tend to be better educated, hold better jobs with higher responsibilities, and garner higher incomes than self-described moderates. Poverty and extremism are entangled in complex ways, and we cannot say that poverty alone accounts for extremism.[39] What we can say with certitude, though, is that poverty can be used most effectively to justify extremism. This is a powerful reason that the West should be working with Middle Eastern governments to encourage and help them to do a much better job of the basic work of social assistance and the provision of economic opportunity for their growing masses of the underprivileged.

To the masses in the Middle East, Islam stands for moral values, and in too many countries, groups that "talk Islamic" are providing what semblance of decent governance there is. When people rally to the fundamentalist battle cry "Islam is the solution" (*Islam hua al-hall*) most of them are doing so in the hope that an Islamic government will deliver what the secular one has not. For Mawdudi, Islam made government good. On the broader Middle Eastern street right now, however, the reverse is true: It is good governance and the provision of social services that are making Islam's case, not calls for violent extremism.

The great hope of the new middle class rising all around the region—pulling itself up out of the poverty that has provided such ripe terrain for the fundamentalist call—is that these business-minded shop-keepers, traders, craftsmen, and civil servants have little or no interest in extremism. The Islam they respect is moderate, and they have generally not thrown their support behind fundamentalist parties in elections— at least not until those parties have abandoned the fundamentalist com-ponent of their stated goals.

During the 1990s, offshoots of the Muslim Brotherhood would show up at the polls in Algeria, Jordan, Yemen, Egypt, and the Pales-tinian Territories. Fundamentalist parties in Malaysia, Bangladesh, and Pakistan that had embraced elections many decades earlier also began to see new promise in democracy. Gone was the fear that embracing god-less democracy would sully fundamentalism's image and give legitimacy to secular regimes. Egypt's Muslim Brotherhood won 22 percent of the seats in parliament in 2005 and in 2006 Hamas, a Muslim Brotherhood offshoot, won in the Palestinian Authority elections.

That rare victory stands out as an exception. The shock of that out-come and the instability—including gang warfare—that wracked Gaza and the West Bank in its wake have amplified fears of what elections might bring if fundamentalists gather a head of steam. But the Palestin-ian Territories are hardly typical of the Arab world, and even less so of the larger Muslim world. In 2006, Palestine was not (and still is not) a state; it lacked (and still lacks) proper political institutions, not to men-tion previous experience with democracy, and wars of liberation hardly make for normal politics.

Even so, fundamentalism was far from a clear favorite with Palestin-ian voters that year. Hamas won only a plurality of the vote (44.5 per-cent against Fatah's 41.5 percent). The Hamas majority in the Palestinian legislature (74 out of 132 seats) was a product of electoral rules designed to hand a decisive win to the party (normally expected to be Fatah) that finished "first past the post." Hamas's popular-vote plurality, moreover, resulted more from its record of providing social services and challeng-ing Israel than from its fundamentalist preaching.

The ballot box has not, in general, been favorable to fundamentalist parties. Fundamentalists in Yemen, Bahrain, Morocco, Kuwait, and Jordan found niches in parliaments dominated by monarchs (or in Yemen's case, a strongman president). Democracy confirmed that fundamentalism had clout, but also showed that it was hardly as popular as followers and critics alike often claimed. Competing in elections has turned out to be tougher—and voters harder to woo—than fundamentalists had anticipated. It seems that many voters may like shariah law as a concept, but are not so sure about actually living under it.

Generally, where Islamic parties have done well, as with Turkey's AKP or its namesake the Justice and Development Party of Morocco (known by its French acronym, PJD), success came only after telltale fundamentalist goals were forgone. This echoes the Western European experience of several decades ago, when the communist parties of Italy and Spain toned down their calls for revolution and joined normal politics under the banner of "Eurocommunism."[40]

The AKP has won successive elections, in 2002 and 2007, on the back of economic and governance issues. The PJD very publicly embraced moderation after terror bombings in Casablanca in 2003 shocked and horrified Moroccans and threatened the crucial tourism sector of their economy. Refusing the fundamentalist label—the PJD prefers to call itself only "a party with an Islamic point of reference"—in 2007 it ran on economic and legal issues in the latest iteration of Morocco's monarchically orchestrated and controlled electoral process.[41]

In Pakistan, a country synonymous in Western minds with everything fearsome about fundamentalism, the coalition of Islamic parties in 2002 managed to turn in fundamentalism's best performance in eight national elections dating back to 1970. But it was still good for just 11 percent of the vote. In the previous elections, held in 1997, fundamentalist parties won a bare handful of seats. In a twist of terrible irony, five years later they wound up with a fifth of the seats because General Musharraf had rigged the system in their favor. With Musharraf on his way out, in the 2008 elections, fundamentalists won just over 2 percent of the vote.

This does not mean that fundamentalist parties should not be of concern. It is too soon to conclude that fundamentalist parties will all moderate and happily coexist with democracy. We have to see yet how fundamentalists over time behave in parliaments.

What the foregoing does strongly indicate, however, is that fundamentalism's hold on the Muslim mind, and on politics, is not as firm as many have feared. Democracy exposes that weakness, and every election further amplifies it. Islam matters to voters in the Middle East—much as does Judaism to many in Israel or Christianity to many in America—but that does not mean automatic support for fundamentalism. Evidence suggests that it is the parties that pay homage to Islam but that actually focus on secular politics that have the edge over those which focus primarily on Islam, period.[42]

If fundamentalism and the shariah are not in fact big vote getters, then what is? The answer is a list familiar from electoral politics the world over: jobs, public services, economic growth, good government, and muscular foreign policy, especially when it comes to America and Israel; in short, secular political concerns. The leaders of Malaysia's largest fundamentalist party reflected on their defeat in 2004 elections saying, "We lost because we emphasized Islam too much instead of social services and governance."[43]

The story of Indonesia's recent set of elections is instructive. In 2004, the fundamentalist Prosperous Justice Party (PKS) surged to tie President Yudhoyono's secular Democrat Party. But PKS's fortunes plummeted five years later in the 2009 elections after the president's party adopted PKS's call for clean and effective government. The Democrat Party won three times as many votes as its fundamentalist rival."[44]

Muslims want rights and representation, honest governance and effective leaders, and yes, they generally prefer that those leaders be true to local values and be good Muslims like themselves. But they also ask of these pious representatives, as they do of the secular ones, "What have you done for me lately?" This pious pragmatism is the most potent force in Middle Eastern politics today, and the most potent foe of extremist fundamentalism too.

CHAPTER 7

THE PROPHETS
OF CHANGE

After Kemalism came fundamentalism; now fundamentalism too is losing ground. What will be the next big idea in the Muslim world? What will the rising middle class hitch its wagon to? With the allure of the state—both secular and Islamic—having lost all of its luster, the Muslim world is embracing something altogether different: pluralism. The region is already well engaged in what journalist Robin Wright describes as a "quiet and profound revolution,"[1] led by bloggers, rappers, fashion designers, televangelists, human rights activists, and self-styled Islamic gurus and thinkers of all stripes. There are secularists in their mix, but this is by and large an Islamic resurgence, which celebrates piety while rejecting violence and extremism. There is no one flavor of Islam dominating; both conservatives and reformists are taking part, with some interested in politics while others are content to leave politics alone and focus on matters of personal faith and practice. Just as the separation of church and state in the United States supported the flourishing of many different Christian denominations, the loosening of the grip of top-down state control and sponsorship of Islam is making room for many Islams. Such is the nature of pluralism.

Though the voices are across a range, however, what is clear is that the revolution is being spearheaded by the rising middle class, which is avidly consuming its many offerings—movies, television programs, music, sermons, blogs, and books. Though this quiet revolution is too nascent for us to conclude that it will inevitably lead to the sort of reform of Islam that the West would like to see—more respect for women's rights, for example—let alone lead the way to more democracy, we can surely take heart that pluralism is taking flight in the Muslim world, and provoking lively debates on all manner of social and political issues, from democracy to the true nature of Islam's teachings to economic reform.

Amr Khalid is one of the widely popular new breed of Islamic preachers. In fact, he is much more, he is a phenomenon. The forty-two-year-old Egyptian, a former accountant, cuts a dashing figure, clean-shaven and dapper in polo shirts and three-piece suits; he is witty, wise, and uplifting. He lectures widely in large halls and auditoriums, and is the host of his own television shows—his latest is called "*Da'wat al-Ta'yish*" or "Call to Coexistence," which broadcasts on four satellite television stations across the Arab world. His sermons reach many more through his website, as well as DVDs and YouTube clips.

Whether in person or on television, he captivates audiences with sermons that present religion and moral instruction in an entertaining format. He gesticulates wildly, cracks jokes, and beseeches his audience through impassioned and lively dialogue.[2] He talks of love and interweaves stories from the life of the Prophet with teaching from the Koran, offering a wealth of scriptural quotes along with his views on current affairs. He rejects extremism and openly criticizes Osama bin Laden, and tells his audience that dialogue is better than destruction and that Muslims can and should coexist with the West. Promoting tolerance, he calls for self-improvement through hard work and faith-based community development, and he regularly speaks out on behalf of women's rights, condemning domestic violence. Islam, he argues, accords women more rights and responsibilities than clerics and the male-dominated Middle Eastern societies acknowledge, reminding his audiences that women were among the first converts to and martyrs in Islam, that they occupy a prominent position in Islamic piety and history. This is one reason among many why he has a particularly strong following among women. Khalid is also, however, an advocate of women wearing the hejab.

His feel-good message is Islamic and modern, one of the most popular of the versions of that blending around the region. He is the closest thing in the Muslim world to the smartly packaged and media-friendly American televangelist, and he commands a following like those of the megachurch preachers. At the same time that al-Qaeda and its atrocities were burning themselves into Americans' mental picture of the Muslim world, Khalid was drawing crowds of more than forty thousand people per sermon with his more moderate brand of Islam, prompting the Mubarak government to ban him—less out of fear of his decidedly moderate Islam than out of anxiety over his sheer popularity. His liberal message of tolerance and coexistence with the West—combined with old-fashioned jealousy—also raised the ire of conservative clerics and even less tolerant extremists, forcing Khalid to leave Egypt in 2002 for life in exile in Britain.

While Amr Khalid is moderate in his preaching, one of the other most popular preachers in the Arab world today is his much older fellow Egyptian, the octogenarian Yusuf Qaradawi, who is staunchly conservative. A cleric trained at Cairo's Al-Azhar University, the leading center of Sunni learning, he joined the Muslim Brotherhood as a devotee of Hasan al-Banna in the 1940s and rose to become an intellectual leader of the organization, but Qaradawi was a dissonant voice within Brotherhood ranks, refusing to abide by party discipline and freely expressing his own views on theological and political issues. After several stints in jail, in 1963 Qaradawi left Egypt and its periodic crackdowns on the Brotherhood for the safer post of dean of Islamic studies at the University of Qatar. From that perch he has gained recognition as the doyen of Sunni clerical scholarship, and communicates with his many followers across the Muslim world through his writings, his widely popular television show on Qatar's al-Jazeera satellite television network, and the website *Islam Online* that he helped found.

Qaradawi holds the lofty titles of head of both the International Association of Muslim Scholars and the European Fatwa Council, a gathering of mainly European-based clerics held in Dublin to minister to the religious needs of Europe's Muslim communities. But those roles are not the primary driver of his fame and popularity among the Islamic

public; that is due to his on-camera gig at al-Jazeera, where he is the host
of a show called *Shariah wa'l-Hayat*, or Shariah and Life. Due to the
enormous popularity of his show, his face is instantly recognizable all
around the Middle East, and he has gained respect for his views on matters large and small from Rabat to Ramallah.

Qaradawi echoes many of the arguments of fundamentalism, advocating the creation of a universal caliphate based on the shariah in place
of ruling secular states, and although he pays lip service to dialogue and
speaks of tolerance, more often than not he speaks of confrontation
with the West and guarding against Jewish conspiracies. On women,
minorities, and cultural freedoms he supports the same set of restrictions on dress and individual rights that also appear on the Muslim
Brotherhood's program. He supports Palestinian suicide bombing and
insurgency attacks in Iraq as self-defense, but he has spoken out strongly
against the renegade teaching of Osama bin Laden and his ilk, defend-
ing the role of trained clerics in interpreting the faith and reminding his
audience that Osama bin Laden is not a cleric and has no authority to
declare jihad, let alone to change the religion's rules in order to suit his
terror campaign. When al-Qaeda claimed responsibility for the bombing of a Tunisian synagogue killing fourteen German tourists, Qaradawi
said, "Civilians, such as the German tourists, should not be killed, or
kept as hostages. . . . Anyone who commits these crimes is punishable
by Islamic Sharia and have committed the sin of killing a soul which
God has prohibited to kill and of spreading corruption on earth. . . .
The only one who could be killed is the murderer or the one who commits a crime punishable by the law. In war . . . Muslims are not allowed
to kill the elderly, women or children. The only legitimate target is the
one who is involved in combat against Muslims."[3]

Qaradawi is a telling representative of just how complex the blending of views in Islam is today. Though he speaks out against the violence
perpetrated by al-Qaeda, he has supported the targeting of Israeli civilians by Hamas as self-defense, arguing that in this case, "Through his
[Allah's] infinite wisdom he has given the weak a weapon the strong
do not have and that is their ability to turn their bodies into bombs as

Palestinians do."[4] Stretching Islamic law's injunction that in jihad only combatants can be targeted, he claims that Israeli civilians can be targets because "they are not like other civilians, they are off-duty soldiers."[5] He has also fanned the flames of anti-Shia rhetoric, warning of a coming Shia invasion of Sunni lands and the Shia intention to conquer and convert all Sunnis. He has also caused a stir by eulogizing Saddam Hussein, and condemning the popular children's cartoon character Pokémon for its employment of Zionist and Masonic symbols and teaching evolution.

Khalid and Qaradawi represent very different trends and that was very clear in the aftermath of the Danish cartoon controversy—when in March 2006 the publication of an inflammatory cartoon of Prophet Muhammad in a Danish newspaper provoked widespread protests across the Muslim world. Khalid proposed dialogue with the West over the issue, suggesting a conference in Copenhagen. He asked Qaradawi for his opinion, and the elder cleric publicly berated Khalid, rejecting the notion that there was any value in dialogue over the issue. What Qaradawi favored then was protest and boycott of Western goods.

Another of the more conservative popular preachers today is the Turk Fethullah Gulen, who left his home country in 1998 for the United States in the face of increasing pressure from the then ardently secular Kemalist establishment. He settled in Pennsylvania and from there has continued to appeal to a sizeable community of devout followers in Turkey and in Turkish communities of Europe who listen to his sermons on CD and DVDs and read his opinions in books and magazines. Gulen advocates Islamic piety, but his message includes neither the hard-nosed fundamentalist call for an Islamic state nor the cut-and-dried puritanism so characteristic of Arab fundamentalists. Gulen encourages personal piety among his followers, but his call to Islam is deeply informed by the Turkish experience. He sees Turkish Islam, shaped by the Ottoman experience and Kemalist modernization, to be both more open to pluralism and dialogue, and accommodating of modernity. He teaches that pious Muslims can and should be full members of modern society and that there is nothing in the shariah that bars them from excelling in it or coexisting with the West.

Gulen is not a televangelist like Khalid and Qaradawi; instead he has received support from pious businessmen, some small merchants and shopkeepers and others big businessmen who made their fortunes in textiles, construction, or food, such as Turkey-based multinational food company, Ulker—which owns Godiva Chocolates. Gulen has also built up a network of civic groups and business ventures. His movement also runs a newspaper, *Zaman*, that is the second largest daily in Turkey.

Gulen is a product of the Nurcu movement, "Nurcu" meaning divine light, which was founded by Bediuzzaman Said Nursi in Turkey's mountainous Anatolian heartland during the early Kemalist years. The Sufi-inspired movement sought to preserve Islamic belief by flying below the radar of Ataturk's secularism, accepting that secularism would rule the government and advocating that Islam should surrender the public space and that believers should withdraw into private spirituality. The Nurcu movement interprets Islam as compatible with modern science and even rationalism, and that has made it spectacularly successful with an estimated 6 million followers, concentrated for the most part in the small towns in "deep Turkey" where tourists seldom visit.

Gulen was a mosque preacher in Izmir, Turkey's second-largest port after Istanbul, on the state payroll, when in the 1970s he began building a following by advocating that Islam should once again become more prominent in the public sphere of Turkish life. He started his network of Islamic associations then, and also opened a number of schools and set up newspapers and television stations. He was modernizing Turkish Islam by first moving it out of the province of mosques, Sufi groups, and religious schools and into the mainstream of Turkish society. By anchoring his call to Islam in modern institutions and using new media to propagate it he infused Turkish Islam with a new entrepreneurial spirit and facility to work in modern society. Gulen also interpreted Islam as science and modernity friendly, emphasizing its values and ethics rather than the enforcement of its rules and regulations. He demanded piety of his followers but also urged them to remain engaged with Turkish society—acting and living modern lives but in accordance with Islamic values and ethics.

Key to the appeal of his message to so many Turks has been its edge of Turkish nationalism; he emphasizes that Turks are natural leaders of the Muslim world, and that Turkish Islam must be propagated—as it was under the Ottomans—for the benefit of all Muslims. His network has opened many schools in Turkey as well as surrounding countries, and even Turks who criticize his efforts to press his Islamic agenda at home look favorably on the training in Turkish-style Islam that Kurdish, Uzbek, Bosnian, or Pakistani students are receiving at these schools.

Even in staunchly conservative Saudi Arabia, new voices are gaining popularity. The young Saudi guru Ahmad al-Shugairi has a popular television show called *Yalla Shabab*, or Let's Go Youth, on which he tells his rapt audience to open their hearts to all Muslims, urging them to break with Wahhabi orthodoxy's rejection of other Islamic schools of thought, and also to accord greater rights to women. Shugairi's message stands in sharp contrast to the preaching of firebrand Wahhabi clerics such as Salman al-Awda of the so-called al-Sahwa or Awakening movement, popular with Salafis and jihadi wannabes who flocked to Afghanistan and Iraq after hearing them. The Awakening very clearly sought to block modernizing reform inside the kingdom and dialogue with the outside world by reviving Wahhabi puritanism.

A key point is that Khalid, Qaradawi, Gulen, and al-Shugairi are not mosque men; they have become men of the people, media men. They reach their audiences through the communications technologies that have become popular with the rising middle class that comprises the bulk of their following. And they are only the tip of the iceberg of a growing number of such media-savvy new voices of Islam in the region who use satellite TV, newspapers, the Internet, and large gatherings at convention halls to build their popularity.

More and more Muslims, especially those in the rising middle class, are going around the mosque and mufti network to take advantage of such choices for engaging with Islam available not only on television and radio but also in cyberspace. It is now possible to get guidance from

on-the-air or online clerics and Islamic sages. *Fatwas*—which are religious decrees that clerics issue to clarify ambiguities in religious practice or to call on Muslims to follow a specific course of action—are a
phone call or an email away. Sites such as IslamOnline, eFatwa.com,
MuftiSays.com, askimam.com or, for Shias, Sistani.org offer lively discussion groups about such hot-button issues as how Muslims should
interpret shariah law, how they ought to behave in the workplace,
and whether the jihadist's call to arms has any religious validity. Such
websites command an impressive number of visitors, and this popular
engagement is generating a democratization of sorts in Islam compa-
rable to the rise of a more populist, and pious, breed of Christianity in
the United States spurred on by the advent of televangelism.[6]

Many of the popular new breed of media-savvy preachers blend tradition with modernity in their style as well as the substance of their messages, wearing Western attire rather than traditional robes, and speaking
to their audiences in the personable, folksy manner of so many popular
American preachers, making use of anecdotes about life's daily struggles.
That recipe has proven enormously popular. The strong appeal of this
blending of modernity and Islam does not mean, however, that there
is strong support for reform of Islam itself. The core of the appeal is in
reassuring the Muslim masses that a modern way of life—the pursuit of
material success, watching television, going out to nightclubs, listening
to pop music—is in no way in conflict with Islam. Muslims can enjoy
the fruits of modernity, they say, and be good Islamic believers at the
same time. They are not, for the most part, championing the kind of
more thoroughgoing reform of the faith that many in the West have
advocated.

We should not kid ourselves: There is very little in the way of liberalizing reform going on in the Muslim world today. If anything, the
phenomenon of rising demand for Islam is disproportionately raising the stock of conservative voices, though there surely are leaders of
movements for democracy—and for women's rights—who are building
followings, as we'll explore shortly. But by and large, while there is a
great deal of engagement with new ways of delivering the message of

Islam, there is not much interest in changing the message itself. For the most part, changing Islamic law or compromising on Islam's values and worldview is not in the cards.

The attacks of 9/11 convinced many Americans that the problem with the Muslim world is that it is "unenlightened," meaning it is pre-Renaissance in its mind-set. To catch up with modernity, Muslims must subject Islam to substantial change—Vatican II at least if not the Reformation *tout court*. But Westerners who are pinning their hopes for better relations with the region on an Islamic Reformation are going to be let down, at least in the near term. The paradox that can be hard to grasp is that the aspirations of the rising middle class have, by contrast, fueled the embrace of traditionalism—the Islamic world's version of old-time religion. The prospect of launching oneself, one's children, and one's society out into the competitive, globalized economy has *increased* rather than decreased interest in tradition—religious tradition very much included—because of the belief that enduring sources of standards and values are needed to help navigate the currents of change. In time, the embrace of tradition may give way to a broader and more vigorous movement for reform, but Western efforts to promote reformism are unlikely to be the impetus. Indeed, they may be even counterproductive, feeding fears that the West wants to subvert Islam.

Many Western observers do not want to hear this. They remain preoccupied with locating the right Islamic reformer, someone who can slingshot Islam onto the fast track toward Reformation and Enlightenment. Why is such a reformer, like Samuel Beckett's Godot, not showing up? Is reform only a matter of time, or is the West wrong to assume that the Muslim world will follow the same historical trajectory that unfolded in the West when capitalism and the scientific revolution forced change on Christianity?

Those advocating a Protestant future for Islam dwell little on the facts that early-modern Christian reformers were hardly liberal or tolerant—and that the Reformation unleashed a century and a half of bloody and even cataclysmic warfare. The Reformation in all its manifestations across Europe enforced narrow puritanical views with great violence. "Knox and his lieutenants," writes the historian Arthur Herman, "imposed the new rules of the Calvinist Sabbath on Scottish society: no working (people could be arrested for plucking a chicken on Sunday), no dancing, and no playing of the pipes. Gambling, card-playing, and the theater were banned."[7] The Reformation's contribution to the rise of capitalism and democracy happened long after the icons of the Reformation, men like Luther, Calvin, and Knox had left the scene, and then only as an unintended consequence.

The twist as regards the argument that Protestant Reformation is needed for Islam is that in the Muslim world today, it is fundamentalism and jihadist extremism that most resemble early Protestantism. After all, it is fundamentalists who, like early Calvinists, believe that God's rule over both the consciences of believers and the ordinances of the state must be as direct and unmediated as possible. Fundamentalism too rejects the authority of clerics and their ancient institutions in favor of direct access to religious texts—every man can read and interpret the Koran and other Islamic sources—and a vigilant and self-policing community of true believers.[8] If there are Muslims today who reject clerics and tradition as did Luther, saying *sola gracia, sola scriptura*, who can stand as the equivalents of Calvin or Knox these days it is Osama bin Laden or Mahmoud Ahmadinejad, who zealously challenge clerics and established political authorities while also calling for a true community of Muslims subservient to God alone. Theirs is a creed of puritanism, with every man reading his own Koran.

What the West wants is not Islamic Reformation, but rather the long-range results of an Islamic Reformation without all the puritanism and rigid theology. What the West really wants is not Islamic Protestantism but the kind of liberal rethinking that swept the Catholic world in the latter part of the twentieth century, producing Christian Democratic parties and the agenda of the Second Vatican Council.

There is, in fact, an Islamic reform movement of sorts, with a number of strong voices putting forth a wide range of arguments about reinterpretations of the faith. These reformers vary in gravitas and seriousness, but together they have written a shelf full of books on the subject—some bestselling—and have made the rounds of Western think tanks and academic institutions. Much attention has gone to writers such as Nurcholis Majid in Indonesia; Abdul-Karim Soroush in Iran; Muhammad Shahrour in Syria; Khalid Abou El Fadl and Abdullahi an-Na'im, Arab thinkers now living and writing in America; and Muhammad Arkoun, a French scholar of Algerian origin. Shahrour, a civil engineer, argues that existing Koranic commentaries are unscientific, and he has authored what he calls a liberal interpretation of the Koran that supports modern political institutions and greater pluralism. El-Fadl and An-Nai'm want to reform Islamic law, doing away with injunctions and interpretations that limit democratic practices. Arkoun draws inspiration from French critical theory to call for "deconstruction" of Islam, which means doing away with layers of interpretation of Islamic texts that have built on one another over the centuries to define Islamic orthodoxy. In its place he wants to put forth a new modernity-friendly interpretation—an exercise that has close parallels in recent Christian and Jewish histories. Soroush has moved from favoring a liberal interpretation of the shariah to advocating a kind of Islamic Protestantism.

The arguments of these reformers have proven much more compelling, however, for Western audiences than with the folks back home. Islamic reformist intellectuals spill more ink in English, French, Dutch, or German than in Arabic, Malay, or Urdu. The fundamental reason for this is probably that their works fail to speak directly to the wants and needs of the majority of Muslim people, especially to the interests of the rising middle class.

The writings of the Islamic reformers have little to say about how to move the Muslim world past its economic stagnation and the grip of dictatorship, or how to end the frustrating impasse of the Arab-Israeli conflict. They also say little about how to restore power to the Muslim world in its dealings with the West. In the end, Muslims may have to accept changes in their faith and its teachings on issues such as the meaning of piety and the status of women and minorities, but they are not there yet. Reform is more likely to come when Muslims by and large begin to believe that it would play a role in solving the problems they want solved.

Take the case of the popularity of the reformer Abdul-Karim Soroush in Iran in the 1990s, when his ideas were embraced because they supported the kinds of reform in the government that many of the political leadership had come to believe were necessary. Soroush did not begin as a reformer; when Khomeini's revolution swept Iran, Soroush was a hard-hitting zealot. He is an accomplished orator with an impressive command of the Koran and Persian literature, and he forcefully articulated revolutionary logic, gaining notoriety as a member of the Council of the Cultural Revolution, which purged universities of secular and leftist professors.[9]

In the 1990s, though, the West met a different Soroush. He was now interested in a reformed Islam, freed from the clutches of the clergy and open to modernist interpretation. While lecturing at Harvard and Georgetown, he talked in long sentences about intellectual debates that changed Christianity during the Reformation, and quoted the pragmatist political philosopher Karl Popper and the voguish German philosopher of civil society activism Jürgen Habermas. He advocated the reform of Islamic law—freeing it of the clergy's supervision and making it easier to accommodate democracy and modernizing social change. In sum, he put forth a Protestant version of Islam that would submit to Western rationalism, pluralism, and democracy. The transformation was striking, as was the size of his following in Iran. His views had changed and had gained popularity because of the widespread perception that change was desperately needed in Iran.

When Khomeini died in 1989, the country lay exhausted from a decade of revolutionary excess, a costly eight-year war with Iraq, and economic stagnation. Khomeini's successors had to address urgent social and economic concerns; in short, they had to govern. The sort of governance they urgently needed to bring about requires institutions, regulations, stable processes, and professionals, and all of that in turn required moving past ideology, revolution, and theocracy. Iran needed new mandarins, and to succeed the mandarins needed freedom from revolutionary ideology and stifling religious control. Soroush became the intellectual voice of this movement for change. The call for reform was not just attractive intellectual speculation; it served a practical and urgent purpose, and for that reason, it developed a constituency—inside the Islamic Republic as well as outside of it. Pragmatists in government, universities, seminaries, and business were looking for ways to loosen the theocracy's hold on policy making, and Soroush's message was music to their ears.

What's more, although he was later hounded and bullied by the Islamic leadership—once the crackdown on reform began—and ended up in exile in America, his ideas have continued to inform debates about change inside Iran. The lesson of Soroush's case is simple: Islamic reformism will grow roots only if and when it relates to pragmatic considerations on the ground in Muslim societies. If its only appeal remains that of an abstract solution to problems that the West sees in the Muslim world, it will continue to go nowhere.

It is perhaps expected that oppressive clerical rule in Iran has provoked anticlerical attitudes among the population. Soroush's ideas appeal to that sentiment, and provide an ayatollah-less Islam that would allow Iran to move forward. But Iran is not alone in this regard. There is unhappiness with clerics in many other Muslim countries, and many more Muslims have taken to reading their own Korans, discussing their own views on Islamic ethics, theology, and law among themselves, and taking control of the interpretation of the faith. They are joining Koran study groups, congregating around particular ideas and thinkers, and taking part in an assortment of self-started study organizations and Islamic associations that meet in small circles in private homes, at mosques, or even at places of work.

This more direct practice of the faith is not seen in terms of Western-oriented reform, but it is doing more to change Islam along the lines of the European Reformation in the sixteenth century than the work of reformers who are more familiar to the West.

Many of these study groups, for one thing, now cater to women. Anthropologist Saba Mahmood writes of Koran study groups in middle-class Cairo whose female leaders not only assert women's claims to religious authority, interpreting Islam and educating other women in religious matters, but do so with the express aim of weaving Islam into the fabric of daily life.[10] Similar developments are evident in Syria, Turkey, Lebanon, Pakistan, and even China, whose Hui Muslims recognize female imams.[11]

In Syria women have been in the forefront of this Islamic revival. Since the 1960s Munira al-Kubaisi, a Sufi-inspired charismatic preacher, has been gathering a dedicated following. The Kubaisi movement is conservative, calling women to the strict observance of their faith, but piety here comes by way of organizing women, and that is something new.

A similar movement in Pakistan, Al-Huda (Guidance) International, is calling urban women to strict Islamic observance. Al-Huda was founded in 1994 by Farhat Hashmi, a self-described female cleric with a doctorate in Islamic Studies from the University of Glasgow. The movement has been gaining strength in recent years—its followers readily identifiable on the streets by their head-to-toe hejab.

As with the Kubaisi movement, Sufism of all sorts is on the rise in various parts of the Muslim world. A Sufi revival in Egypt and Turkey may be expected, but growing interest in Sufism in the Hejaz—the strip of mountains along the Red Sea where Islam was born and where Saudi puritanism now holds firm sway—comes as a surprise.[12] In Iran too, interest in Islamic philosophy, Sufism, and spirituality is on the rise, and along with it calls for Islamic reform. These voices now claim the cutting edge of intellectual discussion in religiously conscious circles. In Iran, the state may be in the hands of Islamic fundamentalism, but the exciting and inspiring ideas are not. Those Iranians who have not opted out of Islam altogether are opting for a different form of it that is decidedly not the regime's preferred variety.

All this religious rethinking is happening at a time of social ferment and political change in the Muslim world. Economies in many countries are doing poorly, while a youth bulge—shifting the demographics dramatically in favor of the up-and-coming generation—has been contributing to restlessness. More and more Muslims believe that what is required for their cultures to contend with these tensions is finding a way to blend faith and modernity. The Holy Grail is not Western-style democratization, but a sustainable balance between Islam and modernity, and this demand for a blending of modernity and conservative, old-time Islam is not likely to recede in the coming years. One indication of that is that the trend in education in recent years has been strongly in favor of providing this blend.

Though a great deal of attention was directed after 9/11 to the problem of extremism being taught in madrasahs (religious schools or seminaries), the truth of the trends in education is once again more complicated than that post-9/11 narrative suggested. The brand of education that is on the rise in the Islamic world is not the extremism taught at some—and only some—madrasahs, but rather a religiously tinged style of education akin to that taught in Catholic schools in the United States. The greatest and fastest growing demand is for high-quality education that will teach children the skills they will need to become successful in the global economy—mathematics, reasoning ability, knowledge of the sciences, and familiarity with the newest trends in technology—but with a strong dose of religious training.

The typical old-school madrasah, with a curriculum heavy on Koranic recitation and rote learning, is simply not well suited to serving the demand of Islam's rising middle class, which is intent on its children being successful in the world of increasing globalization. But quite understandably, many parents feel more confident about their children stepping out in that competitive globalized world if there is reassurance that ties to tradition will be retained. The new modern *and* Islamic style of education serves both of these deeply felt needs.

In the aftermath of 9/11, "madrasah" joined the lexicon of words that roused Americans' fears about extremism and terrorism.[13] Madrasah education was interpreted as bad education; dangerous education that trained young Muslim minds to wage a terrorist jihad, neglecting to teach them math and science, the "real-world skills" in the words of one American lawmaker.[14] Secretary of Defense Donald Rumsfeld said at the time, in an interview on Fox News, that America had to engage in a "battle of ideas" encouraging Muslims to be "learning things like language or math or things that they can provide a living from."[15]

Think tanks and government agencies held conferences and conducted studies of madrasahs, and how to get students into secular schools and also to reform Islamic education. The World Bank, United States Agency for International Development (USAID), U.S. Institute of Peace, the International Crisis Group, RAND Corporation, the Congress, the Pentagon, and various European agencies all weighed in. They found things to be worried about, for sure, from anti-Semitic slanders in Saudi textbooks to the notorious seminary at Akora Khattak, Pakistan, that trained numerous Taliban fighters. But there are aspects of the big picture they missed. Overlooked, for example, was the fact that none of the 9/11 hijackers was a madrasah graduate.

Madrasah is a catchall term. A madrasah can mean something as simple as a Koranic academy where young children learn a few religious basics and practice reciting from Islam's holy book. Or it can mean a primary or secondary school meant to compete with national education; or a seminary established to train proper clerics in classical Islamic religious knowledge.[16] Madrasahs, in other words, vary widely in what they teach, how they teach it, and what view of Islam and its place in the world they impart on their students.

Madrasahs are generally conservative and some are troublingly fanatical—some do indeed harbor and train jihadis and terrorists. These are a minority, however, and the problem is less extensive than is usually thought. To begin with, there are not as many madrasahs as common wisdom holds, and they train relatively few students.[17] A Harvard University and World Bank study of Islamic education in Pakistan found that in 2002, fewer than 1 percent of all students in Pakistan were attending madrasahs. That number has risen but only to 1.9 percent in 2008. The report also found that over the decade leading up to 9/11, madrasah enrollment had risen by 16 percent, which was slower than the increase in overall school enrollment.[18] Madrasahs were not gaining, but instead were losing part of an already small market share. Even in Indonesia, where Islamic education is on the rise, only 13 percent of the country's 44 million students attend some form of Islamic education. The poor do flock to madrasahs, but more so in rural areas than in cities, and studies of students' economic backgrounds reveal too much diversity to see Islamic education as the domain of the poor.[19]

Terrorism experts Peter Bergen and Swati Pandey argue that the link between madrasahs and terrorism is weak.[20] The anthropologist Robert Hefner estimates that of some 46,000 *pesantrans* (as madrasahs are called in Indonesia), no more than forty or so qualify as extremist.[21] Perhaps a larger problem is that in many countries, the so-called secular schools teach a great deal of religion, often interpreted in illiberal ways, and sometimes push hair-raising intolerance. State textbooks in Algeria, Pakistan, Jordan, and Saudi Arabia all stand as cases in point. In Algeria, the battle against Islamic extremism now centers on changing school curricula that have long been under the control of conservative religious leaders.[22] Sometimes, as in Jordan, the problem is that state authorities have tossed fundamentalists the education ministry as a sop. Better to give them that than have them clamoring for the foreign-affairs or finance portfolios, the thinking seems to have run. It is a worrisome reminder of the lack of seriousness with which these governments consider education.

In Pakistan, it was General Musharraf—an avowed secularist and admirer of Kemalism—who changed the law so that a madrasah certificate counts as well as a university degree in qualifying someone to run for parliament. Other rulers seem to feel that a religious formation for young people is preferable to the Marxism or Western decadence that might otherwise vie for youthful attention. Pakistan's national identity is strongly Islamic, and Saudi Arabia sees Wahhabism as its national creed. Neither country can truly envision education as a secular enterprise. In this, they may not be so different from secular-nationalist regimes that seek to infuse young minds with an almost religious sense of national identity and cohesiveness. Madrasah-bashing will not clean up education; that requires pressing the governments not just the clerics.

Since 9/11, many madrasahs have in fact done better than governments when it comes to reform. The overwhelming bulk of madrasahs in Indonesia and Bangladesh have submitted to government oversight and implemented required curricular reforms. In general, madrasah reform progresses slowly, but in the meantime, Islamic education of a hopeful nature has been thriving outside of the madrasahs.

In one Pakistani poll, 70 percent of those surveyed favored reforming madrasahs to root out extremism and boost educational quality but also rejected secular education.[23] That is not a surprise if you consider that secular education in that country has pretty much collapsed. Too many schools lack textbooks, desks, and blackboards, and too many teachers are underpaid and unqualified. There is very little in way of proper education in sciences and math. All around the Islamic world today, in fact, secular education draws little praise. The demand is for high-quality, useful Islamic education but not extremism; for teaching religious values but not political activism; and vitally, for providing children with the knowledge needed to make it in the competition of the modern, globalized economy.

In Pakistan, Islamic high schools cost far less than secular private schools while producing graduates who do better than average on college-entrance exams and standardized tests. Muslim parents can see the value for money here, especially in a country with numerous young people and a tight job market. In Bangladesh, almost a third of university professors are graduates of Alia madrasahs, a network of government-mandated seminaries that combine traditional Islamic education with English and modern subjects. Between 1985 and 2003, the number of Alia madrasahs in Bangladesh grew by 55 percent.[24] If the goal is upward mobility, Islamic education is the rational choice for many parents in many countries.

In too many countries around the Muslim world, political parties have turned campuses into battlegrounds and gutted higher education in the process. A few families looking to avoid this disaster can afford to send their children abroad, while others look to private colleges at home. The booming Qatar Education City, the decade-old 250-

acre campus on the outskirts of Doha, which houses local campuses of American universities such as Georgetown and Texas A&M, appeals to this demand. Also popular are a new crop of American universities in Sharjah, Dubai, and Kuwait. A growing number of parents, though, are turning to locally grown schools that are private and Islamic.

In India, many parents in the Muslim minority believe that the best route to safety in the society for their children is to gain economic power. That belief has supported the growth of a Muslim private education sector with its eye on India's modern globalization-friendly economic sectors.[25] Education is high on the list for these Indian Muslim parents, and since the goal is Muslim power, the education must reflect that identity as well, but it must also teach vital skills. With this in mind, the usually conservative Deobandi madrasahs in the northwest Indian state of Gujarat are now offering computer science and English to their students. Probably not coincidentally, Gujarat is a place where globalization's economic impact is strongly evident, as is the threat to Muslims: Sectarian rioting there in 2002 left many Muslims dead and Muslim homes and businesses in ruins. If Muslim education is seen as something that makes such a fate less likely, the demand for it is easy to understand.

Combining Islamic values with discipline and good education was first pioneered by Fethullah Gulen in Turkey. Gulen's followers now run the Fatih University in Istanbul and a network of high schools from Bosnia to Uzbekistan, with new schools having opened recently in Afghanistan, Pakistan and the Kurdish regions of northern Iraq.[26] Gulen schools resemble Catholic schools and colleges in America, and though these often receive criticism both within the region and in the West for their religious bent, their success at providing solid education is seldom denied.

Gulen graduates typically do well in higher education and the workplace, and other religious movements and entrepreneurs across the Muslim world have been busily copying Gulen's methods. For example, Indonesia's conservative Islamic Prosperous Justice Party (PKS), a small but ambitious group that won 7.3 percent of the nationwide vote in

2004, runs a burgeoning network of modern Islamic schools modeled on the Gulen system.

Higher education in the Muslim world is seeing similar trends. Three decades ago, the governments of Pakistan and Malaysia established the International Islamic Universities of Islamabad and Kuala Lumpur. The idea behind these ventures was to "Islamize knowledge." The best way to explain this ambition is to say that it reflects the fundamentalist goal of Islamizing modernity. The idea has now caught on even in Iran. Mofid University in the great seminary city of Qom, in Iran, trains students with at least two years of seminary education in a modern curriculum heavy on the humanities and social sciences. Tehran's Imam Sadeq University, the alma mater of many of the Islamic Republic's mandarins, combines religion and modern education by teaching both side-by-side. Even traditional seminaries in Qom have taken to teaching modern subjects, whether as electives or required courses seen as necessary for the training of future leaders of the state.

For the most part, it is not government-backed Islamic universities that have been trailblazing here but market-driven, private-sector initiatives. Some have been the brainchildren of Islamic parties and movements eager to promote public piety and gain followers, though increasingly entrepreneurs have been the pioneers. State-of-the-art websites and glossy brochures have become key promotional tools in the work of attracting ambitious students from families who can pay handsome fees. Schools boast of their long waiting lists of applicants eager to gain entrance. The Jamaat-e Islami's computer science and MBA colleges in Bangladesh are immensely popular because of the job prospects their degrees open up. Elsewhere in small but crowded Bangladesh, the state-run University of Dhaka is a war zone where rock-throwing and gun-toting student gangs fight each other on behalf of the country's bitterly divided political parties. In stark contrast to the chaos at UD is the country's newest institution of higher learning, Al-Manarat International University. Established in 2001 under the motto "academic and moral excellence," its promotional literature makes scant reference to Islam—even though its founder is the wife of Bangladesh's most prominent fundamentalist politician—and its course offerings focus on business, computers, law, engineering, and English.

Another hopeful characteristic of the booming brand of Islamic education is that it is increasingly open to women. Formal schooling for females is a rising trend in the Muslim world. Some 60 percent of university students in Iran are now women. Nor is it just upwardly mobile women who are attending class; growing numbers of girls from traditional and conservative backgrounds are going to school, where they study everything from modern subjects to traditional Islamic scholarship. In 1970, there were no Pakistani women studying to become clerics. Now there are multiple women-only madrasahs. In Bangladesh in 1985, 7.8 percent of the students at Alia madrasahs were women; by 2003 the proportion had grown sixfold to 46.8 percent. The same trend is evident in Indonesia, where around half the students in Islamic schools are female.

Female graduates of Islamic schools can become teachers in girls' schools, and some may find a living ministering to the religious needs of women. The combination of upward mobility and growing religiosity has created new educational and career opportunities that were previously the domain of men only. Educated and working women are more engaged in religion and are creating a demand for properly trained female Islamic scholars and teachers. That demand has led to growth in the numbers of women studying religion, and has also created acceptance for this new economic and religious role for women.

The phenomenon of women's education, however, extends beyond only religious training. In Pakistan and Bangladesh, for example, the Jamaat-e Islami runs women-only universities that teach modern subjects under the "seal of approval" of the Jamaat, which is South Asia's leading fundamentalist "brand name." There is growing acceptance of female education, and the desire to stamp it out for which the Taliban in Afghanistan have become notorious fortunately finds no parallel anywhere else in the Muslim world. That this education is also Islamic is reassuring to parents, who associate Islamic schooling with morality and chastity and the rejection of Western libertinism. Girls educated at Islamic schools also have better marriage prospects than those who are uneducated or are trained at government schools. Apparently many men now want educated but religious wives—reflecting their general "modern but also Islamic" consumption preferences.

If decades ago Kemalism looked to education to create a secular and Westernized citizenry, today Islamic education seeks to reverse that process, but not in order to fulfill extremist dreams of making Islam triumphant. Many parents simply genuinely think that being both piously Islamic and modern is possible, and in fact better than being modern and secular.

To a large extent, the same can be said of the booming demographic of those in between the age of parents and their children, the huge segment of Islamic society from teenage through early working age who represent the future of the region.

Even in the strict dictatorship of secular, Baathist Syria, ruled with an iron fist since 1970 by the Asad family, with little patience for Islamic fundamentalism, a striking new interest in Islam is being shown by many young people. As is Turkey, Syria is rapidly succumbing, for example, to the lure of headscarves, and those donning the veil in Damascus are not only small-town "yokels" recently arrived in the big city. If there is one thing that will surprise a visitor to well-to-do neighborhoods of Damascus it is the spectacle of young girls in trendy headscarves and some in full hejab. They bear little resemblance to the traditionally religious lower-class women of their city, who wear a long, uniformlike cover resembling the manteau. These Middle Eastern teens and 'tweens sport blue jeans and display an obvious regard for style and fashion. These are daughters of middle-class and elite families, whose mothers and even grandmothers had cast off the veil and put on Western dress to show their support for secularizing progress. Among well-off Syrians, the veil has become a kind of incipiently post-Baathist fashion statement.

Some of the young women all around the region who are turning to the veil are impressed by fundamentalism's call to piety or belong to Kubaisi women's circles. Others see hejab as a way to rebel against their parents, or to thumb their noses at America and what they take to

be its war against Islam. Still others are merely imbibing popular culture beamed from media outlets in the Persian Gulf, where wealth and
Islamic dress combine to define consumer culture on television screens.
Whatever the motive, enough girls are doing it to support a fashion
industry dedicated to their tastes. Whether you are in Cairo, Amman,
or Beirut, the fashion these days among the young is the headscarf-and-
jeans combo, modernity topped with piety like a cherry on a cupcake,
and piety stylishly accessorized. At the 2008 Summer Olympics in
Beijing, a Bahraini woman sprinter competed in high-tech, head-to-
toe athletic hejab, setting a new standard for how far women can go in
dressing modern and dressing Islamic at the same time. Fashion shows
and magazines cater to the style-conscious hejab wearers. Arab or Turkish girls are not Westernized through and through, nor are they purely
Islamic. Instead, they are something in between, what the author Allegra
Stratton calls "muhajababes," literally, babes in hejab.[27]

Since 9/11, the youth of the Muslim world have been characterized
too often by clichés in the West.[28] They tend to be depicted on the one
hand as jihadis—endless fountains of anger and extremism resembling
the fist-shaking, bewhiskered "Islamic Rage Boy" who became a minor
Internet celebrity by appearing in international wire-service photos
of protests in Kashmir. Or, equally simplistically, they are seen as an
unstoppable force for cultural freedom and Westernizing change. They
are "lipstick jihadis," in the words of the author Azadeh Moaveni;[29]
iconoclasts and the Middle East's "Facebook generation" of Net surf-
ers and bloggers, who are networking, communicating and expressing
themselves in just the ways that their age group does so avidly in the
West.[30] Millions of U.S. taxpayer dollars have been spent to broadcast
pop music into Iran and the Arab world through American-backed television and radio stations in the hope of making these Muslim Millennials become favorable toward the West.

Western music—and local adaptations of it—is indeed popular
with Muslims, middle-aged and even old ones as well as youngsters.
There is plenty of heavy metal in the Arab world, and Iran has thriving acid-rock and rap scenes.[31] Satellite-TV programs from Lebanon to

Pakistan broadcast plenty of Western music, but that has made little dent in the anti-Americanism that rears its head even among Western-educated or Westernized groups. Taste in music or dress is not a good gauge, it turns out, of people's attitudes and political preferences, at least not in the Muslim world.

During the last decade Pakistan has witnessed an explosion of independent television programming beaming all manner of music and soap operas from around the world into Pakistani homes. Yet Pakistan remains a deeply religious place with a dangerous extremist slant. As Washington was talking war with Iran in the summer of 2008, the popular rap group *Hichkas* (Nobody), best known for its brooding numbers on poverty and despair, came out with a defiant rap promising that band members and those who lip-synch its rap would be willing to die for Iran were it attacked. Iran's rebellious youth are as nationalistic as youth everywhere else.[32]

No simple formulation can capture the prevailing attitude of Muslim youth today; they hold a wide range of views about politics and religion and are blending those views in ways that appear paradoxical to Western eyes. At first glance, Amir Hossein Sadeghi fits the bill of what is widely characterized in Western coverage as Iran's West-loving, pro-democracy youth. The twenty-something Sadeghi is a soccer star in a soccer-crazed country. He has plied his trade for the Esteghlal club of Tehran, and also played for the national team. His *GQ* looks—tall, slender, and handsome with shoulder-length hair and a fashionable goatee—have made him something of a local heartthrob. Nothing about his slick appearance or his self-confident swagger says "Islamic Republic." A few years ago, I bumped into him at Germany's Frankfurt airport. He was bantering with his teammates—a group of equally fashion-forward young men wearing gaudy wristwatches, tight T-shirts, and flashy fluorescent sneakers—while waiting for a connecting flight to an international match. We chatted, mostly about soccer, my life in America, and theirs in Iran and Dubai, where two of them played for well-paying clubs. They were jovial and carefree: a little vain, perhaps, but fun-loving free spirits who meant well. It was impossible not to see them as at odds with the rigid theocracy that rules Iran. They were not keen to talk politics, but it is fair to say that they longed for greater freedoms and a different Iran. Their attire alone said that loud and clear.

So it was somewhat surprising when a few months later I saw Sadeghi's picture in a Persian daily celebrating a crucial goal for his club. Surrounded by his jubilant teammates, he had lifted his jersey in the way that goal-scorers the world over do. Beneath was something you don't see every day in the world of pro soccer, however: a white undershirt bearing the visage of the Shia messiah, the Hidden Imam, with the legend "O, Mahdi." Behind Sadeghi's Armani look is simple folk piety; when he plays he counts on Shia saints for help, and when he scores goals he credits them. Sadeghi's patron saint is the same Hidden Imam whom Iran's hard-line President Ahmadinejad also talked about, and in a 2006 speech to the UN General Assembly even claimed to have seen in a vision. That claim gained Ahmadinejad ridicule at home and caused many in the West to fear that he is gunning for Armageddon. Does folk piety make Sadeghi a dangerous extremist or an Ahmadinejad supporter? Definitely not. It is just that he is not the kind of secularist that a Westerner might assume he is, and the future that his generation has in mind is a mixture of modernity and Islam, or in Sadeghi's case, of Giorgio Armani and the Hidden Imam.

A visitor to Tehran can easily find parties where alcohol (and drugs) flow freely, and where young men and women mix without regard to Iran's draconian morals laws. But fun-loving kids eager to explore the extremes of hedonism and social freedoms do not represent the entire younger generation—or in fact even that big a part of it. Millions of young men and women are in the employ of shadowy paramilitaries, such as the Baseej.[33] The Baseejis are the ones who brutally suppressed the 1999, 2003, and 2009 pro-democracy student demonstrations in Iran in youth-on-youth fighting. Largely recruited from the urban poor, they have become the Islamic Republic's domestic shock troops, well-organized and equipped with pagers and motorcycles for rapid response to any call for action. Ahmadinejad emerged from their ranks and has steered state patronage to them in hopes of making them even more formidable. Clearly, not all young Iranians are freedom-loving, pro-Western types.[34]

Neither thoroughgoing secularism nor thoroughgoing religiosity defines Iranian youth. Azadeh Moaveni writes of her encounter with a Baseeji type in Tehran who had a respectable collection of Eminem's rap recordings and thought *A Beautiful Mind* was the best film ever made.[35] The French sociologist Farhad Khosrokhavar concludes from a survey of youth in the holy city of Qom, the seat of clerical power in Iran, that while many youth readily flout restrictions on music, they do not reject religion out of hand.[36] Many more are reading the Koran on their own, while listening less to clerics.

When I visited the Jamkaran Mosque, a little building on the outskirts of the great clerical city of Qom, it was teeming with young people. Jamkaran is special because, according to popular lore, the Hidden Imam once miraculously appeared there. Young boys and girls now come in droves to pray and ask for favors, tying little strings to the iron grid that marks where the Hidden Imam sat. Their concerns are ordinary and touching: Please help me find love, pass my exams, and get a job. More than a few sport stylish headscarves and designer sunglasses, telltale signs of the more affluent and upwardly mobile—the ones whom the West hopes will agitate for democracy and throw off the yoke of clerical rule in their country. They may well hope to do so, but it is not at all clear whether they will want to cast off pious religion in the process.

Youth are a restless bunch. Nearly every civil war, revolution, and transition to democracy in our time has come in youthful societies impatient for change. But what youth thinks and does is not straightforward; there is no one idea or tendency that is associated with them. And in this the youth of the Middle East are not all that different from youth elsewhere in the world. Looking at the population numbers in the Middle East today, it is difficult to see anything but youth in that region of the world. More than half of the Middle East's population of 300 million is under twenty-five years of age.[37] They are the majority in country after country. So it is that they are part of every tendency and movement in that region. The youth want change but what change means today and what shape it will take tomorrow may surprise us. Indeed as the rebellious religion of the Muslim Millennials demonstrates, one can be anticlerical without being antireligious or a Kemalist.

The view so prevalent in the West of the secular division of church and state being a vital step toward not only democratization but also modernization is simply too formulaic to fit the truth of the Middle East today. In countries with more democracy, conservative, pious Islam tends to be on the rise, while, with the exception of Iran, it is in the most autocratic states where Islam is still most suppressed. Arguably, the best-functioning government in the region—that of Turkey—is currently controlled by a party with a distinct Islamic identity, though that party's rise to power in free elections caused great chagrin in both Europe and the United States, where it was feared that the election of an Islamic party would prove a slippery slope to an Islamic state. At the same time, the United States threw its backing—and many billions of dollars—behind the regime of President Pervez Musharraf in Pakistan, feeling confident in his secular leadership. But all too soon, the truth became apparent that he had been deceptive in his efforts to combat Islamic extremists, and he became so reviled by the populace for his authoritarian ways, corruption, and ineffectual stewardship of the country that he was driven from power, leaving a power vacuum that has caused the country to fall into chaos.

The dramatically contrasting stories of Turkey and Pakistan, which will be told in the next two chapters, are cautionary tales about the misplaced fear of all things Islamic that is all too prevalent in the West and has led to horribly flawed decision making about the leaders we will back, and the manner in which we have attempted to exert our influence in the region.

CHAPTER 8

PAKISTAN'S
HORROR AND HOPE

In June 2005, Secretary of State Condoleezza Rice stood before a rapt audience at the American University of Cairo to announce a new dawn in America's relations with the Middle East. Washington would no longer look to secular dictators to protect its interests, she announced, for 9/11 had shown that dictatorship bred extremism. "For sixty years," Rice said, "my country, the United States, pursued stability at the expense of democracy in this region here in the Middle East—and we achieved neither. Now, we are taking a different course. We are supporting the democratic aspirations of all people."[1] These were important words, a rare and sobering admission that American policy had been flawed in propping up authoritarianism; doing so had not led to hope for stability in the region and had in fact played an ironic role in empowering the worst kind of extremism.

Yet even as Rice was speaking of democracy to Egyptians, the Bush administration was busy embracing the secular Pakistani dictator Pervez Musharraf as a vital ally. In 1999, when General Musharraf ordered tanks into Islamabad and seized the reins of government in a coup, the country was mired in corruption, betrayed by self-serving politicians and power-hungry generals, and deeply divided by class and ethnicity. The country's economy was a wreck, due largely to international sanctions imposed in response to Islamabad's 1998 nuclear-weapons test. The Pakistani government had long been a promoter of violent extremism next door in Afghanistan, which had started to cross the border in spillover at home. Taliban warriors and other extremists sympathetic to

al-Qaeda had begun making the country's mountainous northern territories a safe haven.[2] Nuclear-armed Pakistan was spiraling into chaos,
within a stone's throw—or an easy missile shot—of the strategic water-
ways of the Persian Gulf.

In Musharraf, the Bush administration thought it saw a secular,
Kemalist savior. He promised to bring stability to the country and to
set it on the path to both secularization and modernization. When 9/11
placed Pakistan at the front of the so-called War on Terror, Musharraf
was quick to pledge Pakistan's support for the cause. Musharraf would
later claim that the Bush administration had threatened to send Pakistan back to the Stone Age if it didn't agree to support the fight against
the Taliban.[3] Several U.S. policy makers were said to have impressed
that point on Musharraf's intelligence chief, General Ahmad Mahmoud, who was in Washington when the Twin Towers fell. But Musharraf also had his own reasons for accepting the arrangement. When
he summoned his army's nine corps commanders—in effect, his inner
cabinet—he told them that it was in the country's interests to go along,
or at least seem to go along, with American demands. By helping America in Afghanistan, the government would reap billions of dollars in
American and international aid. The regime would also secure American support for its military rule, and an end to the international sanctions that were crippling its economy. More important, the only way in
which Pakistan could protect its position in Afghanistan and in facing
India was to cooperate with the United States. There were dissenters,
but by and large the top brass accepted Musharraf's game plan.

For a time, Musharraf seemed to be making use of the American
backing to make positive reforms in both the government and the economy. He recruited skilled technocrats—some veterans of government
service, others experienced hands from Wall Street, the World Bank, or
the private sector at home—into his cabinet in order to professionalize
the government. Banking reforms, directed at bringing that sector up
to international standards and opening it to direct foreign investment,
helped to provide more seed money for new investments. As business
growth took off, with a boom in start-ups, so did consumption. Rows of

new high-rises sprang up along the boulevards of Karachi and Lahore. The Karachi stock exchange bolted to the top of emerging-market indexes. By 2006, seven years after Musharraf took over, average per capita income had risen by 55 percent, and economic growth averaged 7 percent a year between 2001 and 2007. Car sales grew 20 percent a year, television sales grew 29 percent, and sales of air conditioners grew a whopping 206 percent.[4]

Musharraf cultivated support among secular and liberal intellectuals by protecting them from pressure from religious zealots and providing them with avenues for expression. With government encouragement print media boomed and a slate of private television channels took to the air featuring popular talk shows and soap operas and a new take on covering news. Websites, blogs, and chat rooms also thrived. Political debates became more wide-ranging, breaking with the rigid ways in which politics and religion had been discussed on state television in the past. Musharraf also made a good show of vowing to rein in Islamic extremism, and his interest in doing so seemed perfectly in keeping with his secularism.

At heart, Musharraf was a Kemalist. He had lived in Turkey for a time during his formative years, and spoke some Turkish (he even claims to be a fan of Istanbul's Beşiktaş soccer club). When he first took over the helm in Islamabad, he could not contain his enthusiasm for Ataturk. He would speak warmly of the Turkish military man turned statesman in speeches, hinting that Pakistan's model should be Kemalist Turkey: secular, modern, and dominated by the military. Musharraf also liked to talk of "enlightened moderation" or "Jinnah's Islam," seeking legitimacy through invocations of the name of Pakistan's secular-minded founding father, Muhammad Ali Jinnah.

His call for enlightened moderation was a big hit in Washington. But what Washington policy makers failed to understand was that Musharraf's motives were more complicated than he presented them as being. He had a strong interest in economic progress, and in moderating the role of Islam in Pakistani life. But he also had other goals, which were at cross-purposes with U.S. interests. Among these were providing support to Islamic extremists fighting the Karzai government in Afghanistan.

America gave $11.8 billion in aid to Musharraf's Pakistan, and 90 percent of that went to the military. Though Musharraf had made progress in stimulating the economy, that growth proved short-lived. When he resigned as president late in the summer of 2008, inflation stood at 24 percent, there were acute shortages of food and electricity, and income inequality was at its worst since the end of the Ayub Khan period in 1969, heating up social discontent. Those billions had done little for Pakistan's economy after all, and had also failed to buy America security by breaking the back of extremism in the country's border areas. On the contrary, the extremists had gained a good deal of ground, with the Taliban surging in Afghanistan in 2008, and their Pakistani counterpart, Tahrik-e Taliban (Taliban Movement) in control of large swaths of Pakistan's northwest from where they carried out devastating bombing attacks deeper inside Pakistan. One attack would claim the life of the former Prime Minister Benazir Bhutto in December 2007.

Right after 9/11 Pakistan's private sector had appealed to the U.S. government to open its market to Pakistani products (textiles in particular). That would have generated much-needed export revenue, which, the business community knew, would be the most effective means of growing the economy. But the U.S. government demurred, preferring to invest in Musharraf and Pakistan's military rather than its private sector. The billions of U.S. dollars funneled to the country could have improved education and infrastructure, created jobs and business opportunities, and helped to swell the ranks of the promising, business-minded middle class. This would have been vital in tamping down the power of the extremists who are now threatening the stability of the government.

Fueling the march of the extremists is the fact that Pakistan is still so largely a feudal country, a country of large landlords and poor peasants. The so-called feudals dominate politics outside of the cities, coercing the peasants who live on and farm their land to vote according to their mandates. Gholam Mustafa Jatoi, a large landlord in Sind and Pakistan's one-time prime minister, once expelled his peasants from his land for a whole year because he did not like the way they voted in an election. Few peasants dare risk that sort of punishment by crossing their feudal masters. So it is that Pakistan's parliament is more a house of lords, protecting the prerogative of the elite, than a truly democratic legislature representing the will of the people.

Benazir Bhutto captured the West's imagination as the Oxford- and Harvard-educated face of modern Pakistan, but there was little that was modern in her feudal control of her vast landholdings in Sind. The West has been largely blind to this facet of conflict in Pakistan, failing to anticipate how the seething resentment of the peasantry and the frustration of the urban poor would translate all too readily into support for rebellion and extremism. All through the 1990s, Islamic extremist groups extended their roots in rural Punjab, engaging in class war to bring the population to their cause, just as the Taliban more recently mobilized peasants in Swat to drive out local landlords and gain control over large swaths of territory.[5]

By once again putting its faith in an authoritarian, secular ruler—Pervez Musharraf—rather than cultivating ties with the community of capitalist and reform-minded entrepreneurs and professionals who are the country's greatest hope for eventual political stability and lasting economic progress, the United States inadvertently abetted the descent into mayhem.

The United States had lent its support to a vicious cycle that has long plagued Pakistan, whereby a military dictatorship steps in to take charge after a period of weak civilian rule, setting back whatever scant progress had been made in the building of robust institutions of democracy and of a thriving capitalist business sector.

Once the army first took charge, in a coup in 1958, it never really relinquished its hold on power. Even on those occasions when it has given ground to elected leaders and parliaments it has been enacting a tactical withdrawal rather than anything resembling a principled retreat from control of the political system. Pakistan's military, as is common with armed forces formed under colonialism, looked down from the

start on politics and politicians, and still does, with little time for constitutional rights and democracy. The men in uniform see civilian politics,
to say nothing of democracy, as a mess and a distraction that threatens
to weaken the country. If the generals could have stayed in the presidential palace without interruption they probably would have, but periodic
bouts of civilian resistance have taught the soldiers to punctuate periods
of direct rule with years of subtler management from behind barracks
walls—manipulating politicians and the media to retain control—when
circumstances make such an approach expedient. Most countries have a
military; in Pakistan, the military has a country.

Pakistani politics has settled on a predictable, repetitive sequence:
The army steps in proclaiming that it will restore order, development,
and progress; compiles a mixed record and becomes mired in corrup-
tions of its own; resorts to all manner of dirty pool to hang on; scrambles
for allies, which paradoxically include fundamentalists even as it issues
warnings about jihadi extremism; sees its cynical manipulations increasingly lose credibility with an exasperated populace; gives in to demands
for elections and lets civilian leaders return to power but stays just off-
stage, pulling the strings, dividing the public against one another, and
keeping the door open to another bout of military rule. Civilian leaders
have contributed their share to this charade. They have preferred bickering to effective government and have seldom resisted the temptation to
line their pockets and abuse power.

The worst thing about this pattern of military dictatorship followed
by weak civilian rule is that it is not merely a cycle, but a downward spi-
ral. With every turn, the generals get less done and grow more manipu-
lative, while civilian rule becomes even more ineffectual.

A vital element in understanding why the military has kept the reins
of power, and the often perverse ways in which the military has steered
Pakistani politics and foreign affairs, is appreciating the role of the
country's rivalry with India. Fear of India's encroachment on Pakistani
interests in the region explains a great deal about Pakistan's troubles
through the years, and in dealing with Musharraf, the Bush administration failed to take account of the ways in which Pakistan's history

of conflict with India motivated Musharraf to double-deal.[6] Due to a perceived need to counter India's exercise of influence in Afghanistan, Musharraf—and the secretive Pakistani military intelligence organization, the Inter-Services Intelligence, or ISI for short—calculated that even as they would assist to a certain extent in combating extremists, they would also support the Taliban in its battle against the Karzai government. In the process they allowed extremists to build a power base in Pakistan's mountainous northwestern territory on the border with Afghanistan. This is one legacy of the horrific trauma of the Partition.

———

Pakistan's breakaway from India was a cataclysmic upheaval marked by staggering violence that has left a legacy of intense rivalry—periodically breaking out into outright war—between Pakistan and India. The idea of Pakistan was the brainchild of Muhammad Ali Jinnah, a Muslim lawyer who was a member of the Indian National Congress but also a staunch advocate for protections of Muslim rights in Hindu-dominated India. He went on to become the leader of Pakistan's independence movement, and after the wrenching cataclysm of the Partition became Pakistan's first leader, assuming the position of governor general. The new country also got a prime minister and a cabinet to see to day-to-day affairs of government, while the bureaucracy, judiciary, and military—leftovers of British India—functioned as before. Jinnah might have been able to lead Pakistan to the institution of a stable democratic system, uniting the many ethnic groups, provinces, and tribes that had been cobbled together to form the new state—Bengalis, Punjabis, Pashtuns, Sindhis, and Baluchis, all speaking their own languages and with little binding them but their Islamic faith—but he died in September 1948 from lung cancer, only a year after the Partition. A decade of turmoil followed, with the politicians and bureaucrats, land lords and generals bickering over what shape Pakistan should take. In fact, had it not been for American food aid and financial assistance, Pakistan would not have survived its tumultuous first years.

The most serious point of contention was distribution of power between Pakistan's two wings, separated by the breadth of India. West Pakistan was the capital and political center, but there were many more living in the country's eastern wing and they wanted power commensurate with their numbers. But that was not the only issue at stake. Mawdudi and his Jamaat-e Islami were pushing the state created in Islam's name to live up to that claim. Jinnah saw Pakistan as a Muslim homeland, a secular country that would be a level playing field for Indian Muslims. Mawdudi thought a level playing field was not enough, that only an Islamic state could fulfill the promise of Pakistan. With Jinnah gone and his successors unable to quickly agree on Pakistan's final shape, Mawdudi found ample opportunity to argue his case.

In the face of this political disarray, the prospect of war with India was a constant worry. Pakistan and India had not parted ways amicably—far from it. Large numbers of Hindus, Muslims, and Sikhs had died during the Partition and their pain and suffering clouded relations between the two countries from the moment of their birth on an August midnight in 1947. India and Pakistan also disagreed on the division of territory among them, with Pakistan claiming that the Muslim-majority territory of Kashmir—the idyllic mountainous principality in India's northwest—should have been a part of Pakistan. But Kashmir's ruling prince opted for India just before the Partition. Pakistan refused that outcome and held on to a part of Kashmir. To this day Kashmir sits divided between the two South Asian giants. Three wars have failed to settle the issue, and the conflict is one reason Pakistan has fallen prey to military rule and failed to find its way to stability and prosperity.

In the face of all of the turmoil, the Pakistani military stepped in to take control. While the British had given Pakistan little in the way of a functioning government, a well-oiled economy, or a modern physical infrastructure, they did hand it a formidable army. When the British quit India their fabulous Indian Army—reared in the best traditions of British military service on and off the battlefield and full of units with distinguished combat records from both world wars—was divided roughly evenly, in terms of both matériel and men, between Pakistan and India. Half of the army that had controlled the whole subcontinent was a very big fish in the smaller pond that was Pakistan. In 1958, the generals, under the leadership of General Muhammad Ayub Khan, decided it was time to get down to state building and growing the economy at a rapid clip. Political wrangling ended and industrialization began. Soon the World Bank was hailing Pakistan as a model.

Ayub Khan was a secularizer, believing that religion should be a private matter and that Pakistan must develop free of Islam's influence. He was able to stare down Mawdudi and the Jamaat, and his goal was to build a national identity based not on Islam but on a vision for Pakistan's rapid economic development. His was a Kemalist vision.

Success at development was not enough for Ayub Khan, however; he wanted a larger legacy, as the general who would defeat India and give Pakistan all of Kashmir. Underestimating India's military capability, or perhaps overestimating Pakistan's, Ayub Khan led his forces to war with India in 1965, and the overconfident Pakistani army soon found itself scrambling to stop the Indians from taking Lahore, the country's second-largest city and the capital of the Punjab, Pakistan's most populous province. Pakistan settled for a cease-fire, with the goal of owning Kashmir further out of its reach. Ayub Khan had overreached and was now humiliated.

By 1967, angry and frustrated Pakistanis of all political hues demanded an end to military rule. A robust democracy movement surfaced bringing together secular and religious parties to call for free elections and the return of civilian rule. Those unhappy with growing income inequality, which was the result of rapid economic growth, joined the fray. The opposition took to the streets, and as crowds grew larger, Ayub Khan was pressed by his own generals to leave office. In 1969 he stepped down, handing power over to the army's chief of staff so he could see to elections and the transition to democracy.

Pakistan held its first free and fair elections a year later, in 1970, but even as they ushered in democracy, they exposed all of Pakistan's weaknesses and in fact led to the country's breakup. The Bengali population of East Pakistan was disgruntled over its second-class status. The central government, dominated by West Pakistan, had neglected the country's eastern wing, starving it of economic investment and even denying it proper military defense. East Pakistan lacked representation in the halls of power, and more radical voices claimed the territory was no more than a colony of West Pakistan. It was little surprise then that with the opportunity to register its disgruntlement at the ballot box East Pakistan voted for separatism. The government at the center resisted, and civil war ensued in 1971, as the emerging nation of Bangladesh teamed with India to inflict a humiliating defeat on the Pakistani military.

In what was left of Pakistan, the Sindhi politician Zulfiqar Ali Bhutto, whose Pakistan Peoples Party had won the vote in West Pakistan, became prime minister. A brilliant figure with a gift to inspire and lead, Bhutto promised Pakistan a new beginning (which included, though at the time it was a secret, the start of the country's nuclear weapons program under the young scientist Abdul Qadeer Khan). But Bhutto proved no democrat; no sooner was he in the prime minister's office than he set out to grab all power, railroading any opponent that stood in his way. He was a venerable aristocrat but his politics had a leftist slant. He stood as a populist who crushed capitalism and showered government favor on to the poor. He also nationalized numerous businesses, and put Pakistan's economy in the state's hands, weakening the fledgling private sector and the middle class. Pakistan started to look like many other Third World authoritarian socialist states of the time, where politics was reduced to the cult of personality of the ruler. The thuggish brutality of Bhutto's monopolization of power alienated many in Pakistan. With national elections scheduled for 1977, Bhutto rigged the vote and provoked wide-scale political agitation. With chaos spreading the military once again stepped in, led by General Muhammad Zia ul-Haq, to assume leadership of the country. Bhutto was tried and hanged two years later on dubious murder charges.

General Zia was a staunch fundamentalist who had avidly read Mawdudi, and he was convinced that the Pakistani state must become Islamic. Secularism, to his mind, had failed to bind the disparate groups comprising Pakistan, contributing to the Bengalis' defection. The only reliable force that would bring them together, he believed, was Islam.

He brought once hounded fundamentalists into his cabinet, levied new religious taxes, and instituted new laws based on the shariah. Theft or adultery could cost a perpetrator a flogging, the loss of a hand, or even life itself. Islam flourished not only in government, but on television, in the courts, and in textbooks. There were more public displays of piety, more beards and covered heads, fewer Western suits and a virtual banishment of that classic of subcontinental ladies' wear, the sari—it showed too much skin and was too "Hindu" for the newfound Islamic sensibility.

In General Zia's military, pious officers were promoted faster, and the military paid men in uniform to go on pilgrimage to Mecca. The high command encouraged proselytization in the ranks, and the Kemalist military turned Islamic, a turn of events that would prove consequential for Pakistan's foreign policy for decades to come.

But Zia's Pakistan was not Khomeini's Iran. While Zia believed fundamentalism served as a powerful unifying ideology for the state, he and his military comrades not only retained most of the real power, but even made the military the chief interpreter and implementer of Islam.[7] They embraced fundamentalism in speech, but kept its diehard spokesmen well away from power. Nothing in Pakistan's foreign policy, feudal society, financial institutions, industry, or government administration changed. There were no purges and executions, and no redistribution of wealth or overhaul of the economy and the state. Pakistan remained Western-aligned and under the rule of the generals, land lords, businessmen, and politicians who had run things for years. If anything, leading fundamentalists were co-opted into the fold, joining the ranks of venal and corrupt civilian politicians.

Co-opting fundamentalists served the state well. Though the Islamization of the government—what General Zia called his transformation—drew much international rebuke with its harsh punishments—public floggings and hands being cut off—Pakistan was at its most stable during the Zia years. The state was more powerful, and there were fewer ethnic threats or disruptive social movements than at any time before or since. Beefing up Pakistan's Islamic identity also served the country well when, after the Soviet invasion of Afghanistan in 1979, the Pakistani government elected to throw support behind the mujahideen fighters.

The success of the mujahideen campaign in Afghanistan taught the Pakistani military an unfortunate lesson about the usefulness of backing Islamic extremist groups. The hard-eyed generals and ISI agents who ran the anti-Soviet jihad were not simplistic enough to believe, as many of the foot soldiers did, that the call to Muslim holy war had defeated the Soviets. But the pros from Islamabad did become seduced by the notion that true-believing jihadis can be a highly cost-effective weapons system: cheap to maintain, easy to organize, and lethal on the battlefield. Pakistan's intelligence chiefs believed that while U.S. and Saudi cash had greased the wheels of jihad, it was Pakistani know-how in training and directing the mujahideen that really pushed it over the top to its unlikely-seeming 1989 victory. No matter how lavish the funding, ran this theory, a purely secular war of liberation from Soviet rule could never have succeeded. The Afghans won because the Pakistanis knew how to play on their neighbors' Islamic sensibilities—encouraging talk of jihad to energize the fight against occupation. This highly effective method of meddling in Afghani affairs would be continued in the coming years by the military, even as civilian rule returned to Pakistan— however tentatively—in 1988.

Though secular and pro-democracy forces opposed both the growing Islamization of Pakistan and the lack of political freedoms under Zia, democracy returned to the country only after Zia and a slew of his lieutenants died in a still-mysterious 1988 plane crash. The dictator's death shocked the military, which retreated to its barracks, and elections were held. Once again, the wheel had turned, but Islam would not retreat as readily as the military had, and the military retained its supremacy over the government.

A decade of tumultuous democratic rule followed, with Zulfiqar Ali Bhutto's daughter, Benazir, riding this second wave of democracy to power, elected prime minister after her Pakistan Peoples Party (PPP) won the 1988 elections. She was less keen on pushing ahead with

Islamic programs, but she was not ready, without a better alternative, to change course completely. So Islam continued to hold its grip on public affairs, although less money went to Islamic programs and the government backed away from the more controversial Islamic policies—such as hand-loppings and public floggings—that had given Pakistan a bad name.

The military also began to clean house. The generals still viewed Pakistan as an Islamic state—they too could not think of another glue— but took measures to restore professionalism to their ranks. Gone were the subsidies for officers' trips to Mecca and the counting of Islamic knowledge as a criterion for promotion. But reemphasizing military professionalism was not the same thing as embracing secularism, or the principle of civilian supremacy, or giving up jihadis as a foreign policy tool. Indeed, the military maintained its ties with extremists all through this period.

With uncanny regularity over the next decade, Benazir and her Punjabi archrival Nawaz Sharif, who led a coalition of right-of-center and Islamic parties around his own Pakistan Muslim League, would alternate in the premiership. Neither achieved much in the way of economic progress or political reform; their administrations were characterized by rampant corruption and misrule. All the while the military retained true control of the system, dismissing their governments in turn—either when the hapless prime ministers encroached on the military's turf or when public unhappiness with corruption and mismanagement reached a crescendo. In 1990, 1993, and 1997 the military instructed the president to exercise his constitutional power to dissolve the parliament— thereby unseating the prime minister—and elections followed.

When Benazir Bhutto was elected prime minister in 1988, the generals told her that she would have no say over Afghan or Indian relations or the nuclear program, and just to be sure, they chose her first foreign minister for her. No sooner had she settled in office than the powerful spies at ISI got busy cobbling together a rival political alliance under Nawaz Sharif to agitate against her and spent vast sums luring her allies to the opposition benches with bribes. The seeds of her own corruption were sown when Benazir asked her husband, Asif Ali Zardari (now Pakistan's president), to build a war chest to fight back.

Nor did Nawaz Sharif have more say in foreign affairs. In 1999, shortly before General Musharraf sent his tanks to the presidential palace to stage his coup, he bullied Sharif into signing on to war with India, which nearly touched off a nuclear showdown. Musharraf sent jihadis into the Indian-held part of Kashmir, provoking a limited but brutal war that became history's first direct ground conflict between nuclear-armed states. Jihadi fighters captured the high ground in an area called Kargil and used their perch to attack Indian lines. India retaliated with heavy artillery shelling and aerial bombing, and threatened to take the war across the border into Pakistan.

The United States stepped in to bring the nuclear-armed protagonists back from the brink, and Sharif went to Washington to conclude a cease-fire deal brokered by President Clinton. But no sooner had Sharif returned home than the generals began blaming the humiliation on his alleged readiness to betray Pakistan's interests. Pakistan's economy was then in a bad state, there was growing unhappiness with government corruption, and more so with Sharif's attempt to manage the situation by strong-arming his opponents into submission. Rising tensions with the military were no help. Sharif decided to get rid of the troublemaking Musharraf, but the military was onto him. When in October 1999, while Musharraf was on a foreign visit, Sharif dismissed him as army chief and refused to allow his returning flight to land in Karachi, tanks rolled into the capital.[8] Musharraf got off his plane to once again establish military rule.

The United States was impressed by Musharraf's Kemalist inclinations, but failed to understand his mix of motives. In particular, U.S. policy makers failed to appreciate the danger of his commitment to the Pakistani military's highly destabilizing ongoing support for Islamic fighters in Kashmir and Afghanistan. The generals and lords of the ISI had decided that, having deployed the jihadi weapon with such spectacular results against the Soviets, they would keep the struggle going in a bid to gain dominance over Afghanistan, as well as redirecting extremist attention from their home turf. After 9/11 nothing had changed in how they assessed their strategic interests and in the value they found in using the Taliban to win territory in Afghanistan and jihadis to keep Kashmir on the boil. Pakistan had only to wait until the United States left Afghanistan, and then it could redeploy its jihadi assets to achieve its foreign policy aims.

Pakistan has always had a rocky relationship with Afghanistan.[9] Afghans have never recognized their border with Pakistan—the famous Durand Line, which, in an effort to shore up its rule in northern India, Britain drew up in the late nineteenth century. The demarcation had no basis in history; it was imposed in order to separate what was still the territory of India then from the territory ruled by troublesome Pashtun tribes to the north, and many Afghan Pashtuns hold that the true border is the Indus River, some 120 miles southeast of the Durand Line. The Pakistani military has long feared a Pashtun nationalist uprising that would claim the territory, an especially troubling prospect in light of the large Pashtun population within Pakistan itself.

It was this fear that drove the secular or more moderately Islamic Pakistani military men to support the puritanical Taliban in 1994 in its bid to take over Afghanistan. The Taliban were Pashtun, and it was clearly better for Pakistan to get Pashtuns to fight to the north, in Afghanistan, than to dream of nationalism and set their sights on grabbing Pakistanti territory to the south. In addition, after the Soviets pulled out of Afghanistan, the mujahideen leader who had come out on top of the wrangling for control of the government was the Iran- and India-backed Northern Alliance commander Ahmad Shah Masoud. Pakistan had not supported him during the fight, and because he was a Tajik, a rival ethnic group, he was unacceptable to Pakistan's Pashtuns, who make up about a sixth of the military's officer corps. Pakistan wanted Pashtuns—of the Islamabad-friendly variety—to rule Afghanistan. Of no concern was the fact that the Taliban were laying waste to Afghanistan: destroying the priceless giant Buddhas of Bamiyan, closing schools, brutally punishing people for owning TV sets or having insufficiently long beards, nurturing a drug economy, and sheltering al-Qaeda. These "Islamic students" were serving a larger purpose by keeping Pashtuns preoccupied and fighting against Indian influence.

I remember vividly a talk I had with General Nasirullah Babur in 1996 at the office of the President of Pakistan. He was then Benazir Bhutto's interior minister. Babur was a burly secular Pashtun, a large and imposing man with green eyes and pale skin who cared little for listening and was only too happy to broadcast his very strong opinions, especially on the evils of fundamentalism and the damage that it had done to Pakistan. When the general had finished berating clerics and fundamentalists, I asked him about his pet project; he was reputed to be a champion of the Taliban. He shot back, "They are our Pashtun boys! It is unacceptable for Tajiks [read: Ahmad Shah Masoud] to rule Kabul." As long as the Pashtun boys served a higher cause, of what concern was their violent fanaticism?

At the height of Taliban power, Pakistani generals spoke confidently of the "strategic depth" that proxy control over Afghanistan through their support of the Taliban gave Pakistan in the great game against India. It is little wonder, then, that the generals showed so little real enthusiasm for shutting down the Taliban, and why Islamabad was so suspicious of the independent Afghan state that America propped up after toppling the Taliban in late 2001 and early 2002.

The degree of Pakistani concern about Indian influence in Afghanistan should not be underestimated. For Americans, the most important statistics about Afghanistan since 2001 have been the numbers of Taliban attacks, NATO casualties, and the volume of the drug trade. For Pakistanis, the key figures are the number of Indian consulates in Afghanistan and the number of people they employ. In late 2007, an American television crew interviewed General Musharraf. On camera he was on message, confirming Pakistan's commitment to the War on Terror. Once the cameras were off, he spoke at length about Indian consulates in Afghanistan. The same concern was evident when one senior Pakistani general asked me: "Why does India need so many consulates? How many Indian tourists go to Kandahar to justify 250 Indian personnel at their consulate there? Those 250 people are there for intelligence gathering. We have to think of when it is that we will be facing the Indian army on two fronts [the second front being Afghanistan]."[10]

America wanted a strong Afghan state under Hamid Karzai, while Pakistan saw Karzai as pro-India, and believed a strong Afghan state was a threat. Nothing in American plans for Afghanistan assured Pakistani generals that Kabul would not become a satellite of Delhi, and a pro-Delhi government in Kabul was a bigger worry for the Pakistani military than the Taliban. That calculation has led, however, to the unleashing of extremist mayhem within Pakistan itself.

Countries can do dangerous things in pursuit of national interest. It gets worse when unsupervised generals decide what the national interest is and they alone reckon its costs and benefits. The Taliban helped Pakistan to outface India in the contest over Afghanistan, but the unintended, and so far unstoppable, consequence was that the jihad spilled over into Pakistan, bringing sectarian violence, suicide bombings, and the creation of Taliban "emirates" in the mountain fastnesses of the northwestern region.

In 2000, Bill Clinton warned Musharraf that "terrorism would consume Pakistan if the country continued to back jihadism in the region."[11] Musharraf demurred by claiming that "he could not afford to alienate the powerful Pashtun tribes along the border with Afghanistan."[12]

But as Clinton had perceived, backing the Taliban next door required a degree of tolerance for extremism at home as well.[13] How could Pakistan sustain its "Jihad 2.0" in Afghanistan without nurturing the infrastructure required for recruiting, indoctrinating, training, and managing jihadi fighters? There had to be radical madrasahs, extremist parties, financial networks, training camps, plenty of space to gather and train fighters on Pakistan's borders, and deep ties between jihadis and their ISI handlers. Years after 9/11, that infrastructure remains, and is the bedrock for the persistent extremist menace in Pakistan. It is comforting for the West and convenient for Pakistan to blame all this on rogue elements in the ISI. The truth, however, is that this engineered jihad was far too important to Pakistan for all of it to be a rogue operation.

In 2002, under pressure from Washington, Musharraf did have two thousand extremist suspects arrested, but most were quietly released just weeks later. Many extremists were shipped to Azad Kashmir—Pakistan's portion of Kashmir, which is technically an independent entity—where government bans on extremists did not hold. That was why so many extremists were on hand to help with earthquake relief when massive tremors wreaked havoc in the mountainous region in 2005. Others were sent to the Federally Administered Tribal Areas, or FATA region, of the northwest, the mountainous tribal area outside of government control, where they comingled with the Taliban and al-Qaeda to become only more menacing.

Musharraf made repeated promises that extremist seminaries would be closed and all seminary curriculums reviewed and if need be reformed, but no meaningful steps were taken.[14] Preachers, organizers, and fighters bobbed from one outfit to the next, but stayed very much on the scene. The military cooperated with the United States in suppressing al-Qaeda and its allies inside Pakistan, but protected jihadis fighting in Kashmir, homegrown extremists active in tribal areas, and Taliban leaders holed up in the Pakistani city of Quetta on the Afghan border.

By 2004, there was plenty of evidence that Pakistani intelligence was still in the jihad business, and that the continuing instability in Afghanistan had roots in Pakistani support for the Taliban. There were camps and safe havens on the Pakistani side of the Durand Line, and American commanders could tell that Pakistan was holding back in fighting al-Qaeda along that border.

It was a bit like boxing with a feather bed: Given the deep links between various strands of extremism in the Afghan-Pakistan corridor, hitting the extremists in one spot simply meant causing jihadis to shift from one organization to another. The process also gave extremist groups plenty of time to go underground and, ominously, to gain a measure of autonomy from Pakistani intelligence.

You did not have to go too far out of your way in those days to bump into such groups. When I was in Lahore in 2004, I saw plenty of activity on the part of Lashkar-e Tayiba, a violent group with ties to al-Qaeda and a record of mayhem in Kashmir, which gained notoriety for its brazen attack on Mumbai in November 2008. President Bush had named them as a terrorist organization in a speech and Pakistan had ostensibly banned them in 2002, but there they were, holding a large rally outside Lahore in the spring of that year and bragging that they had just bought a big tract of land to house their new training facilities.

In fact, it was not until September 2008, after Musharraf had left the scene, that the State Bank of Pakistan froze the accounts of Tahrik-e Taliban, the Afghan Taliban's Pakistani counterpart. Its leader, Baitullah Mehsud, was accused by Musharraf of having ties to al-Qaeda and of assassinating Benazir Bhutto in December 2007. Mehsud's followers overran an army fort in January 2008, killing sixteen soldiers and kidnapping another twenty-four.[15] Apparently this sort of record was not an impediment to doing banking in Musharraf's Pakistan.

Musharraf's most important accomplishment in the eyes of his fellow generals was to convince Washington that all this was not happening, and that he was a reliable ally safeguarding Western interests. As one senior general put it to me in 2005, "Muharraf is the best man for the job at this point in time; for getting for Pakistan the most out of this short-run alliance with America."[16] But the military failed to assess the true danger of the extremists. No one seems to have told the fanatics what a limited role they were meant to play. Over time, Musharraf could not control them, either at home or abroad. Baitullah Mehsud and his Tahrik-e Taliban visited increasingly brazen terror on Pakistani cities and military bases in a cascade of suicide attacks on military, police, and civilian targets. Taliban armies showed up on the outskirts of Peshawar—and would eventually take over Swat. By 2007, Pakistan was more at risk than it had been in 2001.

It should not have come as such a surprise when thousands of extremists based in Islamabad's Red Mosque and its attached seminary complex created a national crisis in April 2007. These domestic jihadis had taken it upon themselves to purge Pakistan's debonair capital of all vice and un-Islamic behavior by imposing draconian Islamic laws on its citizens. Armed activists, including young women hidden under head-to-toe *burqas*, attacked video stores and barber shops, and commanded the city's residents to start living like Kabulis under the Taliban. When the extremists kidnapped a number of Chinese nationals whom they accused of running a brothel, the embarrassment grew to be more than Musharraf could stand. Here were thousands of aggressive fanatics who had somehow managed to stow huge arms caches in a mosque less than a mile from the headquarters of the all-seeing ISI—in fact, the Red Mosque was where many of the agency's officers went for daily prayers. Clinton's warning had proved prescient.

After months of official dithering over what to do about the Red Mosque, Musharraf decided to act. In July, he ordered elite troops to storm the complex. Televised mayhem and scores of deaths ensued. Even secular Pakistanis were shocked at how badly Musharraf had handled the whole affair. Enraged extremists hit back with waves of urban suicide bombings targeting police and military facilities. The total number of suicide attacks for 2007 was fifty-six, and all but four happened after the Red Mosque siege.

By the time the general fell from power in the summer of 2008, the extremist surge was in full swing. Local fanatics led by clerics such as Sufi Muhammad and Mawlana Fazlullah (better known as Mawlana Radio for his fiery sermons on his private FM station) or tribal commanders such as Pakistani Taliban warlord Baitullah Mehsud began teaming up with al-Qaeda fighters holed up in the Pashtun tribal no-man's land on the Afghan border. They killed Benazir Bhutto not long after her return from exile, laid siege to the once-popular highland tourist destination of Swat, and menacingly surrounded Peshawar, the Pashtun capital of the North-West Frontier Province (NWFP) and Pakistan's fourth-largest city. The military fought back, was bloodied, and then turned to talks. No approach was of much avail. The Frankenstein's monster that the military had created was now out of control. An army and air force equipped and trained to fight a conventional war against India on the flatlands of the Rajasthan desert could not adapt to guerrilla warfare amid the mountains of the Pashtun-dominated northwest.

The military has been at wit's end. It inflicted heavy casualties at first, but also suffered embarrassingly high casualty rates. Worse yet, the conflict caused unhappiness on the Pakistani streets and even within the military's own ranks. Pakistanis saw extremism as America's problem and the war on jihadis who occupy Pakistani soil as "America's war." With that sort of public attitude the country was unwilling to accept the costs and consequences of fighting extremism. It therefore did not take long for the military to throw in the towel and sue for peace, as if to tell the extremists: We don't want to crush you; we just want to remind you that your mission is to fight *beyond* and not within Pakistan's borders. This suited the extremists; they found ample space and time to build their capabilities and continue to pursue jihad in Afghanistan and extend their reach into Pakistani society. "Having redirected the chaos" back north at least for a time, to use *New York Times* reporter Dexter Filkins's memorable phrase, the generals now in charge of Pakistan's military became the custodians of an uneasy quasi-peace.[17] That peace broke down in the spring of 2009 when, embarrassed by the Taliban's brazen take-over of Swat—no more than eighty miles from the capital Islamabad—the military had to use tanks and artillery to push back the Taliban. Thousands were killed and close to 2 million became refugees in their own country. Pakistan had not faced such calamity since 1947. This is the Pakistan that the notionally Kemalist Pervez Musharraf has left in his wake.

The truth is that the West's best ally against fundamentalism and extremism in Pakistan is not, and never was, that country's incorrigibly double-dealing military and intelligence establishment, but rather civil society and pro-democracy forces that Musharraf fought to suppress.

Musharraf became determined to break the cycle in Pakistan whereby military rule eventually gave way to protests for democracy; he wanted to make military rule stick. He came to believe that Pakistan's destiny lay in his hands, and he basked in the comfort of the billions of dollars of aid money and new respectability that flowed to him.

Soon after the coup in 1999 Musharraf retired senior generals who might stand in his way, replacing them with pliant younger officers. With his position in the military secured, he then expanded that institution's role in society and the economy, handing over to colonels and generals slews of jobs that once had gone to civilians. By 2004, every dean at the University of Punjab was in uniform, and former and serving officers became governors, diplomats, civil servants, and captains of industry.[18] When asked if India should be worried about Pakistan's generals, former Indian premier A. B. Vajpayee mockingly asked, "What do we have to fear from these property dealers?"

Musharraf also fiddled with election laws, broke up Sharif's Pakistan Muslim League to create out of it his own "king's party," and tampered with ballot results. To weaken secular parties and keep both Benazir Bhutto and Nawaz Sharif on their toes—and perhaps also to scare Washington that without military rule Pakistan would turn fundamentalist—he helped religious parties score big in the 2002 elections. New election rules required all candidates to have higher education degrees—which disqualified many secular candidates—and then accepted seminary degrees as fulfilling the requirement. This made it easier for religious parties to contest. ISI also encouraged Islamic parties to set aside their differences and contest the elections as a united bloc. There were many more accusations of foul play, improper government intervention in the election process, and vote rigging that tainted the results. Prior to the 1999 coup, the secular parties had been doing a good job of routing fundamentalists. In elections held between 1988 and 1997, the fundamentalists' seat share in parliament steadily shrank, reaching its lowest to below 1 percent in 1997. Musharraf's scheming boosted them to 20 percent in 2002.

By 2007, the judiciary was looking like the last hurdle in Musharraf's way, and the general decided it was time to do away with it. The constitution said that the same person could not be both president and chief of the army, but the general was determined to hold on to both offices. Generals had bullied judges before, so Musharraf thought little of shuffling the Supreme Court to make sure that it would not interfere with his plan to lock himself in as president and army chief for life. There were prickly judges to be dismissed and friendly ones to be promoted. In Musharraf's estimation, some sixty jurists had to go, beginning with Chief Justice Iftikhar Chaudhry of the Supreme Court.

In his post only since 2005, Chaudhry had lost little time in becoming a thorn in Musharraf's side. That had been unexpected. Chaudhry was from Baluchistan, which is more or less Pakistan's "Wild West" and also its most thinly populated and least influential province. On paper, he did not have the legal background and pedigree to stand up to Musharraf, but he did.[19] He had the inconvenient habit of deciding what cases to hear *suo moto*, or on his own motion. He looked into allegations of government corruption and agreed to hear complaints of families of the "disappeared," the Pakistani equivalents of the *desaparecidos* of Argentina—hundreds of people, guilty and innocent, accused of involvement with terrorism who had vanished into government custody.[20] But Chaudhry's greatest sin was challenging the legality of General Musharraf's government, and in particular taking on Sensitive Question Number One, the issue of whether the general could be both president and army chief.

Families of the disappeared, backed by human rights activists and even Islamic parties, brought suit to force the government to provide information about the disappeared. Chaudhry decided the Supreme Court would hear their complaint. Fearing a negative court ruling, Musharraf summoned Chaudhry in March 2007 and demanded his resignation, but the little-known Baluchi judge would not give in. The government accused him of being soft on terrorism (to sully his image abroad in case anyone took notice of the spat) and of misconduct, and then fired him (along with the sixty or so other judges whose loyalty could not be ascertained). Chaudhry was then put under house arrest. But Musharraf had miscalculated in making this move.

The blatant attack on judicial independence brought thousands of lawyers into the streets and fired up the pro-democracy movement. Chaudhry's principled stance captured the public's imagination and they rallied to his cause. This was not a secular or religious issue; it was about the independence of the judiciary and checking a dictator's abuse of power. Chaudhry's cause brought together the religious and the secular around a common political goal: keeping Pakistan on track toward democracy.

Between March 2007 and January 2008, Pakistan was front-page news around the world. But there was something peculiar about the photos that went with the stories. The pictures showed lawyers in black business suits, white shirts, and ties calling for democracy and the rule of law while braving ranks of baton-wielding riot police and clouds of tear gas under the charge of General Musharraf.

In April 2007, people from every walk of life swarmed the caravan of cars that drove Chaudhry, just freed from custody, from Islamabad to Lahore. The two-hour drive took thirty-six hours. Pakistan had not seen anything like this; never before had the people come in such numbers to cheer for a judge and defend the judiciary. It was as strong an expression of belief in liberal democracy and rejection of dictatorship at the grassroots level as has ever been witnessed in the Muslim world, and it came where least expected. Up to then, the West had generally perceived Pakistan as caught in a tug-of-war between extremism and Musharraf's moderation, between fanatical fundamentalism and his secularism. But what Pakistan was fighting over in the spring of 2007 was something quite different; Pakistan was struggling to free itself from the clutches of a cynical military dictatorship that promised Kemalism even while nurturing fundamentalism and extremism.

Which Pakistan was this that came out into the streets, in Western attire no less, to demand democracy, that evoked sympathy and drew the American Bar Association to its support? Where had it been until now? That Pakistan has always been there. It long pre-dates Musharraf, it has outlasted him, and it remains by far the best hope for setting Pakistan on a better course.

The lawyers' movement rewrote Pakistan's history: It denied a military dictator complete control over the country, paved the way for the return of elected civilian rule, and sowed the seeds of a genuinely popular liberal-democratic movement. During the protest, day after day the lawyers braved batons and tear gas to march down the streets of Pakistan, and every day more and more Pakistanis joined their ranks. The lawyers gave such strong voice to anti-Musharraf feelings that by the time Pakistanis went to the ballot box in February 2008, the general had no leg to stand on. He yielded power to the people's representatives, and Benazir Bhutto's PPP formed the government, with the parliament then electing her husband, Asif Ali Zardari, president. The end for Musharraf came quickly and ignobly.

The lawyers' cause was Pakistan's cause; in the summer of 2008, fully 83 percent of Pakistanis strongly favored the judges' speedy reinstatement.[21] But Zardari feared that Chaudhry might open old corruption cases against him and was not keen to put the judge back on the bench. Nonetheless he was forced to do just that in March of 2009. Zardari had never been popular with Pakistanis, and cooperation with the United States in the fight against Taliban and al-Qaeda had plunged his approval ratings into single digits. Fearing that Nawaz Sharif may pounce at power, in March, Zardari took away control of Punjab from Sharif's party, and used a dubious court ruling to bar him and his brother, Shahbaz Sharif, who was running Punjab, from holding office. The overreach backfired. The lawyers' movement sprang into action and joined hands with protestors from all walks of life to pressure Zardari to back off. Facing a crisis and now also under pressure from the Obama administration, which was not willing to give a green light to undermining democracy, Zardari reinstated Chaudhry in his old position and lifted the ban on the Sharifs.

The civil society activism that the lawyers' movement has been leading draws professionals, merchants, students, and political activists of all persuasions, as well as common folk. There is ample evidence that what is true of the rising middle class elsewhere in the Middle East is true of Pakistan as well: that given the chance to pursue business growth without stifling government control, a capitalist flourishing will follow, and a thriving middle class will serve as the impetus for moderation and democracy. Despite all of the impediments, under Musharraf and up to the recent global economic crisis, private-sector activity ranging from manufacturing to finance, trade, and services, was on the rise. Religious or secular, the growing Pakistani middle class has been overwhelmingly pro-democracy and pro-free enterprise.

———

Though Musharraf ultimately sought to rein in the momentum of this movement for free enterprise and democracy, he also did much, early in his tenure, to spur it. Both Nawaz Sharif, who comes from a family of Punjabi industrialists and is generally pro-business, and Musharraf helped to stimulate economic growth. Both increased investment in infrastructure and privatized many businesses that had long been run by the government.

After 9/11, the international sanctions imposed on the country for having tested a nuclear device in 1998 were lifted and Western markets were opened to Pakistani goods. Exports doubled from around $9 billion in 1999 to the high mark of $18.5 billion in 2007. Some $5.5 billion in labor remittances (from those working in the Persian Gulf or Europe) complemented $5.1 billion in new foreign direct investment.[22] Unofficial estimates of the flow of cash out of Pakistan in prior years indicated that upward of $15 billion a year was leaving Pakistan for Dubai. Money flowing in the opposite direction was a welcome development, and Pakistani entrepreneurs and businesses leaders made good use of the money. Small cities in Punjab such as Sialkot or Gujranwala saw fresh investments and started growing rapidly on the back of small-scale enterprises that make everything from carpets to soccer balls to surgical tools.[23] More women became entrepreneurs, with women accounting for a growing share of workers in the expanding business sector as well, from financial services to software development, private media, and private education. The economic vitality of middle class has shown that when given a chance to build its business—even despite so many restrictions and political instability—their spirit of enterprise has a strong foothold in the country, and given the right support, business development can flourish.

Pakistan has a great deal of ground to cover to catch up with what one recent author has called "the strange [extraordinary] rise of modern India,"[24] but the economic growth that followed positive stimulus has shown that such expectations are not altogether misplaced. Two decades ago, Pakistan's private sector was doing better than its Indian counterpart and the Pakistani middle class could claim to be more prosperous than the same class across the border. India too suffered—and still does—from fractious politics and a society that is deeply divided by caste, class, region, and ethnicity. India too has harbored religious fanaticism and suffered from fits of extremism. Only twenty years ago some observers of Indian affairs thought that there might be no India in the twenty-first century. Yet India managed to turn the corner. Economic reform integrated India into the global economy, creating new business opportunities at home, and a booming middle class demanded more political and economic reforms.

Pakistan is still a poor country. Most of its people live in rural areas under the yoke of feudalism and rigid tribal structures, while the cities teem with poor slum dwellers. Only a fraction of the 175 million Pakistanis, perhaps no more than 10 to 15 percent or about 20 million people, have the financial means to fuel economic growth. But that slice of the population has been growing in size and purchasing power. This is both a promise and a peril. A widening chasm between the vast majority of the poor and the far smaller middle and upper classes could spell trouble. The middle must grow faster—and wealth must spread more quickly and widely—if Pakistan is to avoid continuing chaos.

The end of Musharraf's rule has brought anything but a straight path to economic growth and middle-class domination. Instead the country has been wracked by the effects of rising oil prices and increased political instability—manifested in political wrangling in the midst of as yet uncertain civilian rule, a slate of suicide bombings, and war to break extremist hold over territory in the country's northwest. Tourism, which earned the country $267 million in 2007, dwindled to virtually nothing in 2008, and foreign investment fell by 39 percent between 2007 and 2008.[25]

The economy has begun to unravel. Inflation surged from 8.8 percent to 24 percent between January and October 2008, pushing the rupee down by 23 percent. Energy shortages have been acute, and food prices have soared. The root causes of some of these problems were outside of Pakistan, in the global oil and food markets; and the global financial crisis has brought on a deep recession, with the GDP falling from between 7 and 8 percent in 2007 to 3 to 4 percent in 2008. Unemployment rose to around 40 percent in urban areas and 60 percent in rural areas.[26] By the fall of 2008 Pakistan faced default on its national debt, having drawn heavily on its reserves to keep the economy afloat. The country was facing bankruptcy, and was forced to go hat in hand to the IMF.

The international body was willing to help, but only if Pakistan agreed to reform its economy—raise taxes, cut spending, and encourage private-sector growth with an eye to export earnings—but also reduce its commitment to its military by shrinking the defense budget by 30 percent over ten years.[27] The IMF pill is difficult to swallow. The military will not take kindly to slashing its budget. But it is only by just this sort of radical shift in the direction of development driven governance that Pakistan can hope to turn the corner.

Where does Pakistan go from here? Its government is failing and the Taliban are knocking on the door. If the rot of extremism and political decay continues to corrode the state, Pakistan may eventually unravel. Things have been getting worse but they have not reached the tipping point. When that happens, events could take a dramatic turn for the worse, cracking the state and pulverizing society. That would be a catastrophe for everyone. One nightmare scenario that worries the world is that some or all of Pakistan's many nuclear weapons will fall into the wrong hands.

But it is also possible for Pakistan to find its way out of the woods to a better place where its state and society live not in the shadow of failure and collapse but look to the future with great expectations. The country has a new leadership both on the civilian and military sides. There is a chance, small as it may be, that they may find their way to stability. But if the country is to head toward stability and prosperity—if it is to stay whole and escape the scourge of a failed state—it will have to do so on the back of its pro-capitalism, pro-democracy forces. There is much Islam at the heart of Pakistani society, but that society is more interested in development and prosperity than jihad and foreign adventures, and when they get to choose governments at the polls Pakistanis tend to show more interest in bread and butter issues than foreign rivalry with India or expanding into Afghanistan. Muslim Pakistan can be engaged by secular liberal-democratic values, as the popularity of Chaudhry shows.

The West can work to help strengthen the vital center in Pakistan by focusing not just on its military and political elite, but on strengthening the middle class that is the true force for moderation and a pillar of democracy. That requires a stable and growing Pakistan economy, but more important is strengthening entrepreneurs and businessmen by providing them with financial support and the access to global markets that they desperately need. Pakistanis are capable of getting the job done. When outside their own country, in Dubai, London, or New York, they are every bit as competitive as Indian or Chinese businesspeople. It is back at home that constraints hobble them.

If the United States does not want to keep worrying about nightmare scenarios involving a nuclear-armed, jihadi-ridden Pakistan, then it must work to assist the forces of the center in the country to get on this course. To determine the best methods for doing so, the West should look to the lessons of Turkey—not as that country was in the 1930s or 1950s, but as it is today. Turkey is the exemplary case of capitalist and democratic development in the region, and it got to where it is today largely with the European Union's help. The EU took the long view and in building ties with Ankara required measures to be taken by the Turkish government that have stimulated development. This is the constructive role that the United States must emulate not only in aiding Pakistan, but all around the troubled region.

CHAPTER 9

THE TURKISH MODEL

A discussion I had over dinner in Ankara in March 2004 with a Turkish colonel close to the top brass speaks to the irony of events in recent years in Turkey, as the Islamically oriented AKP party has taken charge of the government and gained widespread popularity for its success in managing the economy. I was in Turkey on a research trip, talking with politicians, intellectuals, and academics about how the country was faring under the leadership of the AKP since a watershed parliamentary election swept the party into power in late 2002. What did he think of the AKP? I asked the colonel, and where did the military see Turkey going? What was the mood among his superiors? He kept his cool, but it was obvious that he thought little of the AKP and its leaders. To him they were nothing more than a better-packaged version of the Egyptian Muslim Brotherhood, poised to shatter the achievements of Turkish secularism and turn the country into an Islamic republic.

I then asked him how he would explain the AKP's business-friendly image in the West, its push for Turkey to become a full-fledged member of the European Union, and the facility with which so many of its members spoke the language of economic globalization. This question struck a nerve. "Business!" he exclaimed. "What is this 'business'? Everybody has become an expert on business. What about nationalism, security, and secularism?"

The mere suggestion that the AKP was on the cutting edge of producing economic prosperity was an affront. The colonel knew that Kemalism's top-down version of development, which went hand in hand with the tight grip of the military over the political system for so many years, was hopelessly outdated. That model was an ossified relic reflecting that state of European rationalism circa 1900. But accepting that the AKP was doing a better job of development was too much for him. In Turkey today, an intense struggle is playing out between those who still support the secularism of Kemalism and those who have thrown their votes behind the AKP.

Kemalism's guardians, who include not only military officers but also the bureaucrats of what Turks call "the deep state"—a shady group of antidemocratic high officials, judges, journalists, intellectuals, and military men that Turks believe will stop at nothing to protect Kemalism—see the struggle as a culture war, a vital battle against the encroachment of Islamic fundamentalism. The AKP and its followers, however, see matters quite differently. They assert that they have abandoned any designs on transforming Turkey into a fundamentalist state, and are instead the shepherds of building an ever more open society based on liberal democracy, and economic development based on entrepreneurial capitalism and globalization.

Turkey's secularists feel cornered, seeing an Islamic wave sweeping over their country. Islamic observance has gone up, with more Turks taking breaks from work at midday to perform the ritual prayers, and more as well going on hajj to Mecca. Headscarves are more visible not just in poor neighborhoods and small towns but also in trendy sections of Istanbul. In the secularists' nightmares, Turkey will become another Iran. But the true course on which the AKP leadership has set the country could not be more different from that of the leadership in Tehran. Indeed, the path they have championed is the most hopeful model in the region for both economic development and the liberalization of politics.

The story of Turkey's progress over the past decade should serve as the model for the ways in which the United States and Western powers can most effectively encourage positive change. Turkey's great progress in the last decade toward capitalist growth and increasing political pluralism has not been contingent on the benevolence of authoritarian leadership or on wads of oil money. Turkey's success has followed from liberalizing, free-market reforms that have unleashed the entrepreneurial energies of the same provincial, religiously conservative rising middle class that is gaining ground all around the region. Also vitally important have been constitutional requirements set by the European Union— including regular elections, civilian government, smaller military with no involvement in politics, and a better human rights record—as conditions of Turkey's hoped-for entry into the EU.

The Kemalist establishment kept a tight grip on the reins of power for decades after Ataturk's death in 1938, with the military serving as the arbiter of who would be the stewards of Kemalism and strictly enforcing Ataturk's top-down secularism in state and society. Under Ataturk's leadership, Turkey was established as a republic, with a president and parliament, and the ruling party in parliament determining by vote who would be the prime minister, usually the head of the party. But while Ataturk was president, he ruled as an autocrat, and his Republican People's Party was for long the only party established. Ataturk envisioned the evolution of a true parliamentarian democracy, however, and even spearheaded the formation of opposition parties during his tenure, though these parties never gained enough momentum to take power. It wasn't until 1950 that an opposition party with sustainable power, the Democratic Party, won control of parliament, on a platform of tempering Kemalism's militant secularism and reducing the state's footprint in the economy. But the evolution of Turkish democracy was fraught with tension. The Democratic Party won two more elections, in 1954 and 1957, but was eventually banned in 1960 for talking too much about Islam; and its leader, Prime Minister Adnan Menderes, was tried and executed for treason the next year. The Kemalist establishment jealously guarded the state's secularist ideology and was quick to shut down any meaningful deviation from the official orthodoxy. As in Pakistan, the military stepped in several times to take power, staging coups in 1960, 1971, and 1980—and since the 1990s, the generals have acted surreptitiously, using the office of the president or the Constitutional Court to dismiss governments they do not like. In the most recent instance of the military's muscle-flexing, in April 2007, threat of a coup came in the form of a message on the website of the Turkish general staff.

Ironically, the resurgence of Islam in the country's public life was due in large part to the military. During the 1980s, the military eased up on its suppression of Islam. As in so many other Middle Eastern countries, in the 1970s radical leftism had gained a strong following in Turkey—provoking a backlash on the right—and the decade was one of severe tumult. Secular ideologies of the right (fascist-like nationalism) and especially the left (a mixed brew of Marxism-Leninism) were feeding off of growing social unrest and clamoring for revolution and radical social change. Students and workers led marches and called strikes, waging large-scale street protests. The opposing factions on the left and right engaged in increasingly violent clashes on campuses and in city streets, and bloody confrontations and assassinations claimed scores of lives. This is when the military staged its third coup, in 1980, jailing thousands of militants and restoring a degree of calm.

As a strategic calculation, the military leadership turned to Islam, viewing it as a bulwark against the radicals. By condoning the reentry of a modicum of religious conservatism into the public sphere, the generals hoped to divert youthful energies away from sedition and revolution. The ban on Islamic education was lifted, in the hope that piety in the classroom would make students less susceptible to recruitment by secular extremists. Once banished to the margins of society, Islamic groups associated with the Nurcu movement and Sufi orders came out of the closet. It was at this time that Fethullah Gulen gained so much popularity with his message. New political parties were formed to take advantage of the Islamic revival and channel its social influence into politics. The generals may have thought that they could make good use of Islam for a while and then reverse course, but the genie would not go back into the bottle.

What the generals failed to realize was the extent to which Islam had remained a vital force below the secular surface of Turkish life— a force that, once released, would swiftly become formidable. In the words of one leading Islamic opposition leader, "secular Kemalism . . .

is an aberration, not the norm. . . . Kemalism never took root beyond the thin sliver of university-educated elites in urban centers of Ankara and Istanbul . . . Turkey has always been an Ottoman Muslim state."[1]

The great irony of Turkey's push in the years since for economic development and entry into the European Union is that the conservative "provincials" who so strongly supported the Islamic resurgence and began voting in droves for Islamic parties have been the strongest supporters of this liberalization.[2] They have not demanded the imposition of a fundamentalist Islamic state—far from it. They have been leading the charge for political pluralism and economic globalization.

———

Throughout the long, tumultuous post-Ataturk period, the predominant approach to management of the economy was one of the state doing all the planning, and managing trade and investment to decide who would produce what—favoring large industry at the cost of limiting private-sector growth. This degree of state control was expected of Kemalism, but Ataturk himself had recognized the need for a degree of liberalization of state control over business, and had allowed for the creation of the Liberal Republican Party in 1930 to push for that. But such nods to liberalism had done little to reduce the state's strict control of the economy. Over time the Turkish economy came to look like an unhappy blend of capitalism and socialism.

In the 1980s, once the Kemalist generals had crushed the radical agitators of the left and the right, they turned their attention to reforming the economy. Growth had been anemic for too long, and the country had fallen on hard economic times, staggering under the weight of masses of foreign debt and the insidious rampages of hyperinflation. The bloated public sector was at a loss to generate growth and to create jobs, an especially vexing issue in light of the tide of jobless migrants that had begun pouring into the country's already teeming cities.

The military leadership conceded that the loosening of state control and creation of more robust capitalism was needed, and the task of freeing up the economy fell to Turgut Ozal, an able, affable technocrat voted in as prime minister with the backing of the generals. An electrical engineer by training, he had worked as a bureaucrat for many years before becoming a manager at the World Bank and chairman of a number of private-sector companies in Turkey, and he had a firm grasp of business and economic policy. He was right-of-center politically and he had ties to Islamic groups, but he was secular enough to suit the military's taste. He ushered in a distinctive new blending of Muslim piety and business-friendly policy. While he legalized Islamic banking and was the first serving prime minister to go on hajj, it was also he who submitted Turkey's application to join the European Union in 1987. He defined a new and also more viable center in Turkish politics: economically liberal, right-of-center, and mildly Islamic, all caged under Kemalism. Many Turks see him as the most significant figure in Turkish history since Ataturk.

When Ozal took charge in 1983, the economy was still plagued by the legacy of Kemalism.[3] Massive red-ink-generating industrialization efforts had benefited the Istanbul business elite but provided few opportunities for small businesses, not to mention jobs for the growing lower- and middle-class workforce. Industries relied on imports and assembly-line manufacturing, with little attempt to produce finished goods suitable for export. The state protected favored industries with high tariffs and favorable exchange rates, as well as subsidies.[4] Ozal secured loans from the World Bank and the IMF, with whom he worked to craft a restructuring plan that hinged on a "neoliberal" shift to decentralization, privatization, a focus on export-led growth, and a redistribution of power away from the state and toward the market.[5] There would be a new emphasis as well on social openness and citizen participation. Many industries were privatized and others that could not be made profitable were closed down. Ozal resolutely redirected government support to those who could export and generate badly needed foreign-exchange revenue. Tariff rules, exchange rates, and subsidies were all changed to promote exports. Among those who thrived especially well were makers of textiles and furniture, clustered mostly in industrial zones in the Anatolian heartland far from Istanbul.[6]

The Ankara-to-Istanbul axis of high-level bureaucrats and top busi-. nessmen began losing ground in control of the economy to a new breed of entrepreneurs working out of smaller cities and towns in Anatolia, which is roughly the Turkish equivalent of the American Midwest, with Istanbul cognate to New York City. These newly successful entrepreneurs were conservative and pious, but they were also well aware that the growth of their businesses depended on joining the global economy through increasing trade. The old economic regime had never supported them, so they had little interest in its state-led model. By contrast, they tended to favor diluting state control through building up true democracy and establishing a truly free-market economy. Somewhat akin to a breed of Republicans in the United States, these "Anatolian tigers" hewed to conservative and religious social values but favored open competition in politics and the economy.

Ozal's reforms led the way to booming export-led growth. The economic transformation ran wide and deep as globalization transformed Turkish economic and social life.[7] Economic power shifted to small and medium-sized businesses and the Anatolian heartland overshadowed Istanbul as engine of growth. By 2004, smaller and midsized enterprises accounted for a quarter of all Turkish exports. Fully 80 percent of such firms had not even existed at the time Ozal became prime minister.[8] These changes over time produced both a new business elite and a new middle class, of the same basic persuasion as that of the rising middle class all over the region.[9] The AKP is the political choice of this emergent class, not only because they like the party's Islamic values, but above all, because they believe the AKP's policies serve their business interests.

That has certainly been true. In 2001, the year that the AKP was formed and one year before it became the governing party, Turkey's economy was in free fall under a coalition government headed by elderly Prime Minister Bulent Eçevit. The Turkish lira had collapsed, losing 54 percent of its value. Eçevit's government had jacked up interest rates in response—in effect, raising the price of money in order to make it more scarce and thereby tame inflation—but this intended cure had caused a sharp economic contraction. The GDP shrank by 10 percent, rendering three million Turks jobless. Many Turks blamed not only government mismanagement but corruption for the crisis. The AKP (whose shortened name in Turkish, "Ak Partisi," means "clean party"), was well positioned to take advantage of the sour mood. The party promised good and clean government and a fresh start.

Once in office, however, the AKP faced an uphill battle. Its first order of business was to impose a tough belt-tightening package demanded by the International Monetary Fund as the price of restructuring Turkey's massive foreign debts. Many expected the party to fail, but they would be disappointed. The AKP wisely privatized many industries, promoted globalization, and particularly deepened Turkey's economic and political ties to Europe. Between 2002 and 2007, thanks to fiscal discipline and wise macroeconomic management, GDP nearly tripled, going from $230 billion to $660 billion and raising Turkey to number seven in the size rankings of European economies and number sixteen in the world. Over the same period, exports went from $30 billion to $125 billion, while Foreign Direct Investment grew at a mind-boggling rate, skyrocketing from just $1 billion to $42 billion by the end of 2007.[10]

The road to the AKP's ascendance, and to the powerful economic growth of the last seven years under its leadership, has surely been rocky. The resurgence of Islam and its infusion into Turkish politics has been highly controversial and has provoked howls of protest, and military crackdowns, all along the way. The fear has been of a fundamentalist takeover, though from the start, the leaders of Turkey's Islamic political revival have been a very different breed from the fundamentalists who have wreaked so much havoc around the region.

The rise of Islamic parties was led by Neçmettin Erbakan, who started the Milli Goruş—National Outlook—movement. A wily old politician, Erbakan was no Sayyid Qutb but he was clearly influenced by fundamentalism. In 1983 he founded the Welfare Party, the ideology of which mixed economic populism with anchoring government in Islamic values and principles. As vague and harmless as this may sound it was revolutionary for the ardently secular Turkey. The party took time to gain ground, but Erbakan would lead the party into a major electoral victory in municipal elections around the country in 1994. When the party took majority seats in parliament two years later, he became prime minister. But Erbakan soon made fatal missteps. His emphasis on Islamic themes, including a promise to roll back Kemalism and enshrine Islam in Turkish society and politics, alarmed not just the Kemalist establishment but also many in the middle class as well. He also did himself serious damage by traveling to Libya in 1996 and meeting with Muammar Qadaffi—who assailed him on Turkey's ties with United States and Israel and membership in NATO and urged dismembering Turkey to create an independent Kurdish state. Many Turks were offended. They scoffed at Qadaffi as a "barefoot Bedouin" who enjoyed sleeping in a tent; but few were charitable to Erbakan for naively walking into Qadaffi's trap.

In 1997, after the military successfully maneuvered to ban the Welfare Party and sent Erbakan's government packing,[11] his followers formed the Islamic Fezilat (Virtue) Party. The Supreme Court thought that too was too Islamic and relying on constitutional ban on religious parties dismantled it. But Islamic activists defied the court sanctions by forming another Islamic party, the Selamat (Felicity) Party, to contest in the new rounds of elections.[12] In the face of this staunch resistance, some among Erbakan's troops softened their Islamic message, and in 2001 a group of younger figures led by Abdullah Gul (now Turkey's president) and Reçep Tayyip Erdogan formed the AKP, whose name in Turkish—Adalet ve Kalkinma Partisi—means Justice and Development Party.

Gone was the combative rhetoric and the demand for shariah government. In their place, the AKP touted a pro-Western outlook, conservative but also favorable to democracy and markets.[13] Though the party would be led by devout Muslims, they accepted secularism and vowed a firm commitment to Ataturk's legacy of modernization. The AKP also claimed as its own the goal of joining the EU.

The Kemalist establishment was unimpressed, and the AKP was no more popular with fundamentalists than it was with secularists. Fundamentalists disapproved of giving up the goal of creating an Islamic

Turkish state based on the shariah. By backing away from the Islamic state, the AKP had placed itself outside fundamentalism's circle of trust, looking for support rather by harking to the nostalgic appeal of Ottoman notions of Muslim society—which celebrated cultural diversity and religious freedom.

The AKP's leaders do not sport long beards, favoring instead either a clean-shaven look or neatly trimmed moustaches of the sort that many Turkish men wear. They wear suits and ties, and they tout the benefits of joining Europe. They have also allied themselves with the United States, and they have been willing to work with Israel. The AKP has expanded Turkey's defense pact with Israel, increased the volume of trade between the two countries, party leaders have visited Israel, and Erdogan has led mediation efforts between Israel and Syria.

Fundamentalists do not seem to doubt the distance between them and the AKP. When I asked the Jamaat-e Islami's leader in Pakistan in 2002 what he thought of the AKP, he first said that he disagreed with the compromises that the party had made, and then added with more scorn that perhaps the AKP's errors stemmed from the Turks' late (eleventh-century) adoption of Islam and consequent difficulty in understanding the faith (a clear put-down). He ended by asserting emphatically that the AKP was not a true Islamic party. The Muslim Brotherhood has similarly rejected the AKP model, arguing that it will chart its own path to Islamic democracy.

The AKP has built its power base not among fundamentalists, but in the Anatolian heartland through the kind of conservative family values rhetoric that has been so popular with more conservative Republican voters in the United States. Party leaders prefer to be called "conservative" rather than "Muslim" or "Islamic" democrats.[14] To them, the term "conservative" evokes in equal measure national-patriotic values, a high regard for the family, religious piety, and a respect for Ottoman as well as local traditions. The AKP's secularist detractors dismiss all this talk as a smokescreen for fundamentalism, but the distinction between "conservative" and "Islamic" that the AKP makes is real. The AKP's notion of "conservative democracy" has stood it in good stead in Europe as well, where it is perceived as akin to the conservative Christian Democratic parties.[15]

The AKP has also been a strong advocate of pluralism. Ataturk's party's mantra in the 1920s was "For the people, despite the people," and he used the state to define social values. The AKP wants to deny the state that monopoly, allowing society to open up to a range of values other than those of Kemalism—including more cultural rights for the country's Kurdish minority. The dispute between the AKP and the Kemalist establishment should be seen as a quarrel over society's demands for openness and pluralism as much as a debate over religious rights.

Islamic activism in Turkey has never been as hard-nosed as Arab or Pakistani fundamentalism. The popular Nurcu movement imbibed Kemalism's love of science, and Fethullah Gulen has harkened back more to Ottoman history than to fundamentalist writings in his preaching. This is probably at least in part due to the doggedness with which the Kemalist state hounded fundamentalists. Some observers argue that the AKP's moderation is the product of the systematic pressure the military put on the Welfare Party and its offshoots. Dismissed from power and banned time and again, those Islamic activists who formed the AKP concluded that Islamic parties' path to power would be permanently blocked by the Kemalist establishment. The only way to get around this problem was to agree to fundamental compromises, to become "Muslim Kemalists," and to push for change from within the system.

Whatever the truth of its motivations, the AKP has been shrewd in its emphasis on economic development, and particularly on its push for membership in the EU. This has surely been a factor mitigating the military's willingness to clamp down on the AKP. Turkey's 1993 agreement with the EU to conditions set for full Turkish membership in that body was a national triumph, strongly supported by the vast majority of Turks. Those conditions include the demand that Turkey remain a democracy, with open politics and civilian supremacy over the military. The soldiers can fume over their shish kebab about the party, as my colonel friend did that evening in Istanbul, but they know that the days of rolling tanks into the streets and arresting elected officials are over.

The EU agreement has also been a mitigating force against Islamification, however, as the EU will not put up with a theocracy either. But the AKP's stance in favor of pluralist democracy does not in itself explain the party's great success. Since its formation in 2001, the party has gone from strength to strength, winning decisive parliamentary victories in 2002 and 2007 and putting an end to what once seemed the permanent Turkish condition of divided, unstable coalition governments. No party in recent memory has found so much favor in every corner of Turkey, from cosmopolitan Istanbul to the Kurdish-dominated, economically depressed southeast, and it has done so because of its success in managing the government and shepherding the economy.[16]

Much of the credit goes to the party's leader, Reçep Tayyip Erdogan, who has made effectiveness the party's mantra and set the pace for achieving it. The tall, charismatic mayor of Istanbul from 1994 to 1998 was wildly popular for his management skills and the fact that during his tenure he solved many of the city nagging infrastructure problems. Erdogan was a fervent Islamic activist when he first became mayor in 1994, but despite much talk on his part about mosque building and Islamic observance, he made no moves to turn Turkey's cosmopolitan business hub into an Islamic emirate. On the contrary, Istanbul prospered during his time in office, drawing increasing tourism and business investment. If he could do for Turkey what he had done for Istanbul, then many Turks were all for AKP.

Indeed, it was abject government failure that pushed the AKP over the top in the elections of 2002. When a massive earthquake laid waste to a heavily populated region of the country about an hour east of Istanbul in August 1999, killing as many as 25,000 people, the government's response was slow. In inquiries into the failures later, it became evident that corruption had facilitated shoddy construction methods that had made the devastation far more extensive and deadly than it should have been. Islamic groups on the other hand, reacted quickly and made a major contribution to the relief effort. The public's anger at secular politicians and the good impression made by self-described Muslim organizations translated into AKP votes in 2002.[17]

The irony of the disdain expressed by Istanbul's debonair secularists toward the small-town, "yokel" businessmen who so strongly support the AKP is that those small-towners are far more at home with globalization than the cosseted government-supported business elite of old ever was or could be. Today's Turkish entrepreneurs do business directly with European and American companies and are sensitive to global economic trends. Their interests are tied to the health of Western markets and financial institutions. This means in addition that they are sensitive to Western concerns about Turkey's image and understand Western sensitivities when it comes to things Islamic. The AKP's soft Islam is not only handy for backing off Kemalist stifling of the economy at home, but is good for business abroad too.

Perhaps nowhere in Turkey is the attitude of this new business class more clearly on display than in the Anatolian city of Kayseri. About 550 miles east of Istanbul, spread out on a volcanic plateau and surrounded by rich agricultural plains that stretch for hundreds of miles in all directions, Kayseri came late to industrialization. The town was awarded an aircraft factory in 1926, shortly after the birth of modern Turkey, and over the years other factories came to Kayseri, but the city remained something of a backwater, displaying none of Istanbul and western Turkey's sophistication or business vitality. Kayseri was a place for small-scale manufacturing that drew little attention or support from the big-city bureaucrats who ran the economy and favored large enterprises.

All that began to change in the 1980s, when Ozal's economic restructuring tilted the balance in favor of Kayseri's small businesses. Money flowed into the town's industrial zone, credit became far easier to obtain, and trade policy as well as exchange rates favored exports. Small Anatolian manufacturers began taking orders from Europe and America and quickly became part of globalization's supply chain. Furniture making and textiles did particularly well. Kayseri began booming and grew rapidly into one of the largest Turkish industrial zones. The pace of growth was so fast that in 2004 the city applied to the *Guinness Book of World Records* for the most new businesses started in a single day: 139.[18]

Kayseri had no obvious comparative advantage in the manufacture of furniture. The landlocked town was not close to the forests of the Black Sea nor to rivers, canals, or highway arteries that would cheaply bring wood to its factories. Nevertheless the city has emerged as the most successful furniture-making hub in Turkey, where some 3,500 companies make an average of 20,000 sofas and 8,000 armchairs a day, employing some 40,000 people.[19] (From those numbers alone you can tell that the average firm size is quite small.) Firms such as Boydak, which was an early mover and is now an industry heavyweight, have grown into global producers, doing for Kayseri and Turkey what IT did for Bangalore and India. The Kayseri furniture-making industry earned more than a billion dollars in export revenues in 2007.[20]

Americans would more readily recognize the other major Kayseri export, Levi Strauss blue jeans. Orta Anadolu (the name means "Mid-Anatolia") is today Kayseri's number one exporter and one of Turkey's most profitable companies. It is a giant in the denim business, supplying Levi's European operations. Orta was established in 1953 by thirteen Kayseri traders. They imported weaving machines from East Germany to supply textiles to the home market. Protected by high tariffs and with easy access to Turkey's ample cotton crops, the company had little competition and almost no need to be efficient. Then in the 1980s Ozal ended its government protection. Inefficient and exposed to competition, Orta fell on hard times and was almost bankrupt when two wealthy, thirtysomething Kayseri businessmen bought the company.

The new management revamped operations, trimming costs and cutting fat. Production shifted to exports and the company worked its way back into the black. By the mid-1980s, Orta was producing denim for the export market. Levi Strauss took note, came to Kayseri to take a closer look and liked what it saw. The American company sent engineers to teach Orta the tricks of the trade and help it retool its plants taking advantage of cheap government credit set aside for exporters. By 1990, the Turkish company was producing world-class denim in quantities large enough to make it one of Levi's three European suppliers.[21] Levi's then helped Orta with design and marketing, and more generally turning Orta into a global player. The company now supplies several other global brands, including Wrangler, Rifle, and Diesel.

Orta is not alone in making a killing in denim in Kayseri: Five of the city's top twenty exporters are textile manufacturers and produce world-quality denim. The $2 billion Turkish denim industry accounts for 6.5 percent of the world's production and clothes some 200 million people.[22] Orta alone makes 1 percent of the world's denim.[23] Virtually every major brand of jeans on earth today uses Turkish denim. What's more, the lessons the industry has learned about doing business in the global market are benefiting other areas of textile manufacturing as well. The business acumen developed in Kayseri is also leading the way in construction, services, transport, and tourism. Textiles and furniture have led the way to a much broader industrial revolution.

The up-and-coming business elite of Kayseri are conservative but fiercely pro-market and firmly committed to globalization. They rely on foreign investment and produce for Western markets but are also expanding their businesses into the Middle East, the Balkans, Caucasus, and Central Asia. The Kayseri-based food products manufacturing giant, Ulker—the owner of Godiva Chocolatier—now has a vast business empire stretching from Europe into Central Asia in everything from construction to food products and media outlets. These business leaders believe in entrepreneurship and hard work rather than government patronage, and even the city's only non-AKP member of parliament said of his country in 2005, "Today Turkey is governed in the way in which Kayseri was governed for the past fifteen years."[24] No wonder, then, that the AKP sweeps elections in Kayseri. For these businessmen, Islam is simply a way of life, not a matter of political mission. They grew up in praying and mosque-going households, and many got to know one another, and still network, in Nurcu circles. In fact, Islamic gatherings in Anatolia's small towns and cities act pretty much as do the Lions or Rotary clubs in countless American counties and cities. The Islamic institutions in Turkey function well as places where businessmen can mingle, network, and make deals. Secular businessmen, meanwhile, find it difficult to succeed in Kayseri because they are not in the right networks.

There is a grand new mosque in the heart of Kayseri's business district, a testament to the city's wealth along with its piety. But the Islam on display in Kayseri and towns and cities like it across Anatolia is not hard-edged fundamentalism and even less so an echo of extremism that inspires radicalism in Pakistan and the Arab world. Islam here is conservative but pro-Europe, pro-democracy, and above all pro-capitalism. Anatolian businessmen combine religion, hard work, and economic innovation in much the same way as did Calvinist Burghers of Northern Europe in the sixteenth century when capitalism was just starting out. What is at play is an Islamic version of that, an "Islamic Calvinism" as some have come to call it: an ethic of hard work and savings, investment, and economic growth, combining strict piety with raging entrepreneurship.[25] The description sits well with many in Kayseri, who readily identify with how Calvinists worked hard, prayed hard, saved money, and then invested it in their businesses, and were comfortable being both rich and pious.[26] It is a common refrain in Turkey that work is a form of worship, and as Pope Benedict learned at the Blue Mosque, God loves businessmen. The political scientist Hakan Yavuz calls the ascent of these provincial businessmen the triumph of the "Anatolian-based Islamic bourgeoisie."[27]

The old business establishment has not ceded ground without resistance. There is a national clash ongoing between this new business class and the old business elite, which is best captured by the competition between Turkey's two largest business associations: The Turkish Industrialist and Businessmen's Association (TUSIAD), which represents the large industrialists once nurtured by the state, and the Association of Independent Industrialists and Businessmen (MUSIAD) which was formed to help the many small businesses that emerged in the 1980s following Ozal's reforms, and nowadays looks after the interests of the new breed of small and medium-sized businesses.[28] TUSIAD is partial to Kemalism and MUSIAD to the market-friendly AKP. It is not the prayer break in MUSIAD meetings that distinguishes it from the secular TUSIAD, but their respective relations with government and outlooks on the economy—big government versus markets, state control versus democracy. TUSIAD is tied to official chambers of commerce, whereas MUSIAD works through voluntary associations. Their differences have come out in the open since the AKP became the governing party, giving more power to small and medium-sized businesses mostly located well east of Istanbul in the Anatolian heartland.[29] The competition between TUSIAD and MUSIAD is now also a tug-of-war between the Istanbul region and Anatolian industrial centers like Kayseri, and is every bit as important as the more visible political fight between the Kemalist establishment and the AKP.

Turkey today hosts little in the form of class warfare, poor versus the rich; all that has been replaced by the clash of two middle classes, their tastes and habits, political preferences, and their contending visions of society and the economy.

The success of the AKP's leadership has not quelled all discontent with the party by any means. Military officers, the keepers *par excellence* of the Kemalist flame, have tried in vain to torpedo the AKP, and continuing suspicions that the party has a hidden fundamentalist agenda fueled an effort to unseat the party in 2007. When that spring the AKP put forward the fifty-seven-year-old Abdullah Gul, party leader and foreign minister at the time, for the presidency of Turkey, the Kemalist establishment reacted viscerally.

First, tens of thousands of Turks took to the streets to object. On April 27, a statement appeared on the website of the military's general staff attacking "the fundamentalist thinking, which is anti-republic and harbors no aim other than eroding the basic characteristics of the state." The statement made clear that "the armed forces will act in a clear and unambiguous manner if necessary."[30] The "e-coup," as the statement was quickly dubbed, was followed by a Constitutional Court ruling that parliament, missing its boycotting secular members, did not have the necessary quorum to elect a president.

To this, the AKP cried foul. Prime Minister Erdogan complained that the court had in effect "fired a shot at democracy" and argued that "it is murder to suggest that there are two Turkeys, one religious and one secular. . . . We are all a part of the same glorious nation."[31] There was only one way for AKP to prove that: Go to the polls to test the AKP's mandate and let the voters settle the dispute. Throughout the 2007 campaign, members of the AKP camp spoke of how well their party had managed the economy. Voters, they suggested, should focus on prosperity and sound governance rather than on worries about Islam and secularism. The voters overwhelmingly agreed. Turks handed the AKP a decisive victory.

Gul, a practicing Muslim with a fundamentalist past whose wife wears a headscarf, thus became president, and to smooth anxieties he has promised to abide by Turkey's constitution and to protect its secularism, proclaiming that he wants to be the president of all Turks. He will focus, he has said, on getting Turkey into the EU, a goal embraced in nearly every quarter of Turkish public life. But many secularists remain skeptical, worried that with the presidential home—known as Çankaya—under the AKP's control, the party will now feel free to aggressively pursue a fundamentalist agenda. Gul's presidency is especially stinging to some because Çankaya was Ataturk's house, where he lived while he was launching his campaign to build modern Turkey. It was there that he charted Turkey's course to the future, where secularism was born and became triumphant. And now its occupant is a devout Muslim.[32]

Secularists' worst fears about AKP rule seemed to be coming true in January 2008, when it became known that the party's draft of a new Turkish constitution—which had long been in the works as part of Turkey's efforts to bring its laws into alignment with the EUs demands—would omit the ban—dating to Ataturk—on the wearing of headscarves in universities. Once again this long-standing hot-button issue flared up. Secularists see the ban as a litmus test of loyalty to Kemalism, while the religiously minded see nullifying the ban as a matter of religious freedom, pointing out that nearly two-thirds of Turkish women wear a headscarf daily, while 70 percent of Turks think that college women who want to wear the scarf on campus and in class should be allowed to do so.[33] Unimpressed by those appeals, the Kemalist establishment decided to dig in for a fight, and in March, the chief prosecutor of Turkey's Court of Appeals, citing the AKP as "the focal point of anti-secular activities," asked the country's Supreme Court to ban the party and banish seventy-one of its top figures, Gul and Erdogan included, from politics.[34]

The court agreed to hear the case, and for a time it looked like that might be the end for the AKP. But under pressure from the United States and the EU, and in the face of fears of an economic backlash and political crisis, the court backed down, merely issuing a censure.

The fate of the AKP is anything but secure, and yet the truth is also undeniable that Kemalist ideology has decisively lost its grip on the Turkish public because the economic coalition that stood behind it has come undone. Small-town values have combined with raw capitalism to become a powerful force in the culture; commerce has both shackled state power and softened Islam's hard edges. The secularists fearing the AKP should take note that commerce has also tied the hands of the AKP. There are many more businessmen in AKP's ranks these days, and it is rapidly becoming a party of tycoons.

Many challenges lie ahead for Turkey. Global recession will slow economic growth, and that may destabilize the political system, challenging the AKP's primacy. The EU may also close its doors to full Turkish membership. Kurdish nationalism may flare up, causing a crisis. The Turkish experiment is also threatened by the rise of a new brand of virulent nationalism that has been gaining ground over the past decade in reaction to Kurdish nationalism and separatism. The rising nationalism is intolerant and xenophobic. If it grows unchecked it will threaten state and society, democracy and capitalism.[35]

But with all that said, Turkey has shown a promising way forward for the wider region. If Turkey stays on its current course, it will become a Muslim capitalist democracy, and the face of Turkish modernity today will become the face of the wider Muslim world tomorrow if the rising business leadership and its attendant new middle class get their way. The United States and its allies should do all that we can to help bring this outcome to pass.

CHAPTER 10

WINNING THE FUTURE

In April 2006, I traveled to Istanbul to attend the biennial meeting of the World Movement for Democracy, a gathering of democratic activists, scholars, and public figures from around the world sponsored by the U.S. National Endowment for Democracy. There were participants from every corner of the globe comparing notes and exploring ways to help build new democracies. As the meeting was being held in a Muslim-majority country, there were plenty of lectures and workshops on Islam and democracy. Fundamentalists and secularists from Morocco to Malaysia had many chances to debate how to balance faith and freedom or to ask whether that was even possible. I sat through many of those sessions listening to fundamentalists—mostly from the Arab world—wax poetic about the democracy of the Islamic state while their incredulous detractors insisted that a shariah state must inevitably be an antidemocratic theocracy. The debate had a familiar quality; the dispute stood pretty much where Mawdudi and his critics had left it decades before.

All this was somewhat amusing to our Turkish hosts. Murat Merçan, a senior Turkish parliamentarian and one of the founders of Turkey's AKP, sat stoically through a particularly heated session in which the discussion never moved past dueling Koran quotes and clashing historical anecdotes from seventh-century Arabia. When it was Merçan's turn to talk, he slowly leaned forward and, with a smirk and a touch of patronizing indulgence in his voice, said "Here in Turkey, we are fortunate that we don't have debates like this. We are past all this talk of what to with the shariah and the Islamic state. We have a democracy and we are in the government, and our voters judge us by our economic achievements."

Merçan was overstating the case; Turks do still passionately debate Islam's role in their society and politics. But his call to focus not on conjectured contradictions between Islam and democracy, but rather on the practical, daily issues of providing economic opportunity was dead-on. The reconciliation of Islam and capitalism that the "critical middle" is voting decisively for is the only way forward toward a wider reconciliation of Islam and democracy. But the evolution of full democracy in the Middle East will take time.

The irony is that the idea of democracy is not alien to the Middle East; it is just that the practice has never taken root. Iranians were among the first non-Western people to fight for democracy, winning for their country a fairly liberal constitution in 1906 that provided for free elections, a parliament, the rule of law, and many political freedoms. But that document failed to truly shape the state and society in Iran. Other than brief periods of democracy in the 1910s and the late 1940s and early 1950s, Iran has been ruled by authoritarianism of one kind or another. It has been the same story in Pakistan and the Arab world—short-lived experiments with elections, parliaments, and democracy have been followed by long stretches of dictatorship—longer and more brutal in the Arab world's case. Only Turkey seems to have escaped this vicious cycle. The country had its last coup in 1980 and since then, despite the military's menacing posture, democracy has gained strength. But then Turkey is different from Iran, Pakistan, and the Arab world in that there, democracy is built on the solid foundation of a real economic revolution.

The West has recently placed a high premium on instilling democracy in the Middle East, after long years of first imposing colonial rule and then supporting autocratic rulers in the region. But as the wrenching exercise of "nation building" in Iraq and disappointments with elections in the Palestinian Territories have exposed, in the course of pushing for Middle Eastern democracy, vital lessons about the steps in the evolution of democracy in the West have been overlooked. The prevailing narrative in the West tends to emphasize that the rights that we hold so dear—the right to vote, freedom of speech, freedom of worship, freedom of association, and the rule of law—were established by the institution of democracy. Less attention is paid to the prerequisites of democracy, and the West has become too enamored of the notion that democracy will flower spontaneously once there are free and fair elections. This discounts the vital importance of fundamental changes in society, law, and the relations between states and their citizens that are necessary for democracy to succeed.[1]

Western history clearly shows that those fundamental changes follow on the evolution of commerce. In Europe it was the mandates of commerce that called into being the bourgeoisie and its insistence on setting limits on the power of kings and the influence of clergy. It was that critical business-minded class that transformed how Europe thought and lived, softening the extremism of puritanical religious reformers and their Catholic adversaries following the horrific violence of the Reformation. Far from a call to liberalism, the Reformation itself was a brutal reign of terror, a century and a half of all-out religious warfare. It was not the Reformation that transformed Scotland, once arguably the most backward part of Europe, into the "inventor of modernity."[2] Only when commerce—and hand in hand with it widening trade—took hold in the country did Scotland became home to the early Industrial Revolution, spawning a new intellectual class of the likes of Adam Smith and David Hume, who gave voice to the aspirations of the rising commercial classes. Commerce and the social changes it requires and stimulates changed mind-sets, not the other way around.

The recent sweep of democracy over Asia, Eastern Europe, and Latin America also came on the back of rising commercial classes. Their business activities now account for most of the real economic growth in those regions.[3] Ambitious and resourceful, they fill the ranks of the professionals, the entrepreneurs, the businessmen, and the traders, and it is they who have established for the next generation a new economic model.

Tony Blair, the former British prime minister, tells audiences that the problems we face today—prominent among them terrorism coming from the Muslim world—require global alliances, and those alliances have to be built on the basis of shared global values, by which he means peace, security, democracy, freedom and human rights, moderation, and religious tolerance. When Muslims too embrace these values and rely on them to reject the culture of violence, he argues, then extremism will stand defeated. His point is well taken, but its corollary must be that values are not embraced in a vacuum; they do not become ubiquitous because one side wins a debating contest.

Values gain currency when they serve the economic and social interests of people, and they shape the governance of nations when those who hold them garner power. If those global values have not been fully embraced in Muslim lands as of yet, that is not because of the fundamental nature of Islam, but primarily because the commercial class that must spearhead the process of propagating them is still too small. Helping that bourgeoisie to grow and come to dominate their societies is the best way of making sure those global values will take deep root as Muslim values, paving the way to democracy. That will require that we in the West learn to see past fundamentalism's hard-hitting rhetoric and the venom spewed by extremists, whose power is by and large on the wane across the Muslim world.

We fear Iran's ruling clerics and their designs for the Middle East, and rightly so. Their suppression of freedoms at home; support of radical militias and violence in Iraq, Lebanon, and the Gaza Strip; and their inflammatory calls for the annihilation of Israel are unacceptable. Their unwavering determination to obtain nuclear capability threatens to set off a nuclear arms race in the region. For all these reasons, we must vigilantly work to rein in their power, but the best way to do so is not by our own version of saber rattling. If we can see through the smokescreen of their rhetoric, we can come to appreciate the opportunity presented by the fact that the lair of the ayatollahs is also the "Islamic Republic, Inc.," where a dynamic sector of society dreams of democracy replacing theocracy and the rules of business trumping ideology. So, too, in Pakistan we must support the energies of the lawyers' movement by working to stimulate the growth of the country's promising private sector.

In revitalizing the global economy in the wake of the current financial crisis, the West should work to empower the budding commercial forces all around the Muslim world. That will not only be good for the global economy—which will get a boost from harnessing the economic energies and purchasing power of 1.2 billion Muslims—it will expedite the process of liberalization through capitalism. Whenever constraints on these new capitalists have been loosened they have made great strides: In Iran, when the clerical rulers sued for privatization and reform in the 1990s; in Turkey's Anatolian heartland, when the Kemalist state relented; and even in strife-riven Pakistan, when pro-business policies were put in place, the entrepreneurial spirit came alive. The West can help this development by encouraging states to loosen their holds on their economies and free their markets. We have to accept that this is the necessary historical process that the Middle East must go through if it is to get to the next stage—the Holy Grail of freedom and prosperity.

For decades we have put much too much stock in the authoritarian states. We say we would like to see the Middle East catch up with Asia and Latin America, in both the nurturing of democracy and economic growth, but by investing so much in authoritarian regimes across the region we have worked at cross-purposes to that good.

The Western powers are capable of providing powerful stimulus for this transformation, but our engagement with the Middle East must follow a coherent plan of using our influence and aid to reduce the state's footprint. We must demand of political leaders in the region—first among them the allies who rely on our aid—to submit to the rule of law, accept constitutional checks and balances, and free up commercial activity from the clutches of restrictive laws and bureaucratic red tape. We must push for fewer and smaller state-run enterprises, smaller public sectors, fewer people on government payrolls, and more in the employ of private sectors. We must also encourage Middle Eastern economies to open up to direct foreign investment, trade, and the free flow of goods and resources. More of the money we pour into the region must go to support entrepreneurship and commerce, and we must open our markets to the many goods that these changes are bound to produce. Let us not forget that rising India owes much of its success to its booming software industry—which in 2007 recorded a whopping $32 billion in exports. That industry found its footing thanks to its direct link to America's Silicon Valley. Bangalore prospered on the back of technology and business ties nurtured mutually by American and Indian companies, and the success in Bangalore led the way for other Indian cities to cultivate similar global links, generating powerful growth.

Economic bonds that will prove far stronger than the current ones between Western capitals and Middle Eastern royal and presidential palaces will, in time, prove far more consequential in setting the Middle East on the path to freedom and prosperity than all the preaching we do, or the military aid and hand holding of dictators. Trying to reform other people's religions is a fool's game, and when it comes to nation building, our record is spotty at best. But if there is one thing America is good at, it is unleashing the transformative power of business. This is what the IMF and EU did so successfully in Turkey. The EU did not preach democracy to Turkey; it put on the table a long-run plan for reforms that would turn Turkey into a democracy with a thriving economy. The plan took a decade to bear fruit—democracy did not come to Turkey because of one free and fair election imposed on the generals. Turkey has gotten to where it is because the EU stuck to its guns and, over time, reforms freed Turkish commerce from suffocating state control. With a booming commercial sector, democracy had a real chance to succeed.

The Middle East presents more challenges than any other region of the world. For one thing, governments such as those in Iran or Pakistan have not indicated that they wish to open up and join the world. The task here, unlike in India or Turkey, is not helping elites eager to change to complete the transformation. The West has to nudge and cajole clerics in Iran and generals in Pakistan to rethink their national interests. That is a difficult task, but by no means an impossible one. These countries have already reached the limit of what they can accomplish with their current strategies. Dialogue, incentives, and concerted pressure by the international community can all help these countries see the light. But equally important, there has to be pressure from below.

Populations—and more specifically rising middle classes—in these countries must see the wisdom of new ways and ask their leaders to change course. That pressure will come sooner rather than later, and it will be far more decisive, if that critical portion of society is to take flight in these countries. For that to happen there has to be more rather than less trade and business engagement with them. That Iran or Pakistan worry the West so much is exactly why we should engage them more rather than less.

America cannot hope to turn the tide in the Middle East in just a few years. There are too many intractable problems and negative trends at work to expect a quick turnaround. Pakistan is infested with radical extremism, which has also reared its head across the Arab world. The Gordian knot of the Israeli-Palestinian problem shows no signs of untangling, and that will keep the region in flux. Economic growth across the region is sluggish and the rate of population growth worrisome. Meanwhile Iran, Egypt, Syria, Lebanon, and Pakistan each has its own set of complex problems. We know that a good deal of the fury in this region has to do with economics, but we must also realize that the solution too lies in economics. Even where least expected any rays of hope we see have to do with economics.

Take the case of Egypt, the stolid and unchanging bastion of authoritarianism at the heart of the Arab world. Over the past decade it has opened its economy somewhat, submitting to IMF strictures and World Trade Organization mandates, which has led to modest steps in the direction of legal reform and greater transparency.[4] Egypt is far from becoming a free capitalist society, but whatever positive change takes place is the result of pressure from market forces. The same goes for the Palestinian Territories. The bell that wasn't ringing, so to speak, during the lead up to the Gaza War was the good news that double-digit economic growth was changing the tide in the West Bank.[5] This is not to say that economics will solve the Israel-Palestinian problem, but economic growth would go a long way in making a solution possible. The lesson here is that the right sort of politics follows the right sort of economy.

We have committed countless trillions of dollars and tens of thousands of our troops to protect our interests in the greater Middle East. And yet Turkey aside, we do very little real business with the region. There has been no trade of any kind between the United States and Iran for the past thirty years, and that gap is increasingly filled by Russia and China, who are unlikely champions of the kinds of reform we would like to see. If we discount oil and weapons sales, in 2007 U.S. trade with the whole Arab world was barely more than $20 billion. The United States now has free-trade deals with Jordan and Morocco, and Europe is considering an economic partnership with the Arab countries of the Mediterranean rim. These are positive steps, but there are still very few "made in the Arab world" goods on America's shelves. By comparison America's trade with Latin America in 2008 was $255 billion, with India $44 billion, Eastern Europe $62 billion, Brazil $63 billion, and Turkey $15 billion. Is it a surprise then that these countries are heeding Mr. Blair's call to endorse global values and the Middle East is not?

The rising business class in the Middle East does not stand against the West; these pragmatic businesspeople do not in general express hatred of America, although many are irked by both U.S. support for Israel and the continuing support of dictators that stand in their way. Neither do they, by and large, stand *with* the West; we should make no mistake in that regard. Their opinions are in tune with the mood in the Muslim world. A recent poll of the Arab world showed that "83% of the [Arab] public has an unfavorable view of the US and 70% express no confidence in the US. Still, Arabs continue to rank the US among the top countries with freedom and democracy for their own people." A particularly telling statistic is that 65 percent of the respondents said they did not believe the United States to be serious about democracy promotion in their countries.[6]

We have to face the fact that the new Middle East being reshaped by the rising middle class is going to be—at least in the short run—Islamic, conservative, and all too often prudish and misogynist. It is certainly not looking for advice or guidance from the West about which of its traditional values should be abandoned. But that does not mean that this middle class will not welcome reforms and that there is no desire among them to fight for more freedom and rights. In Pakistan the spontaneous eruption of the lawyers' movement stood up to dictatorship and brought tens of thousands of religious and secular Pakistanis to the streets. There were people in jeans and traditional *shalwar kameez*, day laborers, students, professionals, and housewives, shoulder to shoulder in defense of democracy. These protests were just about the only thing that had brought Pakistanis together as one nation for as long as many could remember. The world must take heed of this powerful expression of craving for democracy and the protection of liberal values among so many ordinary Pakistanis.

In Iran for the past two years hundreds of thousands of women, and surprisingly also men—both religious and secular—have rallied behind the One Million Signatures campaign to demand rights for women in divorce, in child custody cases, at work, at home, and in the labor market. The movement energized civil society activism and collected its signatures in record time, and made women's rights a hot-button campaign issue in the 2009 presidential elections. In June 2009 those fighting for women's rights joined hands with many more men and women of the middle class to form the Green Movement—so-called for the ubiquitous green headscarves and wristbands that all of sudden seemed to be everywhere to mark support for Mir Hossein Moussavi's campaign, and to protest the outcome of the presidential elections and demand political freedoms and social reforms. But such hopeful signs of political vitality, cutting across the religious–secular divide, could take time to bear fruit. That is to be expected; we know from the experience of the civil rights movement in the United States that change comes only slowly. There will be many hard-fought battles and setbacks.

The provincial lower and rising middle classes have been strong proponents of the institution of Islamic law in Egypt, the wearing of headscarves in Turkey, Islamic education in Pakistan, and Islamic finance in

Dubai. These developments may strike some as setbacks, as signs of the culture of the Middle East moving in the wrong direction. But we in the West do ourselves a grave disservice by focusing with such disdain on these expressions of devotion to Islam. There is little evidence that the growing conservatism of Muslim societies is a bar to fighting for freedom and prosperity—one need not look any farther than Turkey.

Those in the teeming lower classes—but also many among the rising middle class—especially will not be won over by a culture war. As long as those in the lower classes feel their core values are under assault by the West, they will continue to rally to their own hard-line culture warriors. If this happens moderates will lose. At the end of the day, after sanctions and conflicts, the only way we will get less rather than more rejection and extremism—fewer rather than more Ahmadinejads or Qaradawis—is not with more sanctions and conflict but with more business and interaction. We can contain the aggression of those countries we perceive as threats by going to war—as costly as wars may be—but if we really want to change those countries, then we must do more rather than less business with them.

Over time the profit motive will be our strongest ally; it will lead the growing middle class to push increasingly for business-friendly economic reform and the reliable rule of law, as well as the opening up of their economies to trade with the world. They will push with increasing clout for good government, just as the business communities in India and China have forced the hands of their governments in instituting wide-ranging reforms and opening up to the global economy. Of course not every corner of the Muslim world is ready for business, but by achieving success where possible, we can strengthen first movers who can then lead the rest.

The new Middle Eastern middle class is still comparatively small; its numbers do not equal those of China and India, not even where those countries were ten years ago. The great transformation in the Middle East is just beginning, but let us not forget that all great transformations start small, and they are driven by trends that are little noticed before they gather full steam. The economic and social changes that I have pointed to tell of the strong potential for a very different future for the region than the one imagined by Mahmoud Ahmadinejad or Osama bin Laden. There is no question that the balance of power in the Middle East is for now decided by hard power, but the signs for the future are that it will be recalibrated by economics.

We are at a critical historical moment. The Muslim world—and more so its Middle East heartland—is at a crossroads. The region has been living through a dangerous era of popular agitation, spasmodic violence, and brutal crackdown. Wars, large and small, have plagued the region, and occupations and insurgencies, extremism and terrorism are grave threats. In addition, the seething frustration of increasingly youthful populations may push the region into chaos. Shackled by inefficient and brutal dictatorships, mired in corruption, and frustrated with economic stagnation, the Middle East is the focal point of global political instability, and this is largely because the region is not fully integrated into the global economy. If we do not make the effort to assist the region in unleashing its economic potential, then we can very well expect the worst from it. The Islamic threat began with the Iranian Revolution in 1979, and it may very well be that Iran will also decide the region's future; many observers argue that "as Iran goes so will the region." Iran is today a tired dictatorship with a failing economy, and under pressure from a restless population. The ruling clerics may opt to continue down the path of confrontation with the West, but they also have incentives to improve relations, and that is especially so due to economic realities. For years, the West has been looking at Iran only through the prism of its nuclear program, and to a lesser extent its provocations in Lebanon, the Palestinian Territories, Iraq, and Afghanistan, opting for sanctions and isolation to bend Iran's will. Those measures have produced no progress. The United States has as of late softened this approach, balancing pressure with incentives, but as of now, Iran is still surging ahead with its nuclear program and does not look to be changing course on other fronts either. More must be done to stimulate the growth of the commercial sector, building ties through trade, in order for the pressure for reform from within the society to lend the necessary force to the West's efforts. This is what the businessmen all around the region would counsel must be the way forward in all of the region. What sanctions and isolations are achieving, however, is making it more difficult for commerce to flourish, and the historical force that alone can change the Middle East to start that process in the one country that perhaps matters most. As goes Iran so will the Middle East; we had better take good care where we send Iran.

When in March 2009 Tahrik-e Taliban (Pakistan's homegrown Taliban) brazenly attacked a police academy outside Lahore, killing several recruits and leaving little doubt that extremism was determined to take down the Pakistani government, I called an old friend in the city to see how he was and what had happened. My friend is a big businessman, with holdings in textiles and food products, American-educated but also religious. "They are murdering this country one bullet at a time" he told me forlornly. "What can be done?" I asked. "I don't know what we can do," he responded, "but I know what you can do [referring to America]. Lift all those tariffs; that will help." He had explained to me many times before, "Grow the economy; the rest will sort itself out."

NOTES

CHAPTER 1. THE POWER OF COMMERCE

1   Joshua Cooper Ramo, *The Age of the Unthinkable: Why the New World Disorder Constantly Surprises Us and What We Can Do About It* (Boston: Little, Brown and Company, 2009).

2   Ray Takeyh, *Guardians of the Revolution: Iran and the World in the Age of the Ayatollahs* (New York: Oxford University Press, 2009); Shahram Chubin, "Iran's Power in Context," *Survival* 51, 1 (February–March 2009): 165–90, and Mohsen M. Milani, "Tehran's Take: Understanding Iran's U.S. Policy," *Foreign Affairs*, July/August 2009, 46–62.

3   "Iran Has Become an Extra-Regional Power: General," *Tehran Times* (24 September 2007); http://62.193.18.228/indexView .asp?code=153632; and Mohsen Rezaie, "Iran, the Regional Power," *Baztab* (27 March 2005); http://www.baztab.com/ news/22659.php.

4   Personal Interview with President Muhammad Khatami, Davos, Switzerland, January 2007.

5   Personal correspondence with Robert Kaplan.

6   Afshin Molavi, "The Star Students of the Islamic Republic," *Newsweek*, August 9, 2008; http://www.newsweek.com/id/151684.

7   "To excel in today's world," former chief nuclear negotiator and now Speaker of Parliament Ali Larijani told the Arab Strategy Forum in Dubai in December 2006, "you have to be good in either nuclear technology, nanotechnology, or

biotechnology. The West would prefer that we just make tomato paste, but we have our sights set on being a global economic leader."

8 "Iran Invests $2.5 Billion in Stem Cell Research," *Press TV*, November 6, 2008; http://www.presstv.ir/Detail.aspx?id=74490& sectionid=3510210.

9 Interview with Djavad Salehi-Isfahani.

10 Ervand Abrahamian, "Who's in Charge?" *London Review of Books*, November 6, 2008; http://www.lrb.co.uk/v30/n21/abra01_.html.

11 See "Key Excerpts: The Pope's Speech," *BBC News*, September 15, 2006; http://news.bbc.co.uk/2/hi/europe/5348456.stm.

12 Patrick Haenni, *L'islam de marché* (Paris, Seuil, 2005); and Amel Boubekeur, "L'Islam est-il soluble dans le Mecca Cola? Marché de la culture Islamique et nouveaux supports de religiosité en Occident," *Maghreb Machrek* 183 (Spring 2005): 12–13; and Amel Boubekeur, "Cool and Competitive: New Islamic Culture in the West," *ISIM Newsletter*, 16 (Autumn 2005): 45–66.

13 Ibrahim Warde, *The Price of Fear: The Truth Behind the Financial War on Terror* (Berkeley: University of California Press, 2007).

14 Kristin Smith, "From Petrodollars to Islamic Dollars: The Strategic Construction of Islamic Banking in the Arab Gulf," Ph.D. dissertation submitted to the Department of Government, Harvard University, 2006, p. 8; and Michael Maiello, "Managed by God," *Forbes*, April 21, 2008; http://www.forbes.com/2008/04/21/islamic-mutual-funds-cz_mm_islamicfinance08_0421amana.html.

15 S.V.R. Nasr, "Islamic Economics: Novel Perspectives," *Middle Eastern Studies*, 25,4 (October 1989): 516–30.

16 "Understanding Islamic Finance: Local Innovation and Global Integration," *Asia Policy*, 6 (July 2008): 5.

17 "FACTBOX: Key facts about Islamic finance," *Reuters*, February 3, 2008; http://www.reuters.com/article/summitNews/idUSL0122621620080203.

18 "Savings and Souls," *The Economist*, September 6, 2008, p. 81.

19 Andrew Cunningham, "How Big Is 'Islamic Banking'?
    A Snapshot from Saudi Arabia," *Middle East Economic Survey*,
    50,41, October 8, 2007; http://www.mees.com/postedarticles/
    oped/v50n41-5OD01.htm.

20 "Savings and Souls," p. 82.

21 Wayne Arnold, "Adapting Finance to Islam," *The New York Times*,
    November 22, 2007, p. C1; and "FACTBOX: Key facts about
    Islamic finance."

22 Christopher Watts, "Is Islamic Finance at Tipping Point?" *Qatar
    Financial Center Authority*; http://www.economist.com/sponsor/
    qfc/index.cfm?pageid=article104.

23 "Savings and Souls," p. 82.

24 Joanna Slater, "When Hedge Funds Meet Islamic Finance," *The
    Wall Street Journal*, August 9, 2007, p. A1.

25 Rachel Ehrenfeld and Alyssa A. Lappen, "Economic Jihad
    and US Ports?" *The Washington Times*, March 13, 2006;
    http://www.washingtontimes.com/news/2006/mar/12/
    20060312-101234-5706r/.

26 "East Cameron Gas Sukuk: Dawn of A New Frontier,"
    http://www.islamicfinancenews.com/HandbookPDF/32
    .East.pdf.

27 Elisabeth Eaves, "God and Mammon," *Forbes*, April 21, 2008;
    http://www.forbes.com/2008/04/21/islamic-banking-interest-
    islamic-finance-cx_ee_islamicfinance08_0421intro.html.

28 Charles Beard, "Challenges to Mainstreaming Islamic Finance:
    Steps Already Taken and What Needs to Occur for the Future,"
    Arab Financial Forum, http://www.arabfinancialforum.org.

29 Mushtak Parker, "Saxony-Anhalt to Launch Europe's
    Debut Islamic Bond," *Arab News*, July 19, 2004;
    http://www.arabnews.com/?page=6&section=0&article=
    48589&d=19&m=7&y=2004.

30 C. K. Prahalad, *The Fortune at the Bottom of the Pyramid:
    Eradicating Poverty Through Profits* (Philadelphia: Wharton
    School Publishing, 2006).

31 Rodney Wilson, "Arab Governments Respond to Islamic Finance: the Cases of Egypt and Saudi Arabia," *Mediterranean Profile*, 7, 3 (2002): 158.

32 "Economic Developments, Second Quarter of 2007," Saudi Arabian Monetary Agency; http://www.sama.gov.sa/en/ publications/en_2007q2_bulletin_eco.pdf.

33 Smith, "From Petrodollars to Islamic Dollars," pp. 89 and 106.

34 *Ibid*, p. 84.

35 See http://www.accenture.com/Global/Research_and_Insights/ By_Industry/Financial_Services/Banking/IslamicMainstream.htm.

36 Slater, "When Hedge Funds Meet Islamic Finance," p. A1.

37 "Gender Gulf," *The Economist*, April 12, 2008, p. 86.

38 Haris Anwar, "Islamic Bond Decree Cripples Sukuk, Imperils Projects," *Bloomberg News*, September 3, 2008; http://www.bloomberg.com/apps/news?pid=20601109& sid=a_Zh0q70aPxY&refer=exclusive.

39 "Savings and Souls," p. 81.

40 Faiza Saleh Ambah, "Islamic Banking: Steady in Shaky Times," *The Washington Post*, October 31, 2008, p. A16.

41 "Indonesian President Challenges Islamic Banks to Lead in Global Economy," *AHN Global News*; http://www.allheadlinenews.com/ articles/7014267534.

42 John Parker, "Burgeoning Bourgeoisie: A Special Report on the New Middle Class in Emerging Markets," *The Economist*, February 14, 2009, p. 6.

43 Aasiya Lodhi, "Turkish Toil Brings New Form of Faith," *BBC News*, March 13, 2006; http://news.bbc.co.uk/2/hi/business/ 4788712.stm.

44 Dan Bilefsky, " 'Protestant Work Ethic' in Muslim Turkey," *International Herald Tribune*, August 15, 2006; http://www.iht.com/articles/2006/08/11/business/wbturkey.php.

45 Arthur Herman, *How the Scots Invented the Modern World: The True Story of How Western Europe's Poorest Nation Created Our World and Everything in It* (New York: Random House, 2001).

46 Thomas P. M. Barnett, *Blueprint for Action: A Future Worth Creating* (New York: Penguin, 2005).

CHAPTER 2. THE WORLD ACCORDING TO DUBAI

1 Ahmed Kanna and Arang Keshavarzian, "The UAE's Space Race: Sheikhs and Starchitects Envision the Future," *Middle East Report*, 248 (Fall 2008): 34–39.

2 Afshin Molavi, "Sudden City," *National Geographic*, January 2007; http://ngm.nationalgeographic.com/2007/01/dubai/molavi-text .html.

3 Landon Thomas, "Boom Times Take Root in Dubai," *The New York Times*, July 18, 2008; p. C1.

4 Afshin Molavi, "Rising Gulf," *Newsweek*, August 6, 2007; http://www.newsweek.com/id/32632/page/1.

5 "How to Spend It," *The Economist*, April 26, 2008, p. 37.

6 Ibid.

7 "Has the Bubble Burst?" *The Economist*, November 29, 2008, p. 53.

8 Abdulkhaleq Abdulla, "Dubai: An Arab City Going Global," *Journal of Social Affairs*, 23,92 (Winter 2006): 58.

9 Sufyan Alissa, "The Challenge of Economic Reform in the Arab World," *Carnegie Papers*, 1 (Washington: D.C.: Carnegie Endowment for International Peace, 2007), p. 4.

10 Christopher Davidson, *Dubai: The Vulnerability of Success* (New York: Columbia University Press, 2008), pp. 67–98.

11 Michael Slackman, "Young and Arab in the Land of Mosques and Bars," *The New York Times*, September 22, 2008, pp. A1 and A12.

12 Salim al-Zabbal, *I Was a Witness: The Emirates from 1960–1974* (Abu Dhabi: Cultural Foundation, 2001), pp. 95–140.

13 Abdulla, "Dubai: An Arab City Going Global," pp. 68–69.

14 Afshin Molavi, "The CEO Sheikh," *Newsweek*, August 6, 2007; http://www.newsweek.com/id/32716.

15 Niall Ferguson, *The Ascent of Money: A Financial History of the World* (New York: Penguin, 2008), pp. 283–340.

16 Robert Kaplan, "Center Stage for the Twenty-First Century: Power Plays in the Indian Ocean," *Foreign Affairs*, March/April 2009, pp. 19–20.

17 Afshin Molavi, "The New Silk Road," *The Washington Post*, April 9, 2007, p. A13.

18 Ibid.

19 "How to Spend It," p. 38.

20 Chip Cummins, "Dubai Faces Hit as Property Boom Fades," *The Wall Street Journal*, November 13, 2008; http://online.wsj.com/article/SB122649558637520553.html.

21 Jason DeParle, "Fearful of Restive Foreign Labor, Dubai Eyes Reforms," *The New York Times*, August 6, 2007; http://www.nytimes.com/2007/08/06/world/middleeast/06dubai.html?_r=1&scp=6&sq=dubai%20workers&st=cse&oref=slogin.

22 "Dubai Population Makes a Big Surge," *UAE Interact*; http://uaeinteract.com/docs/Dubai_population_makes_big_surge/24196.htm.

23 Ahmed Kanna, "Dubai in a Jagged World," *Middle East Report*, 243 (Summer 2007); http://www.merip.org/mer/mer243/kanna.html.

24 Davidson, *Dubai*, p. 76.

25 Preeti Kannan and Anwar Ahmed, "Iranians Look at UAE as 'Second Home,' " *Khaleej Times*, February, 19, 2008; http://www.khaleejtimes.com/DisplayArticleNew.asp?xfile=data/theuae/2008/February/theuae_February636.xml&section=theuae&col=.

26 Susan Taylor Martin, "Discontented Iranians Have a Place to Call Home," *St. Petersburg Times*, October 24, 2006; http://www.sptimes.com/2006/10/24/Worldandnation/Discontented_Iranians.shtml.

27 Salman Dossari, "Persian Presences in the UAE," *Asharq Alawsat*, February 1, 2007; http://aawsat.com/english/news.asp?section=3&id=7860.

28 Christopher Stewart, "The Axis of Commerce," *Condé Nast Portfolio.com*, September 2008; http://www.portfolio.com/ news-markets/international-news/portfolio/2008/08/13/ US-Trades-With-Iran-Via-Dubai/?refer=email.

29 "A Report on an Invisible Piers," *Iran Emrooz*, http://www.emrooz.org/pages/date/81-12/04/report02.htm; and "Revelations about the Seventh Majlis According to Karrubi," *Sharq*, http://www.sharghnewspaper.com/830119/ parlim.htm.

30 John Irish, "Dubai-Iran Ties Thrive Against Odds," *Arab News*, March 22, 2007; http://www.arabnews.com/?page=4&section=0 &article=94029&d=22&m=3&y=2007.

31 Ibid.

32 Ivan Watson, "Iran's Neighbor Dubai a Place of Intrigue," *National Public Radio*, May 9, 2007; http://www.npr.org/ templates/story/story.php?storyId=10089956.

33 Robin Wright, "Stuart Levey's War," *The New York Times Magazine*, November 2, 2008; http://www.nytimes.com/2008/ 11/02/magazine/02IRAN-t.html?pagewanted=1&_r=1&sq= robin%20wright&st=cse&scp=1.

CHAPTER 3. IRAN'S PREDICAMENT

1 Augustus Richard Norton, *Hezbollah: A Short History* (Princeton: Princeton University Press, 2007).

2 Nir Rosen, "Hizb Allah, Party of God," *Truthdig*, October 3, 2006; http://www.truthdig.com/report/item/200601003_hiz_ ballah_party_of_god/.

3 H. E. Chehabi, "Iran and Lebanon in the Revolutionary Decade" and "Iran and Lebanon After Khomeini," in H. E. Chehabi, ed., *Distant Relations: Iran and Lebanon in the Last 500 Years* (London: I.B. Tauris, 2006), pp. 201–30 and 287–308.

4 Roschanack Shaery-Eisenlohr, *Shi'ite Lebanon: Transnational Religion and the Making of National Identities* (New York: Columbia University Press, 2008).

5 Ervand Abrahamian, "Who's in Charge?" *London Review of Books*, November 6, 2008; http://www.lrb.co.uk/v30/n21/abra01_.html.

6 Ray Takeyh, "A Profile in Defiance: Being Mahmoud Ahmadinejad," *The National Interest*, 83 (Spring 2006), 16–21.

7 Kasra Naji, *Ahmadinejad: The Secret History of Iran's Radical Leader* (London: I.B. Tauris, 2008), p. 5.

8 Fatemeh Rajabi, *Ahmadinejad: Mojezeh-e Hezareh-e Sevvom* (Ahmadinejad: Miracle of the Third Millennium), 2nd ed., (Tehran: Nashr-e Danesh Amouz, 2006).

9 Ali Gheissari and Vali Nasr, *Democracy in Iran: History and the Quest for Liberty* (New York: Oxford University Press, 2006), pp. 147–58.

10 James Dobbins, "How to Talk to Iran," *The Washington Post*, July 22, 2007, p. B07.

11 Trita Parsi, *Treacherous Alliance: The Secret Dealings of Israel, Iran and the United States* (New Haven: Yale University Press, 2007), pp. 238–60 and 341–42. For a broader discussion of this issue see Barbara Slavin, *Bitter Friends, Bosom Enemies: Iran, the U.S., and the Twisted Path to Confrontation* (New York: St. Martin's Press, 2007), pp. 175–208.

12 Vali Nasr and Ray Takeyh, "The Costs of Containing Iran: Washington's Misguided New Middle East Policy," *Foreign Affairs* (January/February 2008), pp. 85–94.

13 "Zawahiri Terms Iran Common Enemy of Al-Qaeda, US," *Fars News Agency*, April 5, 2008; http://english.farsnews.com/newstext.php?nn=8701170513.

14 Gheissari and Nasr, *Democracy in Iran*, pp. 77–104.

15 Ervand Abrahamian, *A History of Modern Iran* (New York: Cambridge University Press, 2008), p. 169.

16 Ibid., p. 180.

17 Sohrab Behdad, "From Populism to Economic Liberalism: The Iranian Predicament," in Parvin Alizadeh, ed., *The Economy of Iran: the Dilemmas of an Islamic State* (London: I.B. Tauris, 2000), p. 130.

18 Suzanne Maloney, "Agents or Obstacles? Parastatal Foundations and Challenges for Iranian Development," in Alizadeh, *The Economy of Iran*, pp. 145–76.

19 Paul Klebnikov, "Millionaire Mullahs," *Forbes*, July 21, 2003; http://www.forbes.com/forbes/2003/0721/056.html.

20 Laura Secor, "The Rationalist: A Dissident Economist's Attempts to Reform the Revolution," *The New Yorker*, February 2, 2009, pp. 34–35.

21 I am grateful to Djavad Salehi-Isfahani for these figures.

22 Afshin Molavi, "Buying Time in Tehran: Iran and the China Model," *Foreign Affairs*, 83, 6 (September/October 2004): 9–16. Gholam-Ali Haddad Adel, the former Speaker of the Parliament and closer adviser to the Supreme Leader, talked of Iran becoming an Islamic Japan in an interview with Agence France-Press, "Profile of Developers of Islamic Iran Alliance," *Iran*, 9, 2734, (February 25, 2004), pp. 3–6.

23 Ali Gheissari and Vali Nasr, "The Conservative Consolidation in Iran," *Survival*, 47, 2 (Summer 2005): 175–90.

24 Akbar Ganji, "Latter-Day Sultan," *Foreign Affairs*, 87, 6 (November/December 2008): 45–66; Karim Sadjadpour, *Reading Khamenei: The World View of Iran's Most Powerful Leader* (Washington, D.C.: Carnegie Endowment for International Peace, 2008).

25 Afshin Molavi, *The Soul of Iran* (New York: W. W. Norton, 2005), pp. 351–55; and Kasra Naji, *Ahmadinejad: The Secret History of Iran's Radical Leader* (London: I.B. Tauris, 2008), pp. 57–90.

26 Nazila Fathi, "Blacksmith's Son Emphasized His Modest Roots," *The New York Times*, June 26, 2005; http://www.nytimes.com/2005/06/26/international/middleeast/26mayor.html.

27 "Iranian Capital Flight to Dubai Continues," *Adnkronos International*, October 1, 2008; http://www.adnkronos.com/AKI/English/Business/?id=3.0.2528276022.

28 "Iran: Ahmadi-Nejad's Tumultuous Presidency," *Middle East Briefing* 21 (Brussels: International Crisis Group, 2007), p. 8.

29 Ibid., p. 12.

30 Ali Ansari, *Iran Under Ahmadinejad: The Politics of Confrontation* (London: International Institute of Strategic Studies, 2007), pp. 67–90.

31 "An Axis in Need of Oiling," *The Economist*, October 25, 2008, p. 72.

32 Najmeh Bozorgmehr, "FT Interview: Mir-Hossein Moussavi," *Financial Times*, April 13, 2009; http://www.ft.com/cms/s/0/a2466224-2824-11de-8dbf-00144feabdc0.html?nclick_check=1.

33 Roshanak Taghavi, "Iran Reformist Eyes Privatization Drive As Vote Looms," *The Wall Street Journal,* June 11, 2009; http://online.wsj.com/article/BT_CO_20090611-703935.html.

34 Steven Weisman, "U.S. Asks Finance Chiefs to Limit Iran's Access to Banks," *The New York Times*, September 17, 2006; http://www.nytimes.com/2006/09/17/world/middleeast/17paulson.html.

35 Najmeh Bozorgmehr, "The Banking Revolutionary," *Financial Times*, November 20, 2007; http://us.ft.com/ftgateway/superpage.ft?news_id=fto112020071527574519.

36 Robin Wright, "Stuart Levey's War," *The New York Times Magazine*, November 2, 2008; http://www.nytimes.com/2008/11/02/magazine/02IRAN-t.html?pagewanted=1&_r=1&sq=robin%20wright&st=cse&scp=1.

CHAPTER 4. THE TRAGIC FAILURES OF SECULARISM

1 See for instance, Bernard Lewis, *What Went Wrong? The Clash Between Islam and Modernity in the Middle East* (New York: Oxford University Press, 2001).

2 Barnaby Rogerson, *The Heirs of Muhammad: Islam's First Century and the Origins of the Sunni-Shia Split* (London: The Overlook Press, 2007).

3 Albert Hourani, *The Emergence of the Modern Middle East* (Los Angeles: University of California Press, 1981), p. 41.

4 Margaret L. Meriwether, *The Kin Who Count: Family and Society*

in Ottoman Aleppo 1170–1840 (Austin: University of Texas Press, 1999).

5 Nikki R. Keddie, with a section by Yann Richard, *Modern Iran: Roots and Results of Revolution*, revised and updated edition (New Haven: Yale University Press, 2003), p. 181.

6 Farhang Rajaee, *Islamism and Modernism: The Changing Discourse in Iran* (Austin, University of Texas Press, 2007), p. 47.

7 Alan Richards and John Waterbury, *A Political Economy of the Middle East* (Boulder, CO: Westview Press, 1990).

8 Said A. Arjomand, *Turban for the Crown: The Islamic Revolution in Iran* (New York: Oxford University Press, 1988), p. 67.

9 Quoted in Peter Evans, *Embedded Autonomy: States and Industrial Transformation* (Princeton: Princeton University Press, 1995), p. 43.

10 Erik J. Zürcher, *Turkey: A Modern History* (New York: I.B. Tauris, 1993), pp. 138–72.

11 M. Hakan Yavuz, *Islamic Political Identity in Turkey* (New York: Oxford University Press, 2003), p. 46.

12 Vamik Volkan and Norman Itzkowitz, *The Immortal Atatürk: A Psychobiology* (Chicago: University of Chicago Press, 1984), p. xx.

13 Houchang Chehabi, "Dress Codes for Men in Turkey and Iran," in Touraj Atabaki and Erik J. Zürcher, *Men of Order: Authoritarian Modernization under Atatürk and Reza Shah* (New York: I.B. Tauris, 2004), p. 228.

14 John R. Perry, "Language Reform in Turkey and Iran," *International Journal of Middle East Studies*, 17 (1985): 295–311.

15 Cyrus Ghani, *Iran and the Rise of the Reza Shah: From Qajar Collapse to Pahlavi Power* (London: I.B. Tauris, 2001), pp. 167–68.

16 Reza Niazmand, *Reza Shah Kabir: Az Tavalod ta Saltanat* (Reza Shah the Great: From Birth to Monarchy) (Washington, DC: Foundation for Iranian Studies, 1996).

17 Amin Banani, *The Modernizaton of Iran, 1921–1941* (Stanford: Stanford University Press, 1961).

18 Shahrough Akhavi, *Religion and Politics in Contemporary Iran:*

Clergy-State Relations in the Pahlavi Period (Albany: SUNY Press, 1980), pp. 36–55.

19 H. E. Chehabi, "Staging the Emperor's New Clothes: Dress Codes and Nation-Building under Reza Shah" *Iranian Studies*, 26, 3–4 (Summer/Fall 1993): 214.

20 Ali Gheissari, *Iranian Intellectuals in the 20th Century* (Austin: University of Texas Press, 1997), pp. 48–49.

21 Gholam R. Afkhami, *The Life and Times of the Shah* (Berkeley: University of California Press, 2008), p. 240.

22 Interview with Princess Ashraf Pahlavi, Oral History Program of Foundation for Iranian Studies (Washington, D.C.: Foundation for Iranian Studies, 1982).

23 Bernard Lewis, *The Emergence of Modern Turkey* (London: Oxford University Press, 1961), p. 293.

24 David Menashri, *Education and the Making of Modern Iran* (Ithaca, NY: Cornell University Press, 1992), p. 106.

25 Barrington Moore, *Social Origins of Dictatorship and Democracy: Lord and Peasant in the Making of the Modern World* (Boston: Beacon Press, 1966), p. 418.

26 For instance, the conservative *Tabnak* routinely refers to Reza Shah as *"padeshah-e faqid"* or "late king."

27 Afshin Molavi, *The Soul of Iran* (New York: W. W. Norton, 2005), pp. 244–47.

28 Paul de Bendern, "Turks Seek Solace in Ataturk at Time of Tension" *Reuters*, April 10, 2007; http://www.reuters.com/article/inDepthNews/idUSL1073129020070411.

CHAPTER 5. THE GREAT ISLAMIC REVOLUTION

1 Francis Fukuyama, *The End of History and the Last Man* (New York: Basic Books, 1992).

2 There are a number of good accounts of the events that led to the Iranian Revolution and shaped politics after its triumph, including Shaul Bakash, *The Reign of the Ayatollahs: Iran and the Islamic Revolution* (New York: Basic Books, 1984); Said A. Arjomand,

The Turban for the Crown: The Islamic Revolution in Iran (New York: Oxford University Press, 1988); Charles Kurzman, *The Unthinkable Revolution in Iran* (Cambridge: Harvard University Press, 2004); and Gholam Reza Afkhami, *The Life and Times of the Shah* (Berkeley: University of California Press, 2008).

3   Hamid, Enayat, "Iran: Khumayni's Concept of the 'Guardianship of the Jurisconsult,' " in James Piscatori, ed., *Islam in the Political Process* (New York: Cambridge University Press, 1983), pp. 160–80.

4   Ervand Abrahamian, *Iran Between Two Revolutions* (Princeton: Princeton University Press, 1982), pp. 156–62; and Fakhreddin Azimi, *The Quest for Democracy in Iran: A Century of Struggle Against Authoritarian Rule* (Cambridge: Harvard University Press, 2008), p. 105.

5   Abrahamian, *Iran Between Two Revolutions*, p. 162.

6   Mostafa Elm, *Oil, Power, and Principle: Iran's Oil Nationalization and Its Aftermath* (Syracuse: Syracuse University Press, 1994).

7   Afkhami, *The Life and Times of the Shah*, pp. 61–186.

8   Farhad Diba, *Mohammad Mossadegh: A Political Biography* (London: Croom Helm, 1986), pp. 158–59.

9   Afkhami, *The Life and Times of the Shah*, pp. 155–84.

10   Maziar Behrooz, *Rebels Without a Cause: The Failure of the Left in Iran* (New York: I.B. Tauris, 2000).

11   Afkhami, *The Life and Times of the Shah*, pp. 187–364.

12   Ibid., p. 224.

13   Personal Interview with Mumtaz Bhutto, March 1990.

14   David Landes, *Bankers and Pashas: International Finance and Economic Imperialism in Egypt* (Cambridge: Harvard University Press, 1980).

15   Keith Kyle, *Suez: Britain's End of Empire in the Middle East* (London: I.B. Tauris, 2003).

16   Vali Nasr, "Politics Within the Late-Pahlavi State: The Ministry of Economy and Industrial Policy, 1963–1969," *International Journal of Middle East Studies*, 32,1 (February 2000): 97–122.

17   Ali Gheissari, *Iranian Intellectuals in the 20th Century* (Austin:

University of Texas Press, 1997), pp. 74–109; and Roy Mottahedeh, *Mantle of the Prophet: Religion and Politics in Iran* (New York: Simon & Schuster, 1985), pp. 287–315.

18 Jalal Al-e Ahmad, *Dar Khedmat va Khianat-e Roshanfekran* (On the Service and Treachery of Intellectuals) (Tehran: Ravaq, 1977), p. 23.

19 Gheissari, *Iranian Intellectuals*, pp. 82–107.

20 Ali Rahnema, *An Islamic Utopian: A Political Biography of Ali Shariati* (London: I.B. Tauris, 1998).

21 Ali Shariati, *Shiah* (Shiism) (Tehran: Elham, 1983), pp. 16 and 114–15.

22 Kim Murphy, "Tehran Contemporary Art Museum Has Picassos in Basement," *Los Angeles Times*, September 26, 2007; http://travel.latimes.com/articles/la-trw-iran-keeps-picassos-in-basement; and Lara Setrakian, "Inside Iran's Billion-Dollar Art Basement," *ABCNews.com*, March 1, 2008; http://abcnews.go.com/Travel/story?id=4372055&page=1.

23 Michael M. J. Fischer, *Iran, from Religious Dispute to Revolution* (Cambridge: Harvard University Press, 1980), pp. 126–27.

24 William Shawcross, *The Shah's Last Ride: The Story of the Exile, Misadventures and Death of the Emperor* (New York: Touchstone, 1989), pp. 43–47.

25 Afkhami, *The Life and Times of the Shah*, pp. 411–12.

26 Mohammad Reza Pahlavi, *Mission for My Country* (New York: McGraw-Hill, 1961), p. 173.

27 Fred Halliday, *Iran: Dictatorship and Development* (New York: Penguin, 1979), pp. 47–48.

28 Azar Salamat, "Of Chance and Choice," in Mahnaz Afkhami, ed., *Women in Exile* (Charlottesville: University of Virginia Press, 1994), p. 86.

29 Bakhash, *The Reign of the Ayatollahs*, p. 75.

30 Ervand Abrahamian, *Tortured Confessions: Prisons and Public Recantations in Modern Iran* (Berkeley: University of California Press, 1999).

31 Shirin Ebadi, *Iran Awakening: A Memoir of Revolution and Hope* (New York: Random House, 2006).

32 S.V.R. Nasr, *Islamic Leviathan: Islam and State Power* (New York: Oxford University Press, 2000), pp. 127–29.

33 Patrick Cockburn, *Muqtada: Muqtada al-Sadr, the Shia Revival, and the Struggle for Iraq* (New York: Scribner, 2008), p. 89.

CHAPTER 6. THE TRUE COURSE OF FUNDAMENTALISM

1 Charles Le Gai Eaton, *Islam and the Destiny of Man* (Albany: SUNY Press, 1985), p. 172.

2 Ann K. S. Lambton, *State and Government in Medieval Islam: An Introduction to the Study of Islamic Political Theory of the Jurists* (London: Oxford University Press, 1981).

3 Seyyed Hossein Nasr, *The Heart of Islam: Enduring Values for Humanity* (San Francisco: HarperOne, 2002), pp. 205–206.

4 Ayesha Jalal, *Partisans of Allah; Jihad in South Asia* (Cambridge: Harvard University Press, 2008), p. 7.

5 Ibid., p. 4.

6 Ibid.

7 Ishtiaq Ahmed, *The Concept of an Islamic State: An Analysis of the Ideological Controversy in Pakistan* (New York: Macmillan, 1987).

8 Noah Feldman, "Why Shariah?" *The New York Times Magazine*, March 6, 2008; http://www.nytimes.com/2008/03/16/magazine/16Shariah-t.html?_r=1&scp=2&sq=noah+feldman&st=nyt&oref=slogin.

9 Steve Coll, *The Bin Ladens: An Arabian Family in the American Century* (New York: Penguin Press, 2008), pp. 198–212; and Peter Bergen, *The Osama bin Laden I Know: An Oral History of al Qaeda's Leader* (New York: Free Press, 2006).

10 Richard P. Mitchell, *Society of Muslim Brothers* (New York: Oxford University Press, 1969); S.V.R. Nasr, *Mawdudi and the Making of Islamic Revivalism* (New York: Oxford University Press, 1996).

11 Asma Afsaruddin, *The First Muslims: History and Memory* (New York: Oneworld, 2007).

12 Nasr, *Mawdudi*, p. 80

13 Ibid., pp. 59–60.

14 Olivier Roy, *Globalized Islam: The Search for a New Ummah* (New York: Columbia University Press, 2004), p. 25.

15 Nasr, *Mawdudi*, p. 71.

16 Ibid., p. 88.

17 "Hasan al-Banna: The New Renaissance," in John J. Donohue and John L. Esposito, eds., *Islam in Transition; Muslim Perspectives*, 2nd ed. (New York: Oxford University Press, 2007), p. 60.

18 Steven Barraclough, "Al-Azhar: Between the Government and Islamists," *Middle East Journal*, 52,2 (Spring 1998): 237.

19 Lawrence Wright, *The Looming Tower: Al-Qaeda and the Road to 9/11* (New York: Knopf, 2006), pp. 7–31.

20 Gilles Kepel, *Muslim Extremism in Egypt: The Prophet and Pharaoh* (Berkeley: University of California Press, 2003), pp. 36–70; and Ahmad S. Moussalli, *Radical Islamic Fundamentalism: The Ideological and Political Discourse of Sayyid Qutb* (Syracuse: Syracuse University Press, 1993).

21 "Sayyid Qutb: Jihad in the Cause of God," in Donohue and Esposito, *Islam in Transition*, pp. 409 and 416.

22 Gilles Kepel, *Jihad: The Trail of Political Islam* (Cambridge: Harvard University Press, 2003), p. 26.

23 Ibid., p. 32.

24 Coll, *The Bin Ladens*, pp. 439–44.

25 Ministry of Hajj, Kingdom of Saudi Arabia. Accessed at http://www.hajinformation.com/main/l.htm.

26 Yaroslav Trofimov, *The Siege of Mecca: The Forgotten Uprising in Islam's Holiest Shrine and the Birth of al-Qaeda* (New York: Doubleday, 2007).

27 Olivier Roy, *Islam and Resistance in Afghanistan* (New York: Cambridge University Press, 1990), pp. 69–70.

28 David B. Edwards, "Summoning Muslims: Print, Politics, and Religious Ideology in Afghanistan," *The Journal of Asian Studies*, 52,3 (August 1993): 609–628.

29 Barnett R. Rubin, "Arab Islamists in Afghanistan," in John L. Esposito, ed., *Political Islam: Revolution, Radicalism, or Reform?* (Boulder: Lynne Rienner, 1997), pp. 179–207.

30 Roy, *Golablized Jihad*, and David Kilcullen, *The Accidental Guerrilla: Fighting Small Wars in the Midst of the Big One* (New York: Oxford University Press, 2009), pp. xxiv–xxviii.

31 Fawaz Gerges, *The Far Enemy: Why Jihad Went Global* (New York: Cambridge University Press, 2005).

32 Rusen Cakir, "The Reemergence of Hizballah in Turkey," *Policy Focus*, 74 (Washington, D.C.: The Washington Institute for Near East Policy, 2007), p. 6.

33 "Poll of the Iranian Public," presentation of World Public Opinion Survey at the Iran Policy Forum of United States Institute of Peace, January 16, 2007.

34 Lawrence Wright, "The Rebellion Within: An Al Qaeda Mastermind Questions Terrorism," *The New Yorker*, June 2, 2008; http://www.newyorker.com/reporting/2008/06/02/080602fa_fact_wright.

35 Janine Clark, *Islam, Charity, and Activism: Middle Class Networks and Social Welfare in Egypt, Jordan and Yemen* (Bloomington: Indiana University Press, 2004); and Asef Bayat, "Activism and Social Development in the Middle East," *International Journal of Middle East Studies*, 34 (2002): 1–28.

36 Michael Gordon, "In Sadr City, Basic Services Are Faltering," *The New York Times*, April 22, 2008, pp. A1 and A10.

37 Clark, *Islam, Charity, and Activism;* and Glenn E. Robinson, "Hamas as a Social Movement," in Quintan Wiktorowicz, ed., *Islamic Activism: A Social Movement Theory Approach* (Bloomington: Indiana University Press, 2004), pp. 112–39.

38 Bayat, "Activism," p. 12.

39 John L. Esposito and Dalia Mogahed, *Who Speaks for Islam? What a Billion Muslims Really Think* (New York: Gallup, 2007), p. 71.

40 Sheri Berman, "Taming Extremist Parties: Lessons From Europe," *Journal of Democracy*, 19,1 (January 2008): 5–18.

41 Michael McFaul and Tamara Cofman Wittes, "The Limits of
    Limited Reforms," *Journal of Democracy*, 19,1 (January 2008):
    19–33; and Amr Hamzamy, "Party for Justice and Development
    in Morocco: Participation and Its Discontents," *Carnegie Papers*,
    93 (Washington, D.C.: Carnegie Endowment for International
    Peace, 2008).

42 Vali Nasr, "The Rise of Muslim Democracy," *Journal of Democracy*.
    16,2 (April 2005): 13–27.

43 From comments by Emile Nakhleh, "How the Intelligence
    Community Understood the Islamic Challenge," at the Council
    on Foreign Relations, New York, April 15, 2009.

44 Sadanand Dhume, "Indonesia Rejects Extremism," *The Wall
    Street Journal*, April 16, 2009; http://online.wsj.com/article/
    SB123984963676123781.html.

CHAPTER 7. THE PROPHETS OF CHANGE

1 Robin Wright, "A Quiet Revolution Grows in the Muslim World,"
   Time, March 19, 2009; http://www.time.com/time/magazine/
   article/0,9171,1886539,00.html.

2 Samantha M. Shapiro, "Ministering to the Upwardly Mobile
   Muslim," *The New York Times Magazine*, April 30, 2006;
   http://www.nytimes.com/2006/04/30/magazine/30televangelist
   .html?_r=1&ei=5070&en=0435ab049955ff40&ex=1146628800
   &pagewanted=all.

3 "Qaradawi Rejects Al-Qaeda's Killing of Innocents," *Islam for
   Today*; http://www.islamfortoday.com/qaradawi02.htm; also see
   Marc Lynch, *Voices of the New Arab Public: Iraq, Al-Jazeera and
   Middle East Politics Today* (New York: Columbia University Press,
   2005), pp. 87–88.

4 Magdi Abdelhadi, "Controversial Preacher With 'Star Status,' "
   BBC News; http://news.bbc.co.uk/2/hi/uk_news/3874893.stm.

5 Ibid.

6 Fareed Zakaria, *The Future of Freedom: Illiberal Democracy at Home
   and Abroad* (New York: W. W. Norton, 2003), pp. 199–238.

7 Arthur Herman, *How the Scots Invented the Modern World: The True Story of How Western Europe's Poorest Nation Created Our World and Everything in It* (New York: Random House, 2001), p. 16.

8 Ellis Goldberg, "Smashing Idols and the State: The Protestant Ethic and Egyptian Sunni Radicalism," in Juan R. I. Cole, ed., *Comparing Muslim Societies: Knowledge and the State in a World Civilization* (Ann Arbor: University of Michigan Press, 1992), p. 195.

9 Abdul-Karim Soroush, *Reason, Freedom, and Democracy in Islam: Essential Writings of Abdolkarim Soroush*, Ahmad Sadri and Mahmoud Sadri, eds. (New York: Oxford University Press, 2000); Valla Vakili, "Abdolkarim Soroush and the Critical Discourse in Iran," in John Esposito and John Voll, eds., *Makers of Contemporary Islam* (New York: Oxford University Press, 2001), pp. 150–76; and Farzin Vahdat, *God and Juggernaut: Iran's Intellectual Encounter with Modernity* (Syracuse: Syracuse University Press, 2002), pp. 198–211.

10 Saba Mahmood, *Politics of Piety: The Islamic Revival and the Feminist Subject* (Princeton: Princeton University Press, 2005).

11 Anne Miller and Dru Gladney, "China's Nu Ahong," *Saudi Aramco World*, July/August 2008, pp. 24–33.

12 Faiza Saleh Ambah, "In Saudi Arabia, a Resurgence of Sufism," *The Washington Post*, May 2, 2006, p. A13.

13 Jessica Stern, "Pakistan's Jihad Culture," *Foreign Affairs*, 79, 6, (2000): 115–26; Peter Singer, "Pakistan's Madrassahs: Ensuring a System of Education not Jihad," *Brookings Institution Analysis Paper* 41 (Washington D.C.: Brookings Institution, 2001).

14 See comments of Representative John F. Tierney, Chairman of the Subcommittee on National Security and Foreign Affairs; http://nationalsecurity.oversight.house.gov/story.asp?ID=1304.

15 See Fox News, November 2, 2003; http://www.foxnews.com/story/0,20933,101956,00.html.

16 Muhammad Qasim Zaman, *The Ulama in Contemporary*

Islam: Custodians of Change (Princeton: Princeton University Press, 2002); and Mumtaz Ahmad, "Continuity and Change in the Traditional System of Islamic Education: The Case of Pakistan," in Craig Baxter and Charles H. Kennedy's, eds., *Pakistan 2000* (Karachi: Oxford University Press, 2001), pp. 129–38.

17 "Madrassa Maths," *The Economist*, May 21, 2005, p. 45.

18 Tahir Andrabi, Jishnu Das, and Asim Ijaz, *Religious School Enrollment in Pakistan: A Look at the Data* (Washington D.C.: The World Bank, February 8, 2005); http://papers.ssrn.com/sol3/papers.cfm?abstract_id=667843.

19 C. Christine Fair, *The Madrassah Challenge: Militancy and Religious Education in Pakistan* (Washington, D.C.: United States Institute of Peace, 2008), pp. 30–35.

20 Peter Bergen and Swati Pandey, "The Madrassa Myth," *The New York Times*, June 14, 2005; http://www.nytimes.com/2005/06/14/opinion/14bergen.html.

21 Robert W. Hefner "Islamic Schools, Social Movements, and Democracy in Indonesia," in Robert W. Hefner, ed., *Making Modern Muslims: The Politics of Islamic Education in Southeast Asia* (Honolulu: University of Hawaii Press, 2009).

22 Michael Slackman, "In Algeria, a Tug of War for Young Minds," *The New York Times*, June 23, 2008, pp. A1 and A8.

23 Fair, *The Madrassah Challenge*, p. 70.

24 I am grateful to Mumtaz Ahmad for these figures.

25 Omar Khalidi, "Entrepreneurs From Outside Traditional Mercantile Communities: Muslims in India's Private Sector," *Journal of South Asian and Middle Eastern Studies*, 31, 2 (Winter 2008): 13–42.

26 Sabrina Tavernise, "Turkish Schools Offer Pakistan a Gentler Vision of Islam," *The New York Times*, May 4, 2008; http://www.nytimes.com/2008/05/04/world/asia/04islam.html?_r=1&scp=1&sq=sabrina%20tavernise%20pakistan%20schools&st=cse&oref=slogin.

27 Allegra Stratton, *Muhajababes: Meet the New Middle East—Young, Sexy and Devout* (New York: Melville House, 2008).

28 For a discussion of numbers and their implication see Graham Fuller, "The Youth Factor: The New Demographics of the Middle East and Implications for U.S. Policy," *The Brookings Project on U.S. Policy Toward the Islamic World* (Washington, D.C.: Brookings Institution, 2003), p. 7

29 Azadeh Moaveni, *Lipstick Jihad: A Memoir of Growing Up Iranian in America and American in Iran* (New York: Public Affairs, 2005).

30 Nasrin Alavi, *We Are Iran: The Persian Blogs* (Brooklyn, NY: Soft Skull Press, 2005); Mona Elthawy, "The Middle East's Generation Facebook." *World Policy Journal*, 25, 3 (Fall 2008), pp. 69–77.

31 Mark LeVine, *Heavy Metal Islam: Rock, Resistance, and the Struggle for the Soul of Islam* (New York: Three Rivers Press, 2008); Sholeh Johnston, "Persian Rap: The Voice of Modern Iran's Youth," *Journal of Persianate Studies*, 1,1 (2008), pp. 102–19; and Anuj Chopra, "Rebels of Rap Reign in Iran," *San Francisco Chronicle*, April 16, 2008; http://www.sfgate.com/cgi-bin/article.cgi?f=/c/a/2008/04/16/MNRGUSJSS.DTL&hw=anuj+chopra&sn=002&sc=135.

32 http://www.youtube.com/watch?v=wcZWXX8oc3k.

33 Najmeh Bozorgmehr, "Iran Military Force Fears Threat from Within," *Financial Times*, December 28, 2007; http://www.ft.com/cms/s/0/a21ee6d8-b4ce-11dc-990a-0000779fd2ac.html?nclick_check=1.

34 Borzou Daragahi and Ramin Mostaghim, "Iran's Other Youth Movement," *Los Angeles Times*, June 10, 2007; http://articles.latimes.com/2007/jun/10/world/fg-basiji10.

35 Azadeh Moaveni, *Honeymoon in Tehran: Two Years of Love and Danger in Iran* (New York: Random House, 2009), p. 32.

36 Farhad Khosrokhavar, "The New Religiosity in Iran," *Social Compass*, 54,3 (September 2007): 453–63.

37 Mohammed Bin Rashid Al Maktoum, "Education vs. Extremism," *The Wall Street Journal*, June 3, 2009, p. A15.

CHAPTER 8. PAKISTAN'S HORROR AND HOPE

1 "Remarks at the American University in Cairo," U.S. Department of State, June 20, 2005; http://www.state.gov/secretary/rm/2005/48328.htm.

2 Ahmed Rashid, *Descent into Chaos: The United States and the Failure of Nation Building in Pakistan, Afghanistan, and Central Asia* (New York: Viking, 2008), p. 145.

3 Pervez Musharraf, *In the Line of Fire: A Memoir* (New York: Free Press, 2006), p. 201.

4 Peter Wonacott, "Modern and Muslim: In Turbulent Pakistan, Start-Ups Drive a Boom," *The Wall Street Journal,* September 5, 2007, p. A14.

5 Jane Perlez and Pir Zubair Shah, "Taliban Exploit Class Rifts in Pakistan," *The New York Times,* April 16, 2009, p. A1.

6 David Sanger, *The Inheritance: The World Obama Confronts and the Challenges to American Power* (New York: Harmony, 2009), pp. 173–265.

7 Hassan Abbas, *Pakistan's Drift Into Extremism: Allah, the Army, and America's War on Terror* (Armonk, NY: M.E. Sharpe, 2004), pp. 169–75.

8 For a detailed account of this sordid affair, see Owen Bennett Jones, *Pakistan: The Eye of the Storm* (New Haven: Yale University Press, 2002), pp. 34–55.

9 Barnett R. Rubin and Ahmed Rashid, "From Great Game to Grand Bargain: Ending Chaos in Afghanistan and Pakistan," *Foreign Affairs* (November/December 2008): 30–44.

10 Personal interview, Lahore, Pakistan, May 2005.

11 Bruce Riedel, "Musharraf's Departure Is Good for Pakistan but Is It Too Late?" *Brookings Brief,* August 18, 2008; http://www.brookings.edu/opinions/2008/0818_pakistan_riedel.aspx.

12 Ibid.

13 The best account of the war and Pakistan's role in it is Steve Coll, *Ghost Wars: The Secret History of the CIA, Afghanistan, and Bin*

Laden, from the Soviet Invasion to September 10, 2001 (New York: Penguin Press, 2004).

14 Dexter Filkins, "The Long Road to Chaos in Pakistan," *The New York Times Magazine*, September 28, 2008; http://www.nytimes.com/2008/09/28/weekinreview/ 28filkins.html?_r=1&scp=2&sq=dexter%20filkins&st= cse&oref=slogin.

15 "SBP Directs Banks to Freeze TTP Accounts," *Daily Times*, September 2, 2008; http://www.dailytimes.com.pk/default.asp ?page=2008%5C09%5C02%5Cstory_2-9-2008_pg1_13; and Ismail Khan, "Pakistan Fort Overrun by Militants," *The New York Times*, January 17, 2008; http://www.nytimes.com/2008/01/17/ world/asia/17pakistan_web.html?_r=1&scp=2&sq=Tehreek%20 Taliban&st=cse&oref=slogin.

16 Personal interview, Lahore, Pakistan, April–May 2005.

17 Dexter Filkins, "Right At the Edge," *The New York Times Magazine*, September 7, 2008; http://www.nytimes.com/2008/09/07/ magazine/07pakistan-t.html.

18 Ayesha Siddiqa, *Military Inc.: Inside Pakistan's Military Economy* (London: Pluto Press, 2007); and Ayaz Amir, "Realtor's Paradise," *Dawn*, December 10, 2004; http://www.dawn.com/weekly/ ayaz/20041210.htm.

19 James Traub, "The Lawyers' Crusade," *The New York Times Magazine*, June 1, 2008; http://www.nytimes.com/2008/06/01/ magazine/01PAKISTAN-t.html?_r=1&scp=3&sq=aitzaz%20 ahsan&st=cse&oref=slogin.

20 Declan Walsh, "Without a Trace," *The Guardian*, March 16, 2007; http://www.guardian.co.uk/world/2007/mar/16/alqaida.pakistan; and Barbara Plett, "Painful Search For Pakistan's Disappeared," *BBC News*, December 13, 2006; http://news.bbc.co.uk/2/hi/ south_asia/6177057.stm.

21 Zahid Hussain, "Sharif's Party Pulls Out of Pakistani Coalition," *The Wall Street Journal*, August 26, 2008, p. A6.

22 Wonacott, "Modern and Muslim," p. A14.

23 "Gujranwala Business Center," *Pakistan Times*, May 13, 2007;
http://www.pak-times.com/2007/05/13/gujranwala-business
-center/print/; and David Montero, "In Pakistan Entrepreneurs
with a Mission," *The Christian Science Monitor*, October 24, 2006;
http://www.csmonitor.com/2006/1024/p06s02-wosc.htm.

24 Edward Luce, *In Spite of the Gods: The Strange Rise of Modern India*
(New York: Doubleday, 2007).

25 Michael F. Martin and K. Alan Kronstadt, "Pakistan's Capital
Crisis: Implications for U.S. Policy," *Congressional Research Service
Report for Congress* (November 7, 2008), p. 5.

26 Hashim Abro, "Inflation, Unemployment and Recruitment,"
Pakistan News, October 27, 2008; http://paknewsupdate.com/
?p=48.

27 Mazhar Tufail, "Bitter Fruits of IMF Bailout," *The News*, October
24, 2008; http://www.thenews.com.pk/top_story_detail.asp
?Id=17970.

CHAPTER 9. THE TURKISH MODEL

1 Cited in Emile Nakhleh, *A Necessary Engagement: Reinventing
America's Relations with the Muslim World* (Princeton: Princeton
University Press, 2009), p. 5.

2 Hakan Yavuz, *Secularism and Muslim Democracy in Turkey* (New
York: Cambridge University Press, 2009).

3 Feride Acar, "Turgut Özal: Pious Agent of Liberal
Transformation," in Metin Heper and Sabri Sayari, eds.,
Political Leaders and Democracy in Turkey (Lanham, MD:
Lexington Books, 2002), pp. 163–180.

4 Ziya Onis, *State and Market: The Political Economy of Turkey
in Comparative Perspective* (Istanbul: Bogazici University Press,
1998).

5 Ziya Onis, "The Evolution of Privatization in Turkey:
The Institutional Context of Public-Enterprise Reform,"
International Journal of Middle East Studies, 23,2 (May, 1991):
163–176.

6 Haldun Gulalp, "Globalization and Political Islam: The Social Bases of Turkey's Welfare Party," *International Journal of Middle East Studies*, 33,3 (August 2001): 433–48.

7 John Waterbury, "Export-Led Growth and the Center-Right Coalition in Turkey," *Comparative Politics*, 24, 2 (January, 1992): 127–145.

8 Gulalp, "Globalization and Political Islam," p. 437.

9 Ahmet Insel, "The AKP and Normalizing Democracy in Turkey," *South Atlantic Quarterly*, 102, 2–3 (Spring-Summer 2003): 297–298.

10 "A Conversation with Ali Babacan," *Charlie Rose*, September 23, 2008; http://www.charlierose.com/shows/2008/09/23/2/ a-conversation-with-ali-babacan-minister-of-foreign-affairs-of -turkey.

11 Hakan Yavuz, "Political Islam and Welfare (Refah) Party in Turkey," *Comparative Politics*, 30,1 (October 1997): 63–82.

12 Berol Yesilda, "The Virtue Party," *Turkish Studies*, 3,1 (Spring 2002): 62–81.

13 Jenny White, "The End of Islamism? Turkey's Muslimhood Model," in Robert Hefner, ed., *Modern Muslim Politics* (Princeton: Princeton University Press, 2005), pp. 87–111.

14 Yalçin Akdogan, "The Meaning of Conservative Democratic Political Identity," in M. Hakan Yavuz, ed., *The Emergence of a New Turkey: Democracy, and the AK Parti* (Salt Lake City: University of Utah Press, 2006), pp. 49–65.

15 Interview with Yalçin Akdogan, Ankara, March 2004.

16 Kerem Oktem, "Harbingers of Turkey's Second Republic," *Middle East Report* (August 1, 2007); http://www.merip.org/mero/ mero080107.html.

17 Soli Ozel, "After the Tsunami," *Journal of Democracy*, 14,2 (April 2003), pp. 80–94.

18 Dan Bilefsky, " 'Protestant Work Ethic' in Muslim Turkey," *International Herald Tribune*, August 15, 2006; http://www.iht .com/articles/2006/08/11/business/wbturkey.php.

19 "Islamic Calvinists: Change and Conservatism in Central Anatolia," (Berlin and Istanbul: European Stability Initiative, 2005), p. 9.

20 Zehra Saygin, "Office Furniture Industry Booming in Turkey," *Today's Zaman*, September 21, 2008; http://www.todayszaman.com/tz-web/detaylar.do?load=detay&link=153828&bolum=105.

21 "Islamic Calvinists," pp. 14–15.

22 Hasan Gulveren, "Turkey Chases Away the Denim Blues," *Just-Style*, August 5, 2005; http://www.just-style.com/article.aspx?id=92475.

23 Bilefsky, " 'Protestant Work Ethic' in Muslim Turkey."

24 "Islamic Calvinists," p. 34.

25 Ibid. and Bilefsky, " 'Protestant Work Ethic' in Muslim Turkey."

26 Aasiya Lodhi, "Turkish Toil Brings New Form of Faith," *BBC News*, March 13, 2006; http://news.bbc.co.uk/2/hi/business/4788712.stm.

27 Yavuz, *Secularism and Muslim Democracy in Turkey*. Also see Kamil Yilmaz, "The Emergence and Rise of Conservative Elite in Turkey," *Insight Turkey*, 11,2 (2009): 113–136.

28 Ziya Onis and Umut Turem, "Entrepreneurs, Democracy, and Citizenship in Turkey," *Comparative Politics*, 34,4 (July 2002): 439–456.

29 Ziya Onis, "The Political Economy of Turkey's Justice and Development Party," in Yavuz, *The Emergence of a New Turkey*, pp. 211–28.

30 More of the statement is available at "Excerpts of Turkish Army Statement," *BBC News*, April 28, 2007; http://news.bbc.co.uk/2/hi/europe/6602775.stm.

31 "Turkey's Political Crisis," *The Economist*, May 3, 2007; http://www.economist.com/world/europe/displaystory.cfm?story_id=9116841; and "PM Erdogan: Constitutional Court ruling a 'bullet shot into democracy,' " *Hürriyet*, May 2, 2007; http://www.hurriyet.com.tr/english/6446198.asp?gid=74.

32 Christopher de Bellaigue, "Turkey at the Turning Point?" *New*

York Review of Books, 54,16, October 25, 2007; http://www
.nybooks.com/articles/20707?email.

33 Hilal Elver, "Lawfare and Wearfare in Turkey," *Middle East
Report* (April 2008); http://www.merip.org/mero/interventions/
elverINT.html.

34 Vincent Boland, "Official Wants Turkey's Ruling Party Shut
Down," *Financial Times*, March 15, 2008; http://www.ft.com/
cms/s/0/f62d63ba-f233-11dc-9b45-0000779fd2ac.html?nclick_
check=1.

35 Jenny White, "The Ebbing Power of Turkey's Secularist Elite,"
Current History, 106, 704 (December 2007): 427–33.

CHAPTER 10. WINNING THE FUTURE

1 Larry Diamond, *The Spirit of Democracy: The Struggle to Build Free
Societies Across the World* (New York: Times Books, 2008).

2 Arthur Herman, *How the Scots Invented the Modern World: The
True Story of How Western Europe's Poorest Nation Created Our
World and Everything in It* (New York: Random House, 2001).

3 John Parker, "Burgeoning Bourgeoisie: A Special Report on the
New Middle Class in Emerging Markets" *The Economist*, February
14, 2009, p. 6.

4 Bruce Rutherford, *Egypt after Mubarak: Liberalism, Islam and
Democracy in the Arab World* (Princeton: Princeton University
Press, 2008), pp. 197–230.

5 Jeffrey Goldberg, "Good News from Palestine," *The Atlantic*,
January 9, 2009; http://jeffreygoldberg.theatlantic.com/
archives/2009/01/good_news_from_palestine.php.

6 Shibley Tilhami, "2008 Annual Arab Public Opinion Poll"
(College Park, MD: the Anwar Sadat Chair for Peace and
Development at the University of Maryland, 2008);
http://www.brookings.edu/topics/~/media/Files/events/2008/
0414_middle_east/0414_middle_east_telhami.pdf.

ACKNOWLEDGMENTS

I have incurred many debts in writing this book. First, I am grateful to the Carnegie Corporation of New York for selecting me as a Carnegie Scholar in 2006. The core ideas of this book flowed from research I conducted under the aegis of that fellowship. Several friends and colleagues pointed me to new arguments and sources. I am grateful to Khaleq Abdallah, Jon Alterman, Najmeh Bozorgmehr, Ruşen Çaker, Ginger Dagli-Juhi, John Esposito, Robert Hefner, Ayesha Jalal, Yasar Jarrar, Ibrahim Kalin, Bijan Khajepour, Fareed Mohamedi, Afshin Molavi, Fawzia Naqvi, Richard Norton, Barnett Rubin, Jean-Francois Seznec, Randa Slim, Mohamad Sotoudeh, Alix Van Buren, Hakan Yavuz, and Rochdi Younsi. Mahnaz Afkhami, Mumtaz Ahmad, Leila Fawaz, Ali Gheissari, and Ibrahim Warde deserve a special note of thanks for reading through the early drafts of this book and improving it in important ways. Philip Costopoulos read what I wrote with great care and gave it his full measure of attention and erudition. The manuscript is all the richer for his contribution. My research assistants, Julia Bennett at the Fletcher School of Law and Diplomacy and Arathi Rao at the Council on Foreign Relations, provided invaluable help with locating many of the large and small facts that appear in these pages.

Jamshed Bharucha, the provost at Tufts University, and Stephen Bosworth, the dean at the Fletcher School, provided me with release time and generous funding to complete my research and writing. I am grateful to the fellows and staff of the Dubai School of Government, and especially its dean, Tarik Yousef, for their invaluable help with this book. Throughout the time this project took form and came to fruition I benefited from the support of colleagues at the Council on Foreign Relations, and from the many stimulating discussions I was privy to at roundtables there. I would like to thank in particular CFR's president, Richard Haass, for his keen interest in my work, and for the many ideas he planted in my head. Lisa Shields, friend and supporter extraordinaire of all CFR fellows, never ceased to remind me of the importance of communicating what I thought and wrote to a broader audience. I am grateful for her friendship and good cheer.

I am in debt to my literary agent, Susan Rabiner, for giving direction to this project, and for finding a home for it at Free Press. I could not have wished for a better editor to work with than Emily Loose. She took great interest in this book and read closely everything I wrote, honing my arguments in more ways than one. The book's organization, style, and structure all owe much to the clarity of her vision. Thanks also to Emily's assistant, Maura O'Brien, my publicist at Free Press, Nicole Kalian, and the entire team at Free Press for their wonderful work.

Finally, this book would not have been without my family's support. I am grateful to my wife, Darya, sons, Amir and Hossein, and daughter, Donia, for their patience and good humor during the many months of manic writing. I hope they will find the result worthy of that indulgence.

INDEX

About the Author

VALI NASR is a professor of international politics at the Fletcher School of Law and Diplomacy of Tufts University and an adjunct senior fellow for Middle Eastern studies at the Council on Foreign Relations, as well as a senior fellow of The Dubai Initiative at Harvard University's John F. Kennedy School of Government. He is the author of *The Shia Revival; Democracy in Iran;* and *The Islamic Leviathan.* He appears regularly on major network news shows as an expert on Middle Eastern affairs and writes for *The New York Times, The Washington Post* and *The Wall Street Journal.* He lives in Washington, D.C. with his wife, two sons, and a daughter.